# Perspectives on Economic Development - Public Policy, Culture, and Economic Development

*Edited by Ryan Merlin Yonk and Vito Bobek*

Published in London, United Kingdom

IntechOpen

*Supporting open minds since 2005*

Perspectives on Economic Development - Public Policy, Culture, and Economic Development
http://dx.doi.org/10.5772/intechopen.82996
Edited by Ryan Merlin Yonk and Vito Bobek

Contributors
Itumeleng Pleasure Mongale, Livhuani Baloyi, Elwasila Mohamed, Vito Bobek, Moritz Jellenz, Tatjana Horvat, Emiliano Gil-Blanco, Mohamed Aslam, Irina A. Zhuravleva, Panagiotis E. Petrakis, Kyriaki I. Kafka, Pantelis C. Kostis, Ryan Merlin Yonk



First published in London, United Kingdom, 2020 by IntechOpen
IntechOpen is the global imprint of INTECHOPEN LIMITED, registered in England and Wales, registration number: 11086078, 7th floor, 10 Lower Thames Street, London, EC3R 6AF, United Kingdom
Printed in Croatia

British Library Cataloguing-in-Publication Data
A catalogue record for this book is available from the British Library

Additional hard and PDF copies can be obtained from orders@intechopen.com

Perspectives on Economic Development - Public Policy, Culture, and Economic Development
Edited by Ryan Merlin Yonk and Vito Bobek
p. cm.
Print ISBN 978-1-78985-937-9
Online ISBN 978-1-78985-938-6
eBook (PDF) ISBN 978-1-78984-647-8

# Meet the editors

Ryan M. Yonk is the Undergraduate Programs Director in the Center for the Study of Public Choice and Political Economy at North Dakota State University. He is also a lecturer in the Department of Agribusiness and Applied Economics. Dr. Yonk received his PhD in Political Science from Georgia State University in 2011. He was previously a research assistant professor of economics at Utah State University. His books include *Green V. Green*, *Direct Democracy in the United States*, *Nature Unbound: Bureaucracy vs. the Environment*, *Reality of American Energy*, and *The Political Impact of Quality of Life*. Dr. Yonk is the author of numerous academic journal articles and policy reports focused on the intersection of public policy, economics, and politics.

Vito Bobek works as Professor of International Management at the University of Applied Sciences FH Joanneum (Graz, Austria). During the course of his academic career, he has published more than 400 units and visited twenty-two universities worldwide in the capacity of a visiting professor. He is a member of the editorial board of five international journals and an open access publishing company.  He has a long history of being involved in academia, consulting, and entrepreneurship. In 2008, he founded a consulting company, "Palemid," whereby he managed twelve major projects. He is also co-founder of the Academy of Regional Management in Slovenia. Over the last 17 years, he has also been a member of the supervisory board at KBM Infond Management Company Ltd.

# Contents

# Preface

Among the most discussed and hotly contested areas of policy are those that surround economic development and growth. Robust economic development and the economic growth that underlies that development have long been articulated as the primary aims of governments around the world. Among the wide universe that is public policy, those policies that claim to enhance economic development have long been viewed as particularly important. Discussions over what the best approaches are have been varied, heated, and often at the core of the success or failure of national, regional, and local governments.

Scholarship about economic development has most often mirrored this reality, with focus on approaches and mechanisms dominating the discussion. This volume seeks to build on the robust literature by focusing on the policy approaches for economic development across the world.

Despite the primacy of economic development among the policy aims of most every government, it is important to remember that economic growth is not an end in itself and does not occur in a vacuum. Rather the goal of economic development is the material well-being of individuals, and policy decisions about it happen in a broader policy context. In this light, this volume explores a variety of policy choices that impact economic development and ultimately the well-being of individuals, within that wider context.

The well-being of individuals is not found just in their pocketbooks (although that is often a dominant concern in well-being discussions) but also in the cultural, social, and political realms. Understanding and thoroughly exploring economic development requires an understanding of how policy decisions focused on economic development interplay with these complex realities.

Throughout this volume, chapter authors explore the policy environments of particular cases and seek to better explain how these policy decisions impact economic development in light of the interplay with other factors. From discussion of tax policy in the Russian Federation, to the interplay of economic development and culture in Namibia, to the complex interplay between tourism and extractive industries in the United States, this volume addresses a wide range of circumstances and policy realities.

Despite the variety of policy decisions, one common theme carries across each of the chapters in this volume, the decisions of policy makers continue to play an important and defining role in economic development, and that those policy decisions have real consequences for individuals. Further, this volume illustrates that economic development remains a worthy aim for policy makers in materially improving the lives individuals.

My own background is heavily tilted toward public policy in the United States. The policy questions that surround economic development in developed nations like the United States differ substantially from those faced by less developed nations.

The nature of the economic system and its level of development greatly influence the policy options available to foster economic development. Thus, a full understanding of how policy decisions will impact economic development requires a robust knowledge of the institutions, economies, and culture of the area being studied. Throughout this volume, our authors explore the impact of policy decisions within those cultural, political, and economic realties.

It would be difficult to underestimate the importance of economic development and the policies that attempt to foster it. The impact of these policy decisions are among those that have the most direct and immediate effect on the daily lives and well-being of individuals. Most often the impact of these policies are felt not by the policymakers but by those who must live with the policies they make.

Collectively, this and other work on economic development serves an important purpose in better enlightening the impact of policy decisions on economic development and can highlight what has worked and what has not in the particular cultural, economic, and political context. Our hope is that those who explore the chapters gain a better understanding of economic development policy and its impact on the well-being of individuals.

**Dr. Ryan Merlin Yonk**
North Dakota State University,
United States of America

**Dr. Vito Bobek**
University of Applied Sciences FH Joanneum,
Austria

Section 1

# Understanding Economic Development

Chapter 1

# Why Coevolution of Culture and Institutions Matters for Economic Development and Growth?

*Kyriaki I. Kafka, Pantelis C. Kostis and Panagiotis E. Petrakis*

## Abstract

Theoretical considerations that choose to make reference to the institutional and cultural considerations presuppose that these are in an optimal form. However, this is not the case in the real world. This chapter argues that the coevolution requirements of institutional and culture change are critical for economic outcomes. When institutions and culture coevolve in an optimal pattern, economic development and growth are facilitated. In contrast, when institutions and culture deviate from the optimal pace of coevolution, incompatible alterations of institutions and culture may end up causing an inability of the policy designers to implement the required changes in institutions and/or cultural behaviors. The result can be a series of failing attempts to implement a modernized progrowth framework of institutional settings and cultural behaviors. Using a dataset of 80 countries for the period 1981–2019, the analysis concludes that institutions and culture are complements—and not substitutes—in terms of their role in economic development, as when both sizes are strong it leads to higher levels of GDP per capita. When either or both of them are at a weak level, economic development is much lower.

**Keywords:** culture, institutions, economic development, economic growth, coevolution

## 1. Introduction

Many studies and empirical works have come to conclusions about the important role of the institutional and/or cultural background in economic development and growth. Theoretical constructs that choose to refer to the institutional and cultural background presuppose that both of these backgrounds are in optimal form. However, this is not the case in the real world.

The requirements regarding the coevolution of the institutional and cultural background are crucial to the development process of an economy. When institutions and culture coevolve in an optimal pattern, economic growth is facilitated. In contrast, when institutions and culture deviate from the optimal pace of coevolution, incompatible alterations of institutions and culture may end up causing an inability of the policy designers to implement the required changes in institutions and/or cultural behaviors. The result can be a series of failed attempts to implement a modernized development framework for the institutional and cultural background of societies, leading to the perpetuation of stagnated growth prototypes.

A stagnated growth prototype can be transformed into a progrowth one by introducing ambitious institutional and cultural alterations through structural reforms. These reforms require the optimal coevolution of institutions and culture. However, the process of the reorganization of the institutional background and the change of culture can be seriously interrupted by the so-called coevolution requirements of institutions and cultural background. In fact, the evolution of institutions and culture can be toward the same direction but may not coincide time-wise. Then, the prevailing cultural background, which has not been altered yet, could work as a brake to the new institutional setting or vice versa. Therefore, the implementation of structural reforms can fail, given that institutional and cultural behaviors can be incompatible.

The purpose of this chapter is to highlight the problems arising from the asynchronous change of the institutional and cultural background for the economic development and growth. In that way, the aim is to highlight the interconnection between the institutional and cultural background and how this interconnection affects the economies. In other words, the chapter aims to show whether the institutional and cultural background functions in a complementary or substitutive way in their role in economic development, contributing to the debate on whether or not they coevolve. The analysis is based on a sample of 80 countries for the period from 1981 to 2019.

The structure of the chapter is as follows: In Section 2, the coevolution of institutions and cultural requirements is presented. In Section 3, why institutions and culture usually lead to stagnated growth prototypes is presented. In Section 4, a descriptive analysis on culture is presented and institutions are complements or substitutes, while Section 5 analyses the fact that structural reforms that promote growth need institutional and cultural changes that also promote growth. Finally, the chapter ends with the conclusions.

## 2. The coevolution of institutions and culture

In general, the problem of coevolution in a system, the subparts of which evolve at a different pace, creates imbalances and failures in its effective operation. The evolution of institutions and culture does not always present a compatible path of evolution leading to conflicts when institutions and culture do not match. The issue under investigation has a time dimension, but usually it has a qualitative nature as well. In other words, institutions may change at the same direction with the cultural background, but these changes may not be compatible as far as the end result is concerned.

Thus, incompatibility may arise because either the institutions may change but not the cultural background or the cultural behaviors may change but the institution changes do not follow. In addition, incompatibility may appear because both concepts may evolute but their stationary equilibrium is not characterized by the optimum supplementary combination of institutions and cultural behavior matching.

But there is an even worse situation of incompatibility. This is when a change in institutions may appear and the noncompatible cultural behaviors would act to oppose and cancel these changes and vice versa. This is a very probable situation, which can arise after the implementation of an institutional structural reform, which we usually expect to be enforced and have fruitful results on growth in short- or medium-term horizon, but the prevailing cultural behaviors may sterilize those reforms.

*DOI: http://dx.doi.org/10.5772/intechopen.90631*

On the one hand, the cultural background is usually a slow-moving structure, which evolves in the long and the very long run (sometimes it can take more than 100 years to change). Globalization effects and other megatrends (e.g., the aging) may lead to incremental changes of the cultural background. Norris and Inglehart [1] conclude to the cultural backlash hypothesis in the sense that factors such as generational substitution, increased access to higher education, urbanization, increased gender equality, and increased ethnic diversity have led to cultural background changes in the last decades in the high developed world. Moreover, there may exist several external shocks (like an economic crisis) or migration shocks that can change the cultural background even in the short run [2, 3].

On the other hand, institutions can change at different speeds too. Institutions can be divided into two categories, based on the speed of their evolution: fast-moving institutions (such as political institutions), which can change overnight, either through a legislative intervention or after revolutionary moments; and slow-moving institutions (such as the property rights, cooperation procedures, etc.), which need a long period of time through a gradual and constant process of evolution [4]. A basic question raised is why countries with ineffective institutions do not "copy" the institutions of developed countries [5]. The answer lies in the fact that institutions do not change easily; it takes 10–100 years for formal institutions and 100–1000 years for informal in order to be changed [6]. Thus, the political leadership usually finds it very difficult to innate a similar process of structural reform.

In this way, during the process of their evolution, a vicious cycle of interaction between the institutions and culture can be created. If the two concepts could change at the same rate, that is, when there is coevolution, then the economy could approach a new point of equilibrium, enhancing the efficiency of the economic system.

The relevant literature on the coevolution of institutions and culture focuses on the hypothesis of the natural selection of the institutions [7–11]. According to that, some institutional and behavioral traits might give competitive advantage to individuals or populations within their local environment [12]. Nevertheless, gaining an understanding of the way in which institutions and culture interact is not an easy task, due to the endogenous character of their evolution [13, 14].

Samuel Bowles' contribution to the field of coevolution process [8–10, 15–17] focuses on the impact of the institutions on human behavior through the ways in which particular institutional settings prompt individuals to draw one or another response from their varied behavioral repertoires. Furthermore, the structure of social interactions, both within and between groups, affects the pace and direction of cultural evolution, the economic institutions and policies that influence ingroup-outgroup relationships, and other aspects of preferences, casting doubt on the economists' canonical premise that preferences are exogenous [18]. In addition, some institutions may reduce the variance of reproductive success within groups and, thus, weaken the force of selection on the level of individuals [8]. The emergence of these institutions depends on the existence of such group-beneficial traits and these in turn may only be able to proliferate if these institutions are in place.

According to Veblen [19], institutions shall be understood as the rules, habits, and other culturally transmitted norms that individuals follow when interacting with each other [20]. He shows that evolution may also create institutions that are complementary to the mate choice based on genetically fixed preferences, which can be interpreted as genetically coded information processing. The evolutionary theory of institutional change of [19] centers on the notion of "habits of thought,", where habits are viewed as durable and adaptable—in the long run—propensities on how to think and act. Because these habits reside within individuals, institutional change involves the simultaneous coevolution of both shared prevalent habits of thought (institutions) and the habits of individuals [21]. Endogenous interactions among institutions and culture, and their coevolution are important during economic evolution [13].

However, we do not have adequate critical information on how economic institutions may impact on culture, due to the fact that we know very little about the process of cultural transmission, which means that we do not have adequate information on who acquires what trait from whom, under what conditions, why, how, and how persistent the traits may be once the initiating environment is withdrawn [22]. Furthermore, there is no strong evidence on how culture and institutions evolve over time and whether they mutually reinforce each other or whether one is a precursor to the other [23]. Thus, the question is posed on whether culture and institutions coevolve or they proceed independently or causality is unidirectional.

Bisin and Verdier [24] claim that culture and institutions jointly evolve and interact, and focus on the process as determined by the interaction and not on the cause of the interaction. They define the cultural (or institutional) multiplier as the ratio of the total effect of institutional (or cultural) change on economic prosperity divided by the direct effect, that is, the counterfactual effect that would have occurred had the distribution of cultural traits in the population (or the institutions) remained constant after the institutional (or cultural) change. In that way, they contribute to the analysis of whether culture and institutions coevolve or their change is incompatible in time and quality considerations.

In sum, the coevolution process of institutions and culture is the product of complex interactions between human behavior, preferences, economic performance, and time. How and in which speed the institutions change vis-à-vis the cultural background-and vice versa-is particularly important, as coevolution affects the effectiveness of the growth model, since different degrees of compatibility can be observed.

## 3. The role of institutions and culture in stagnated growth prototypes

The existence of an optimum structure of institutions that is associated with an optimal nexus of cultural values can exist at the theoretical level for the sake of simplifying reality and for improving the analytical tools of comprehension. Thus, in real economy, “stagnated growth prototypes” are created since usually the institutions and culture that prevail interrupt the process of economic development and growth and could be characterized as idiosyncratic [25]. The prevalence of a stagnated growth prototype has crystal-clear effects on the mode of operation of the economies, the most important one being the increase in the level of insecurity and the inefficient allocation of resources. Thus, an optimal growth pattern often cannot be encountered, as the existence of idiosyncratic institutions is one of the most significant reasons for the deviation from the optimal pattern [25].

For instance, a stagnated growth prototype could be described as following[1] [25]: (a) Existence of extractive institutions [26]. The economies that are dominated by extractive institutions are characterized by the absence of established relations between the members of the economic system. This results in the emergence of conditions that favor factors that enhance the existence of idiosyncratic institutions. Factors that enhance the creation of idiosyncratic institutions (hierarchies and high transaction costs) are coordination failures, asymmetries of

[1] It is not the only possible form of deviation from optimality but we chose to concentrate on that due to the fact that it could describe better an emerging economy that faces a long period of stagnation.

information, evolution path dependence, and rent-seeking activities, which all lead to the appearance of high systematic risk. (b) Existence of specific characteristics that act in a peculiar manner, shaping human behavior and preferences. This could be the case when there exist idiosyncratic cultural values like uncertainty avoidance behaviors, in-group collectivism, high time discount preferences, and lack of trust, as well as nondiversified investment attitudes [27, 28] and loss aversion behaviors [29–31].

There is a two-sided effect between idiosyncratic institutions and idiosyncratic cultural background described above, since the existence of idiosyncratic institutions can lead to the formation of an idiosyncratic cultural background and vice versa. This interrelationship perpetuates the existence of idiosyncratic institutions and cultural characteristics. Thus, a stagnated growth prototype is generated and prevails. This stagnated growth prototype has no endogenous energy to break the barriers to growth. Stagnated institutions always affect culture and vice versa, through the coevolution pattern that they follow and that has a long lasting ability to survive. When a stagnated growth prototype is prevailing in an economy, it can experience long periods of stagnation or periods near stagnation. These periods usually can be interrupted only by large waves of foreign incoming capital, which usually take the form of a very large public or private investments in specific sectors.

## 4. Culture and institutions: complements or substitutes?

In this section, we try to examine whether the cultural and the institutional background of the societies and the economies are characterized as substitutes or complemented issues in relation to their effects on economic development. To achieve the objectives of the chapter, a dataset of 80 countries[2] is used for the period of 1981–2019.

Initially, as a measure of economic development, GDP per capita (purchasing power parity; 2011 international dollars) is used derived from the World Economic Outlook (WEO) database of the International Monetary Fund (IMF).

To measure the cultural background, the present chapter makes a selective selection of seven cultural values that express the cultural background of the societies that make up the sample under analysis, based on relevant studies in the literature [2, 32–34]. The data contributing to the cultural background were compiled from the World Values Survey (WVS) and supplemented by data from the European Values Study (EVS) for corresponding questions, on the following waves: 1981–1984, 1990–1994, 1995–1998, 1999–2004, 2005–2009, 2010–2014, and 2017–2019.

Specifically, for the measurement of the cultural background, an overall measure was used that emerges as the first principal component of a principal component analysis (PCA) for the following seven cultural values: generalized trust, control of life, respect, independence, honesty, competition affinity, and

[2] The countries used in the analysis are the following: Albania, Algeria, Argentina, Armenia, Australia, Azerbaijan, Bangladesh, Belarus, Bosnia and Herzegovina, Brazil, Bulgaria, Burkina Faso, Canada, Chile, China, Colombia, Croatia, Cyprus, Czech Republic, Dominican Republic, Ecuador, Egypt, Estonia, Ethiopia, Finland, France, Georgia, Germany, Ghana, Haiti, Hong Kong, Hungary, India, Indonesia, Iran (Islamic Republic of), Italy, Japan, Jordan, Kazakhstan, Republic of Korea, Kuwait, Kyrgyzstan, Latvia, Lebanon, Libya, Lithuania, Malaysia, Mali, Mexico, Republic of Moldova, Morocco, Netherlands, New Zealand, Nigeria, Norway, Pakistan, Peru, Philippines, Poland, Romania, Russian Federation, Rwanda, Serbia, Slovakia, Slovenia, South Africa, Spain, Sweden, Switzerland, Thailand, Tunisia, Turkey, Ukraine, United States, Uruguay, Venezuela, Vietnam, Yemen, Zambia, Zimbabwe.

work ethic. The cultural values of honesty, competition affinity, and work ethic result again as the primary components from specific PCAs—using queries selected by WVS and EVS to express each value. The way generalized trust, control of life, independence, honesty, competition affinity, and work ethic are calculated is described in [2], while for the variable respect in [33]. The first principal component that emerges for the overall measurement of the cultural background follows a normalization on a scale of 0–10 (according to [35]), with 0 signaling a weak cultural background and 10 signaling a strong cultural background.

To measure institutional background, the World Economic Freedom Index is used as reported by the Fraser Institute [36]. The construction of the index is based on 42 subindices and is set on a scale of 0–10, with 10 representing the best performance and 0 the worst performance. Despite the availability of alternative indicators to reflect the institutional background of economies (such as the Heritage Foundation's financial freedom index and the protection against the risk of expropriation of the ICRG), the Fraser Institute Index is used as the most appropriate because of the long period under study as well as due to the sample size of the countries covered by this indicator. The degree of economic freedom, based on this indicator, is calculated on the basis of the institutions and policies applied by each country in five areas: size of state, rule of law, access to a strong currency, freedom of international trade, and regulatory environment in bank credit, employment, and entrepreneurship.

Authoritative research has consistently confirmed that people living in countries with a high degree of economic freedom enjoy a higher level of prosperity, have wider political and social rights, and present longer life expectancy. Hall and Lawson [37] conduct a literature review using the Fraser Financial Freedom Index. They result in 402 articles using this index, 198 of them using it as an independent variable. They note that 134 of these 198 articles conclude that financial freedom leads to faster economic development and growth, better living standards, higher levels of happiness, etc., while only 8 articles conclude that financial freedom has a negative impact to economic growth through increasing economic inequalities. Williamson et al. [35, 38–40]—among others—use the Fraser Financial Freedom Index as a measure of the quality of the institutional background. They note that this is a comprehensive measure that includes the factors that historically economists have found to be significantly related to economic development and growth.

The foundation of the relationship between the cultural and institutional background and their relation to GDP per capita of the economies is outlined in a four-quadrant scatter plot, as shown in **Figure 1**.

The first quadrant (A) brings together countries with strong institutional and weak cultural backgrounds, the second quadrant (B) countries with strong institutional and cultural backgrounds, the third quadrant (C) countries with weak institutional and cultural backgrounds, and the fourth quadrant (D) countries with weak institutional and strong cultural backgrounds.

For each country included in the sample, its average values for the cultural background, institutional background, and GDP per capita are calculated for the entire analysis period, so that for each country, there is one value for each variable. Following the methodology of [41], countries with a strong cultural background/institutional background are those with scores above 7, while those with a weak cultural background/institutional background are those with score below 6.

**Figure 2** illustrates in a descriptive way the relationship between cultural and institutional background and their relation to the level of economic development. Countries in quadrants (A) and (B) clearly outperform those countries in quadrants (C) and (D), as they have a stronger institutional background. Moreover, countries

| | |
|---|---|
| **(A)** **Strong Institutions** **Weak Culture** | **(B)** **Strong Institutions** **Strong Culture** |
| **(C)** **Weak Institutions** **Weak Culture** | **(D)** **Weak Institutions** **Strong Culture** |

**Figure 1.**
*Strength of institutions and culture.*

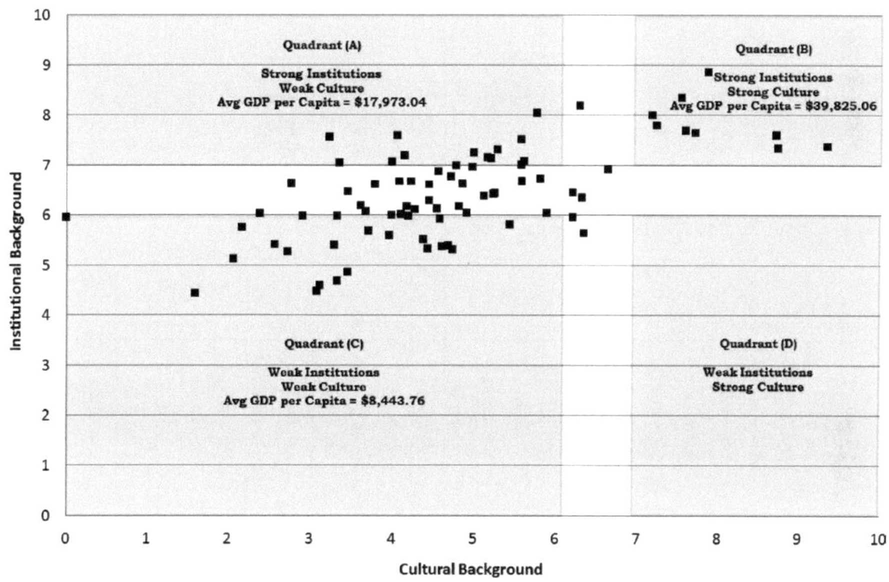


**Figure 2.**
*Descriptive foundation of the cultural/institutional background relationship and the GDP per capita.*

belonging to quadrants (B) and (D) clearly outperform those in quadrants (A) and (C), as they present a stronger cultural background.

Quadrant (B) countries, those with strong institutional (average 7.83) and strong cultural background (average 8.07), have the highest average GDP per capita of $ 39.826. This group includes countries such as Norway, Sweden, Hong Kong, Switzerland, and Canada, countries that are characterized by high economic freedom and at the same time by social behaviors that promote economic development and growth, such as high levels of generalized trust, respect, independence, and honesty. In contrast, countries in quadrant (C), those with weak institutional (average 5.39) and weak cultural background (average 3.41), have the lowest average GDP per capita of $ 8.443. This group includes countries such as Iran, Libya, Zimbabwe, Algeria, and Venezuela, that is, countries with a low degree of economic

| | Country | GDP per capita | Cultural background | Institutional background |
|---|---|---|---|---|
| **Quadrant A: Strong Institutions, Weak Culture** | France | 34558.47 | 5.61 | 7.08 |
| | Spain | 28817.90 | 5.21 | 7.14 |
| | New Zealand | 28268.62 | 5.76 | 8.05 |
| | Czech Republic | 26175.23 | 4.15 | 7.21 |
| | Slovakia | 20558.37 | 4.00 | 7.07 |
| | Lithuania | 19989.40 | 5.16 | 7.16 |
| | Estonia | 19887.70 | 5.57 | 7.52 |
| | Malaysia | 17286.46 | 5.57 | 7.01 |
| | Latvia | 16185.53 | 4.99 | 7.25 |
| | Kazakhstan | 15735.42 | 4.78 | 7.00 |
| | Chile | 15360.80 | 5.28 | 7.31 |
| | Lebanon | 12649.27 | 3.36 | 7.05 |
| | Georgia | 5716.39 | 4.06 | 7.59 |
| | Armenia | 5075.77 | 3.23 | 7.57 |
| | Vietnam | 3330.30 | 5.89 | 6.05 |
| | **Average of Quadrant A** | **17973.04** | **4.84** | **7.21** |
| **Quadrant B: Strong Institutions, Strong Culture** | Norway | 55653.87 | 9.35 | 7.38 |
| | Switzerland | 49494.08 | 7.54 | 8.35 |
| | The Netherlands | 40332.87 | 8.71 | 7.61 |
| | Hong Kong | 37889.14 | 7.87 | 8.86 |
| | Germany | 37573.25 | 7.60 | 7.69 |
| | Sweden | 37068.91 | 8.74 | 7.34 |
| | Canada | 36705.35 | 7.18 | 8.00 |
| | Australia | 36647.47 | 7.24 | 7.81 |
| | Finland | 33646.95 | 8.71 | 7.60 |
| | Japan | 33247.75 | 7.72 | 7.65 |
| | **Average of Quadrant B** | **39825.96** | **8.07** | **7.83** |

DOI: http://dx.doi.org/10.5772/intechopen.90631

| | Country | GDP per capita | Cultural background | Institutional background |
|---|---|---|---|---|
| **Quadrant C: Weak Institutions, Weak Culture** | Libya | 26331.32 | 3.33 | 4.69 |
| | Russian Federation | 19549.52 | 4.58 | 5.94 |
| | Poland | 16716.41 | 5.44 | 5.81 |
| | Argentina | 15807.43 | 4.60 | 5.38 |
| | Venezuela | 15032.13 | 1.60 | 4.45 |
| | Iran | 14920.61 | 3.46 | 4.87 |
| | Brazil | 12418.27 | 2.73 | 5.27 |
| | Algeria | 11667.48 | 3.09 | 4.48 |
| | Dominican Republic | 9441.76 | 4.19 | 5.98 |
| | Egypt | 8778.71 | 4.69 | 5.40 |
| | Ecuador | 8530.45 | 3.72 | 5.69 |
| | Ukraine | 7201.05 | 4.74 | 5.32 |
| | Nigeria | 4075.95 | 2.07 | 5.13 |
| | Pakistan | 3639.66 | 3.97 | 5.59 |
| | Ghana | 3585.80 | 2.17 | 5.75 |
| | India | 3413.81 | 3.33 | 5.99 |
| | Zambia | 2782.47 | 3.29 | 5.41 |
| | Zimbabwe | 2540.86 | 3.12 | 4.60 |
| | Bangladesh | 2180.83 | 4.43 | 5.34 |
| | Haiti | 1777.94 | 0.00 | 5.96 |
| | Mali | 1641.60 | 2.57 | 5.43 |
| | Burkina Faso | 1195.23 | 2.91 | 5.99 |
| | Ethiopia | 977.15 | 4.37 | 5.52 |
| | **Average of Quadrant C** | **8443.76** | **3.41** | **5.39** |
| **Quadrant D: Weak Institutions, Strong Culture** | — | — | — | — |

*Note: Countries not falling into a quadrant are (not characterized by either strong or by weak institutional and cultural background): Albania, Azerbaijan, Belarus, Bosnia and Herzegovina, Bulgaria, China, Colombia, Croatia, Cyprus, Hungary, Indonesia, Italy, Jordan, Republic of Korea, Kuwait, Kyrgyzstan, Mexico, Republic of Moldova, Morocco, Peru, Philippines, Romania, Rwanda, Serbia, Slovenia, South Africa, Thailand, Tunisia, Turkey, the United States, Uruguay, and Yemen.*

**Table 1.**
*Countries belonging in each quadrant and averages.*

freedom and social attitudes that oppose economic development and growth processes. A comparison of these two quadrants highlights that the institutional and cultural backgrounds are complementary, as when both are strong, a significantly higher degree of economic development is achieved. Countries in quadrant (A), those with strong institutional (average 7.21) but weak cultural backgrounds (average 4.84), average GDP per capita of $ 17.973. This group includes countries such as Latvia, the Czech Republic, Georgia, Lebanon, and Kazakhstan, which, while characterized by a high degree of economic freedom, are also characterized by social behaviors that are opposed to economic development and growth processes. A comparison with quadrant (C) shows that the improvement of the institutional background leads to a much higher level of economic growth. Also, the scatter chart does not show countries belonging to quadrant (D) characterized by weak institutional and strong cultural background, while the opposite relationship holds (quadrant A). This demonstrates that the cultural background alone is not sufficient and exists only in a strong form when there is also a strong institutional background, thus reinforcing the hypothesis of complementarity between the two kinds of background.

**Table 1** gives a detailed breakdown of the countries belonging to each quadrant and the average of each country for GDP per capita, cultural background, and institutional background.

## 5. Structural reforms that promote growth need institutional and cultural changes that also promote growth

Structural reforms imply changes both at an institutional and cultural level in order to ensure economic development and growth in the long term by raising the growth potential. This is so because they are able to increase the GDP, reduce unemployment, and 'fortify' the economy against potential shocks. In this direction, what is regarded as structural reform may include the intervention in transaction costs, product and service markets, and the labor market, reducing entry barriers, improving public sector administration, and enhancing the role of private sector over government [42]. Structural reforms usually include policies that make labor markets more adaptable and responsive, liberalizing the service sectors, increasing competition in product and service markets, improving the institutions for the strengthening of market efficiency, improving the entrepreneurial climate, and encouraging innovation [43]. Additionally, structural reforms are the key to sustainable development [44] as the enhancement of productivity constitutes a factor that promotes the improvement of the standard of living in emerging and developing economies, leading to a removal of the obstacles to the efficient utilization of resources. Thus, the need for transformation from a stagnated to an optimal growth model requires structural reforms referring to institutions and culture.

Institutions are one of the most important areas affected by the implementation of structural reforms [45]. This is why structural reforms usually concern institutional reforms that involve market, or even nonmarket, institutions. Essentially, market institutions refer to economic institutions and thus reforms concern institutions such as the labor market, the product market, the taxation, social security and financial system, etc. Reforms in nonmarket institutions may concern political institutions (quality of democracy, politicians/political parties, municipalities, etc.) or social institutions (judicial system, legal system, army, education system, healthcare system, etc.).

Johnson [45] examines the relationship between the time of the implementation of major reforms and the institutional quality index, concluding that countries with more powerful institutions (as they are approached from the perspective of property rights and the rule of law) introduced important reforms earlier. In other words, it seems that there is a negative association between the time of the implementation of structural reforms and the quality of the institutions.

Moreover, Kafka [3] concludes that the only way for economies to improve their institutional background and their innovative performance and to converge with the economies that form the frontier of performance in innovation and institutions is through economic policies to accelerate change in the institutional background, such as structural reforms. Her analysis concludes to the creation of thermal maps that present—for each of the 152 economies included in the analysis—the specific institutions that need to be structurally reformed.

Furthermore, surveys such as those by [46–48] associate political institutions with economic reform effectiveness. Rajan and Zingales [47] note that democracy can obstruct reforms, if special interests prevail in the societies where these reforms are implemented, given that the capitalists are usually fortified in speculative positions and, thus, they often are the primary opponents of economic reforms, which may disrupt their interests. Fernandes and Rodrik [46] reach a similar conclusion, stressing that interest groups may block reforms if there is certainty over the distribution of the benefits of structural reforms. Also, Giuliano et al. [48] note that the increase in the quality of democratic institutions has a positive and statistically significant impact on structural reforms. Haggard [49] claims that the institutions may overcome collective action dilemmas by restricting the selfish behavior of interest groups.

The literature seems to be especially interested in the question of whether the extensive and swift institutional changes lead to a reduction of the output that is produced, even when these changes involve institutions of higher quality and greater effectiveness. For example, Roland and Verdier [50] note that firms do not invest after structural reforms because they wait until the economy is stabilized, and this fact results in a reduction of product produced. Moreover, Blanchard and Kremer [51] explain that the reduction of output produced is the result of the ineffectiveness of negotiations between the firms. While a great deal of institutions can develop in a very short period of time [52], there are other institutions that require a significant amount of time in order to function effectively.

As far as the cultural background is concerned, often this must also change for the impact of structural reforms to be more effective. As Kafka [3] points out, changing the cultural background through economic policy requires a long-term wait for results that can exceed 20 or 30 years, while requiring interventions focused on the education of societies. But what economic policy makers should not miss is to take into account the cultural characteristics of their society before making decisions. Not all societies are ready to accept all economic policies and each economic policy is expected to have different efficiencies based on the cultural characteristics of the society for which it is intended for [3]. Structural reforms must take into account not only the formal rules and procedures but also informal behaviors and deep-rooted models and values that lie between the formal declaration of the intention to implement a particular structural reform and its actual implementation [53]. Ban [54] argues that cultural background is a critical issue in every attempt to implement a structural reform.

An additional problem that arises regarding the cultural background concerns the fact that not all societies are ready to accept the structural reforms that are designed by the political actors. Consequently, reforms must have the appropriate flexibility in order to adapt to the needs of the society; only in this case will the society accept reforms and allow their implementation. Besides, the basic problem is that the changes of the cultural background can only be slow-moving [55–57], even though there are behaviors that change even in a short-term horizon.

## 6. Conclusions

The forces deployed in the society either encourage the prevalence of features that promote a progrowth model or lead to a variety of problematic growth models, or to a mixture of progrowth and antigrowth characteristics with ambiguous results.

The transformation of a stagnated model to a progrowth one is not an easy task, focusing mainly on the coevolution requirements. Since the coevolution requirements cannot be met, there is a possibility that a perpetual stagnated prototype may become stronger. More specifically, the stagnated growth prototype may be transformed into a progrowth optimal prototype through suitable structural reforms on institutional and cultural background. However, the coevolution process taking place between institutions and culture may interrupt this process, having as a result a series of failing attempts to implement a modernized progrowth framework of institution settings and cultural behaviors leading to the salvation of the existing stagnated growth prototype, despite the probable design of ambitious structural reforms.

The analysis of the chapter reveals the complementary relationship between the institutional and cultural background in terms of their role in economic development and growth, as when both sizes are strong it leads to higher levels of GDP per capita. When either or both of them are at a weak level, economic development is much lower.

Thus, the existence of economic freedom is an important condition for economies to thrive. However, when these conditions are accompanied by social behaviors that promote economic development and growth and relate to individuals' trust and independence, the highest possible level of economic growth is achieved.

For instance, the presence of institutional structures that adequately manage property rights and contracts between economic actors has a positive impact on the level of economic development. But when this is accompanied by a high level of generalized trust and respect for other members of the society, the positive impact on economic development multiplies as the performance of the already satisfying cultural background improves. In addition, when there is an institutional background in which government spending, taxation, and the size of state-controlled enterprises are such that state decisions do not replace private choices, financial freedom is increased with significant benefits for economic performance. But when this institutional framework characterizes societies that are independent of choices, the benefits of the institutional and cultural background to the level of economic development are even more crucial.

By presenting in a different way the conclusion about the complementarity of the two sizes, the results of the analysis lead to the fact that even if the institutional background is strong, it depends on whether the cultural background is weak (quadrant A in the analysis) or strong (quadrant B in the analysis) to determine whether or not an economy achieves satisfactory economic development. Thus, the same institutional background may have a different impact on economic development depending on the cultural background.

This relationship gives a good explanation of why economic policies, such as structural reforms, are effective in some countries and noneffective in others. The transformation of a stagnated growth prototype to a progrowth one is not an easy task, focusing on the coevolution requirements. Since the coevolution requirements

*DOI: http://dx.doi.org/10.5772/intechopen.90631*

cannot be met, there is a possibility that a perpetual stagnated prototype may become stronger. More specifically, the stagnated growth prototype may be transformed into a progrowth optimal prototype through suitable structural reforms on institutional and cultural background. However, the coevolution process taking place between institutions and culture may interrupt this process, having as a result a series of failing attempts to implement a modernized progrowth framework of institution settings and cultural behaviors leading to the salvation of the existing stagnated growth prototype, despite the probable design of ambitious structural reforms. Thus, the conclusion on the complementarity of the two sizes is therefore an important contribution for all those who design or pursue economic policy in either developing or developed economies.

## Author details

Kyriaki I. Kafka, Pantelis C. Kostis and Panagiotis E. Petrakis*
Department of Economics, National and Kapodistrian University of Athens, Athens, Greece

*Address all correspondence to: ppetrak@econ.uoa.gr

## References


[1] Norris P, Inglehart R. Cultural Backlash: Trump, Brexit, and Authoritarian Populism. New York: Cambridge University Press; 2019. DOI: 10.1017/9781108595841

[2] Kostis PC, Kafka KI, Petrakis PE. Cultural change and innovation performance. Journal of Business Research. 2018;**88**:306-313. DOI: 10.1016/j.jbusres.2017.12.010

[3] Kafka KI. The relative creditworthiness of development and growth theory [PhD thesis]. Department of Economics, National and Kapodistrian University of Athens; 2020

[4] Roland G. Institutions and economic performance—Fast-moving and slow-moving institutions. CESifo DICE Report. Ifo Institute for Economic Research at the University of Munich. 2004;**2**(2):16-21

[5] Fukuyama F. Culture and economic development: Cultural concerns. In: Smelser NJ, Baltes PB, editors. International Encyclopedia of the Social and Behavioral Sciences. Oxford: Elsevier Internet Publication; 2001. pp. 3130-3134. DOI: 10.1016/B0-08-043076-7/04584-8

[6] Petrakis PE, Kostis PC. Medium term effects of culture, transactions and institutions on opportunity entrepreneurship. Journal of Innovation and Entrepreneurship. 2014;**3**:11

[7] Boyd R, Richerson PJ. Group beneficial norms can spread rapidly in a structured population. Journal of Theoretical Biology. 2002;**215**(3):287-296

[8] Bowles S, Choi JK, Hopfensitz A. The co-evolution of individual behaviors and social institutions. Journal of Theoretical Biology. 2003;**223**(2):135-147

[9] Bowles S. Group competition, reproductive leveling, and the evolution of human altruism. Science. 2006;**314**(5805):1569-1572

[10] Choi JK, Bowles S. The coevolution of parochial altruism and war. Science. 2007;**318**(5850):636-640

[11] Gintis H. A framework for the unification of the behavioral sciences. Behavioral and Brain Sciences. 2007;**30**(01):1-16

[12] Lewis O, Steinmo S. How institutions evolve: Evolutionary theory and institutional change. Polity. 2012;**44**(3):314-339

[13] Tabellini G. The scope of cooperation: Values and incentives. Quarterly Journal of Economics. 2008;**123**(3):905-950

[14] Aghion P, Algan Y, Cahuc P, Shleifer A. Regulation and distrust. Quarterly Journal of Economics. 2010;**125**:1015-1049

[15] Bowles S. Microeconomics: Behavior, Institutions, and Evolution. Princeton: Princeton University Press; 2004

[16] Bowles S. Did warfare among ancestral hunter-gatherers affect the evolution of human social behaviors? Science. 2009;**324**(5932):1293-1298

[17] Bowles S, Gintis H. Walrasian economics in retrospect. Quarterly Journal of Economics. 2000;**115**(4):1411-1439

[18] Bowles S. Group conflicts, individual interactions, and the evolution of preferences. In: Durlauf S,

Young P, editors. Social Dynamics. Cambridge: MIT Press; 2000

[19] Veblen T. The Theory of the Leisure Class: An Economic Study of Institutions. New York: MacMillan; 1898

[20] Antrup AH. Co-evolution of institutions and preferences: The case of the (human) mating market. Journal of Theoretical Biology. 2013;**332**. DOI: 10.1016/j.jtbi.2013.04.009

[21] Kingston C, Caballero G. Comparing theories of institutional change. Journal of Institutional Economics. 2009;**5**(02):151-180

[22] Bowles S. Endogenous preferences: The cultural consequences of markets and other economic institutions. Journal of Economic Literature. 1998;**36**(1):75-111

[23] Murrell P, Schmidt M. The coevolution of culture and institutions in Seventeenth Century England. In: Mimeo. University of Maryland; 2011

[24] Bisin A, Verdier T. On the joint evolution of culture and institutions. In: Working Papers 2017-039. Human Capital and Economic Opportunity Working Group; 2017

[25] Petrakis PE, Valsamis DG, Kafka KI. From an optimal to a stagnated growth prototype: The role of institutions and culture. Journal of Innovation & Knowledge. 2017;**2**(3):97-105

[26] Acemoglu D, Robinson J. Why Nations Fail: The Origins of Power, Prosperity and Poverty. New York: Crown; 2012

[27] Kuznets S. Modern economic growth: Findings and reflections. In: Prize Lecture, Lecture to the Memory of Alfred Nobel. 1971 Available from: http://nobelprize.org/nobel_prizes/economics/laureates/1971/kuznetslecture.html

[28] Grossman GM, Helpman E. Innovation and Growth in the Global Economy. Massachusetts: MIT Press; 1992

[29] Kahneman D, Tversky A. Prospect theory: An analysis of decision under risk. Econometrica. 1979;**47**:263-291

[30] Kahneman D, Tversky A. Choices, Values and Frames. Cambridge University Press; 2000

[31] Ert E, Erev I. On the descriptive value of loss aversion in decisions under risk. In: Working Paper. Harvard School; 2010

[32] Inglehart R. The renaissance of political culture. American Political Science Review. 1988;**82**:1028-1034. DOI: 10.2307/1961756

[33] Tabellini G. Culture and institutions: Economic development in the regions of Europe. Journal of the European Economic Association. 2010;**8**(4):677-716

[34] Bützer S, Jordan C, Stracca L. Macroeconomic imbalances: A question of trust? In: Working Paper. European Central Bank; 2013. p. 1584

[35] Williamson CR, Mathers RL. Economic freedom, culture, and growth. Public Choice. 2011;**148**:313-335

[36] Gwartney J, Lawson R, Hall J. Economic freedom of the world. In: Annual Report. 2019

[37] Hall J, Lawson R. Economic freedom of the world: An accounting of the literature. Contemporary Economic Policy. 2014;**32**(1):1-19

[38] Gwartney JD, Holcombe RG, Lawson RA. Institutions and the impact of investment on growth. Kyklos. 2006;**59**(2):255-273. DOI: 10.1111/j.1467-6435.2006.00327.x

[39] Lothian JR. Institutions, capital flows and financial integration. Journal of International Money and Finance. 2006;**25**(3):358-369

[40] Mathers RL, Williamson CR. Cultural context: Explaining the productivity of capitalism. Kyklos. 2011;**64**(2):231-252. DOI: 10.1111/j.1467-6435.2011.00504.x

[41] Williamson CR. Informal institutions rule: Institutional arrangements and economic performance. Public Choice. 2009;**139**(3):371-387

[42] Rodrik D. Economics Rules: The Rights and Wrongs of the Dismal Science. New York: W.W. Norton and Company; 2015. pp. 213-215

[43] Canton E, Grilo I, Monteagudo J, Pierini F, Turrini A. The role of structural reform for adjustment and growth. ECF in Economic Brief. 2014;**34**

[44] Dabla-Norris E, Ho G, Kochhar K, Kyobe A, Tchaidze R. Anchoring growth: The importance of productivity-enhancing reforms in emerging market and developing economies. IMF Staff Discussion Note. 2013;**13**:08

[45] Johnson S. Structural reforms and economic performance in advanced and developing countries. International Monetary Fund. 2008

[46] Fernandez R, Rodrik D. Resistance to reform: Status quo bias in the presence of individual-specific uncertainty. American Economic Review. 1991;**81**(5):1146-1155

[47] Rajan R, Zingales L. Making capitalism work for everyone. Journal of Applied Corporate Finance. 2004;**16**(4):101-108

[48] Giuliano P, Mishra P, Spilimbergo A. Democracy and reforms: Evidence from a new dataset. American Economic Journal: Macroeconomics. 2013;**5**(4):179-204. DOI: 10.1257/mac.5.4.179

[49] Haggard S. Pathways from the Periphery: The Politics of Growth in the Newly Industrializing Countries. Ithaca: Cornell University Press; 1990

[50] Roland G, Verdier T. Law enforcement and transition. In: Working Papers Series 262. William Davidson Institute, University of Michigan; 1999

[51] Blanchard O, Kremer MR. Disorganization. Quarterly Journal of Economics. 1997;**112**(4):1091-1126

[52] North DC. Institutions, Institutional Change, and Economic Performance. Cambridge University Press; 1990

[53] Bennett L. Policy reform and culture change: Contesting gender, caste, and ethnic exclusion in Nepal. In: Dani AA, de Haan A, editors. Inclusive States: Social Policy and Structural Inequalities. New Frontiers of Social Policy. Washington, DC: World Bank; 2008. pp. 197-224

[54] Ban C. How Do Public Managers Manage? Bureaucratic Constraints, Organizational Culture, and the Potential for Reform. San Francisco: Jossey Bass; 1995

[55] Johnston L. Resisting change: Information-seeking and stereotype change. European Journal of Social Psychology. 1996;**26**:799-825

[56] De Jong E. Culture and Economics: On Values, Economics, and International Business. London: Routledge; 2009

[57] Schwarz SH. Culture matters: National value cultures, sources, and consequences. In: Wyer RS et al., editors. Understanding Culture. New York: Psychology Press; 2009

Chapter 2

# Developing Together? Understanding the Interaction between, Amenity-Based Tourism, Agriculture, and Extractive Industries in the Northern Rockies

*Ryan M. Yonk*

## Abstract

The factors that lead to economic growth at the county level are not always easy to identify or explain, though surely both energy and amenity resources can influence county growth. However, there are many other factors that can also influence growth, such as amenities in surrounding counties, the specifics of oil and gas development, and land-use policies. In examining the factors that affect county economic growth, several key findings emerge: this study examines how counties balance energy extraction and development of amenities on their lands. It is important to note, however, that a county possesses only limited authority with respect to development issues; many dimensions of development lie outside of the county domain at the state or national levels.

**Keywords:** economic development, rural development, local government, energy economics, amenity economics

## 1. Introduction

Many areas of the United States that were previously largely rural have been and continue to be transformed by population growth and increases in the production of oil and natural gas. As a result of population increases cities have grown and expanded and are now abutting areas set aside for forests, national parks, and areas meant to "be held in public ownership because of their other resource values" [1, 2]. This expansion has contributed to growing levels of recreation on many public lands, which foster economic expansion based on those amenities. At the same time, advances in energy extraction, particularly hydraulic fracturing, has made it possible to extract oil and gas from many areas that were previously not economically or technologically feasible.

Throughout this chapter the terms "energy extraction," "energy resources," and "energy development" are used to refer to the exploration and/or production of oil and natural gas. The term "amenity development" was chosen to describe a variety of activities that contribute to the natural attractiveness and value of a given area, including wilderness or other designated lands, recreation opportunities in



IntechOpen

those areas, and agricultural activity. The use of the term "amenity" as a means to describe areas with the presence of natural features comes from the Natural Amenities Scale created by the U.S. Department of Agriculture (USDA), which originally guided our decisions regarding what amenities to describe in this report [3]. The term "amenities" is commonly used to refer to the types of areas and activities discussed in this report, such as "clean beaches, hunting and fishing opportunities, forests to hike in, the view of green farmlands, and clean rivers for recreating in" [4].

It has become common to view energy development and amenity development as mutually exclusive, though this view is by no means dominant in the scholarly literature. This chapter explores the degree to which the two types of activities can coexist and make positive contributions to a county's economic well-being. Three case studies that explore land use and economic outcomes across the spectrum of the energy/amenity plane are presented.

Counties were selected by region based largely on their blend of energy extraction and amenity development. The cases were chosen to illustrate the choices and trade-offs encountered when deciding whether to develop energy, amenities, or both.

### 1.1 Understanding divergent claims about the role of energy and amenities in economic development

There has always been debate about how best to develop energy and amenity resources within a county. Opponents of energy development often argue that the oil and gas industry cannot coexist with amenity-based industries. Further, some argue that amenity activities create better economic and employment opportunities than do extraction activities on public or protected lands.

This view that places amenities and energy extraction in conflict has been in part based on research that extrapolates from the positive correlations between amenity resources and economic growth. For example, using the USDA's Natural Amenities Scale, Gebremariam et al. [5] finds a positive although not statistically significant relationship between employment growth rates and a county's amenity rating and it and other similar literature has been used to suggest that that amenity development must occur without extractive industries. Further those extrapolations have suggested that "footloose" entrepreneurs are moving to areas with access to outdoor recreation and avoid those with extractive industries [6–10].

The evidence, however, is far from conclusive on the role amenities play in economic growth. One widely cited article found no evidence that federal wilderness designations within a county affected population-density or total employment-density growth in the Intermountain West during the 1980s [11, 12]. Further, counties with designated wilderness areas appear to be held back by relatively low-wage and seasonal service-sector jobs [13, 14] Perhaps because of this, counties with primarily amenity-based growth rarely develop into economically and socially vibrant communities [14].

Further, research by Yonk, Simmons, and Steed [15] finds "a significant negative relationship between the presence of [designated wilderness lands] in county total payroll, county tax receipts, and county average household income."

Though some research promotes one type of development as preferable to another, a more nuanced reading of the literature suggests that counties that try to balance energy extraction activities and amenity development have healthier economies [10, 14, 16].

This chapter is part of a larger project identified five states/regions as having counties with varying levels of energy and amenity development: California,

Colorado, Utah, the Northern Rockies, and the Northern Plains, during a period of high oil and gas production, namely the period through 2013. This chapter presents three cases from the Northern Rockies Region, but the full set of cases is available on request.

### 1.2 Data

The data used in this study came primarily from the U.S. Census Bureau and the Bureau of Labor Statistics (BLS). For each case study, data from 2001 through 2011 were compiled on a variety of economic indicators ranging from average annual pay to employment by industry sector. Data were also gathered from the U.S. Geological Survey (USGS), U.S. Energy Information Agency (EIA), and USDA. Other quantitative data, such as tax revenues raised from energy extraction industries, were collected by placing calls to county officials and accessing data on state and county websites.

Qualitative data was gathered from a variety of sources including local newspapers, environmental group publications, and county websites. Personal interviews of local residents were also used when possible to explore local reactions to development in each county over time and to illustrate how development had influenced the lives of residents.

## 2. The Northern Rockies

The states of Montana and Wyoming make up the Northern Rockies area. In these states, whose landscapes and economies are diverse and varied, this study examines Teton County and Sublette County in Wyoming, and Sheridan County in Montana. In the Northern Rockies, the oil and gas industry and the tax revenues it generates play an important role in some county economies. The following cases explore the relationship between amenity development and energy extraction.

### 2.1 Economic development in the Northern Rockies

Amenities play an important role in Teton County, which has no energy extraction activities. While there are considerable amenity resources in Sublette County, they play a small role in the economy relative to oil and gas. Sublette County is the quintessential boomtown and demonstrates the rapid growth that can result during the start of energy extraction activities. Small, rural communities like Sheridan County rely heavily on tax revenues from the oil and gas industry to cover the costs of its school systems and other services.

Sublette County is most focused on energy development, Sheridan County more balanced, and Teton County currently without active oil and gas development. In Wyoming, the oil and gas industry supported[1] 61,065 jobs and contributed $7 billion to the state economy in 2009. The average salary of oil and natural gas workers in Wyoming is $74,538, which is $33,200 higher than the state average of $41,258 [17].

Similar economic benefits are observed in Montana, where 40,276 jobs were supported[2] by energy extraction in 2009, and $4 billion was contributed to the state economy. The average salary of oil and natural gas workers in Montana is $72,886, which is much higher than the state average of $33,244 [18].

[1] This support includes direct, indirect, and induced jobs.

[2] This support includes direct, indirect, and induced jobs.

**Table 1** shows that in Sublette and Sheridan counties, average annual pay (reported in nominal dollars) in the upstream oil and gas sector is significantly higher than in the sectors of hospitality and recreation, and agriculture. Teton County does not have pay information in upstream oil and gas due to the lack of petroleum activity, but its hospitality and recreation workers earn slightly more than workers in this same sector in Sublette and Sheridan counties.

**Table 2** shows employment by sector for the civilian employed population over age 16 in Sheridan, Teton, and Sublette counties. Employment in oil and gas is included in the agriculture, forestry, fishing and hunting, and mining sector. As the table shows, Sublette County has the highest percentage employed in this sector. Sheridan County's employment is more mixed, while Teton County has the highest percentage (25.11%) employed in the arts, entertainment, recreation, accommodation, and food services sector.

Small communities in the Northern Rockies often rely on the natural resources available in the county for developing their economic base. This dependence can lead to an uncertain economic climate and cyclical employment, regardless of the natural resources that are being developed. By diversifying their economies,

| | Upstream Oil and Gas | | Hospitality and Recreation | | Agriculture | |
|---|---|---|---|---|---|---|
| | Employment | Average Annual Pay | Employment | Average Annual Pay | Employment | Average Annual Pay |
| Sublette, WY | 1,408 | $ 76,947 | 458 | $ 22,858 | 72 | $ 34,715 |
| Sheridan, MT | 23 | $ 46,913 | 152 | $ 13,743 | 12 | $ 26,752 |
| Teton, WY | | | 6,633 | $ 24,896 | | |

*Source: BLS 2011*

**Table 1.**
*Employment and average annual pay.*

| | Sheridan | Montana | Teton | Sublette | Wyoming |
|---|---|---|---|---|---|
| Agriculture, forestry, fishing and hunting, and mining (oil and gas is included in this sector) | 20.9% | 7.10% | 3.60% | 32.70% | 11.8% |
| Construction | 8.80% | 8.50% | 13.30% | 10.10% | 8.7% |
| Manufacturing | 1.50% | 4.80% | 1.40% | 1.70% | 5.00% |
| Wholesale trade | 1.70% | 2.70% | 0.80% | 0.70% | 2.20% |
| Retail trade | 11.90% | 12.30% | 8.60% | 8.70% | 11.20% |
| Transportation, warehousing, utilities | 8.60% | 5.00% | 3.90% | 5.60% | 6.60% |
| Information | 1.80% | 1.90% | 2.30% | 1% | 1.70% |
| Finance, insurance, real estate | 6% | 5.69% | 7.66% | 2.30% | 4.42% |
| Professional, scientific management, administrative | 3.88% | 8.14% | 10.97% | 6.20% | 6.55% |
| Educational services, health care, and social assistance | 18.78% | 22.42% | 17.17% | 15.50% | 21.96% |
| Arts, entertainment, recreation, accommodation, and food services | 5.59% | 10.57% | 25.11% | 6.50% | 9.25% |
| Public administration | 5.53% | 4.71% | 3.17% | 4% | 4.26% |
| Other services | 4.89% | 6.11% | 2.13% | 4.90% | 6.41% |

**Table 2.**
*Percent of the civilian population employed by sector.*

communities in the Northern Rockies may improve economic outcomes and reduce the magnitude of cyclical fluctuations.

## 3. Sublette County, Wyoming

Sublette County residents are experiencing the benefits and challenges that come with developing energy and amenity resources in a -rural economy. Surrounded on three sides by wilderness and national forest lands, Sublette County has many amenity opportunities. The county also has concentrated pockets of oil and gas drilling. Both of these industries contribute to the economy, albeit in different ways. County Commissioner Joel Bousman describes the current economic climate of Sublette County as both “exciting and challenging” [19].

Sublette is a small ranching community southeast of Jackson Hole. It has only 6000 residents [20]. The county is part of rural Wyoming—there are no stoplights anywhere in the county—where suburban developments are separated by hundreds of miles. A petroleum boom in the county has driven economic growth. While some drawbacks have accompanied this growth, including a reliance on a non-resident workforce and rising costs of living, Sublette County demonstrates the important role that the oil and gas industry can play in providing tax revenue and boosting the economy.

Oil and natural gas extraction occurs away from areas of the county where designated federal lands and wilderness amenities are located. Most extractive activities occur on lands administered by BLM and non-federal lands in the central and southern parts of the county. Parts of the Bridger Wilderness, Teton National Forest, Gros Ventre Wilderness, and Bridger National Forest are located within Sublette County, as well as some Bureau of Reclamation lands.

### 3.1 Energy development

The Pinedale Anticline Project Area consists of about 197,000 acres in central Sublette County and is the third largest gas field in the United States [21, 22]. The BLM operates 80% of the anticline’s surface. The remaining 20% is divided between the State of Wyoming (5%) and private ownership (15%). Gas reserves in the field are estimated at 40 trillion cubic feet, and the area is one of the most productive fields in the United States [21]. Operators first drilled there in 1939 looking for oil, but abandoned the site when they found gas instead. Subsequent activity in the field was difficult because the tight sandstone formations made conventional drilling methods nearly impossible. However, thanks to improvements in technology and high prices for natural gas in the early 2000s, extraction in the Pinedale Anticline began to flourish. Today, Shell, Ultra Petroleum, and QEP Energy are primary leaseholders in the field. Shell alone has “drilled more than 400 natural gas wells, operating 21,000 acres and producing 350 million cubic feet of natural gas per day” [22].

The Jonah Field, near the Pinedale Anticline, has a similar geographical makeup and was rediscovered in the early 1990s. It is considered one of the most significant recent natural gas discoveries. Covering 21,000 acres, the field is estimated to contain approximately 10.5 trillion cubic feet of natural gas, with 98% of the field managed by the BLM and the remaining portion split between state and private ownership [21].

Production in the Pinedale and Jonah fields began slowly as pipelines and infrastructure were needed to support significant production. However, once the infrastructure was in place, there was a jump from 150 wells in 1999 to 300 wells by July 2001 [21]. This, combined with advances in technology and new methods of extraction, such as hydraulic fracturing, created a boom in gas production from these previously unproductive fields. During the 2008 recession, natural gas prices fell, reducing drilling activities in a slowdown that has persisted since [21].

Oil production in the county grew steadily from 2000 until 2009, peaking just below 8 billion barrels in 2009. Production has dropped off since 2009 to 6.8 million barrels of oil in 2012 [23].

Gas production, has experienced growth similar to oil. Production grew from 2000 to 2010, peaking at 1.2 TCF. Production has since declined, falling to a little under 1.1 TCF in 2012 [23].

### 3.2 Amenity development

In addition to its oil and natural gas resources, Sublette County has numerous amenity opportunities. Over 80% of Sublette County's lands are public [24] Sublette County includes parts of the Bridger National Forest, Bridger Wilderness, Gros Ventre Wilderness, and the Teton National Forest. The Wind River Mountains are also part of the county. The highest peak in Wyoming, Gannett Peak, along with 14 of the state's highest peaks, provides ample opportunities for hiking and recreation [25].

Freemont Lake, Wyoming's second largest natural lake and the seventh deepest in the United States, is located in the county, along with nearly 1300 other lakes, providing fishing and water recreation opportunities. Sublette County is home to more active glacial fields in the contiguous United States than any other county [20]. Big game from the Yellowstone ecosystem winters in the northern part of the county [26]. The natural environment of the county is ideal for backpacking, hiking, biking, four-wheeling, snowmobiling, golfing, hunting, skiing, and wildlife viewing.

Built in 1897, the Gros Ventre Lodge is believed to have been the first full-time dude ranch in Wyoming. Ranching became an industry in Sublette County after 1877, once the railroad made the shipping of stock possible from Wyoming to Oregon [25]. Some of the rancher families that first settled Sublette are still ranching in the county today, five or six generations later [27]. Ranchers continue to walk their cattle along the Green River drift, in use since 1896, to move their herd from summer to winter grazing areas [27].

### 3.3 Economic indicators

Ranching remained the primary source of economic activity in Sublette County until recently, when the petroleum boom caused a shift in the economy. Today, the county describes its major industries as oil and gas, tourism, recreation, and government [28]. Oil and natural gas provide the largest share of the county's revenue.

Increasing demand for natural gas dramatically changed Sublette County's economy. From 2000 to 2005, Sublette County's permanent population grew by 20% and 500 new homes were built [29]. By 2007, 50% of those employed in the county worked in the natural gas industry. Of dollar spent in the county, 50 cents was directly tied to the natural gas industry [29]. This growth spiked the median household income to $70,147 in 2010, 30% higher than the state average. This also reduced the poverty level to less than half of the state average [30]. Today, energy extraction remains an important economic base for Sublette County.

Between 2001 and 2006, sales tax revenue in Sublette County increased by 271%, while use tax revenue increased by over 300% [31]. The mining industry, which includes oil and gas activity, accounted for 51% of the sales tax revenue and 45.6%

of the use tax revenue [31]. In 2006, despite its low population, Sublette County ranked sixth in the state for tax revenue generation and fifth for total taxable sales transactions. Sublette County accounts for 6.5% of sales and use tax revenue in the state and 7.21% of total sales activity in the state [31].

Sublette County sees large contributions to its budget from oil and gas companies. In 2012 oil and gas companies comprised the top 10 taxpayers in Sublette County, with a total assessed value of $3.9 billion [31]. Energy companies in Sublette paid $1.1 billion in taxes on oil and gas production in 2008 and Sublette County and its municipalities received 5.86% of that revenue [19]. Also in 2012, Sublette collected almost $31 million in sales tax from the mining industry, which includes oil and gas. These revenues offset the costs associated with increased energy development. Funding for infrastructure improvements has been identified as the biggest challenge facing local governments in Sublette County [19].

Tax revenue is also generated by the recreation and hospitality sector, though not to the same magnitude as the oil and gas industry. In 2012 agriculture, forestry, fishing and hunting contributed $1523 in sales taxes to Sublette County [32]. The leisure and hospitality sector meanwhile contributed almost $985,000 in sales taxes the same year (p. 27). In 2012 the retail trade, accommodation, and food services sector generated nearly $8.3 million in sales tax revenue for the county [32]. Only Pinedale, Sublette County's seat, imposes a lodging tax, for which it collected about $200,000 in revenue in 2012 [32].

Employment in upstream oil and gas, although only recently publicly available, is much higher than that of agriculture or hospitality and recreation. With over 1400 employees, upstream oil and gas employed 950 more people than did the hospitality and recreation sector in 2011. Employment in hospitality and recreation grew from 2001 to 2006 by 190 employees, but has since slightly declined, employing about 460 people in 2011. Employment in agriculture has been quite steady, with an average of 75 employees [33].

With the advent of energy extraction activity in Sublette County, the nature of employment and wages has changed drastically. For example, before the natural gas boom in the early 2000s, seasonal unemployment was high due to the county's focus on tourism, agriculture, and ranching. Since 2000, however, these fluctuations have been greatly reduced [34]. Sublette County's unemployment rate was has hovered around 4% Wages in the petroleum industry are now some of the highest in Sublette County, even for unskilled workers, and ample opportunities exist for wage advancement and overtime [34]. The cost of living in Sublette County, however, is about 19% higher than the rest of Wyoming, and second only to Teton County [35]. Those employed in upstream oil and gas make far more annually than those employed in amenity sectors—almost three times as much in years for which data is available.

Just over 32.7% of Sublette County's civilian population over age 16 is employed in agriculture, forestry, fishing and hunting, and mining, of which oil and gas is a subset. This percentage is much higher than the Wyoming average of 11.8% for employment in the same sector. Employment in arts, entertainment, recreation, accommodation, and food services at 6.6% is lower in Sublette County than in the state [33].

### 3.4 Development strategies

Sublette County is an example of an area with a booming energy industry that has not detracted from amenity development. The county retains its strong amenity sector thanks to its many natural attractions and its conscious development policies. Mary Lynn Worl, a board member of Wyoming's Citizens United for Responsible Energy

Development, said, "We don't believe that public health and the quality of life in our communities need to be traded away for economic activity. We can have both" [36].

With the arrival of the oil and natural gas boom, Sublette County has seen many positive changes. The county has collected millions of tax dollars as a result of petroleum production, which is money that can be spent on community improvement projects and infrastructure—projects that improve the county now as well as help develop the area for future potential enterprises. Numerous jobs have been created for local residents, and companies active in Sublette County's gas fields have invested heavily in organizations serving the community and improving the environment [21]. Many of these activities have sprung up out of necessity to lessen the impacts of energy development on the environment. For example, a portion of the increased tax revenue the county receives is used to build infrastructure such as underground pipelines for material transport, lessening the need for above-ground transport and its impacts on the community [21].

Energy development has also brought changes to Sublette County's local community. Housing, schools, and public services like law enforcement and health care, have been stretched thin as a large, primarily non-resident and temporary workforce has moved into the community [21]. The county has been able to adjust fairly well to the increased non-resident and temporary workforce, however, and private sector housing and services have experienced rapid growth in response to the increased demand [21]. The petroleum companies operating in Sublette have contributed to the community by funding infrastructure such as road improvement, a drug counseling center, a domestic abuse shelter, a new sheriff's office and jail, and an indoor community swimming pool [26]. Further, natural gas workers book nearly 75% of hotel rooms, helping hoteliers during the winter months [29].

The natural gas boom in Sublette has impacted the environment, but the impacts are being addressed. Though air pollution has significantly increased since 2005 [37], air quality monitoring is now required and actions are in place to help reduce the problem. Companies have generally been responsive to the ozone advisories, reducing or suspending operations until the advisories end. Although natural gas production increased 8% from 2008 to 2010, emissions actually decreased, attributable to increased regulation and voluntary actions from the industry [38].

Wildlife in the county is also being impacted by the development. The Pinedale Anticline includes important migration corridors and habitat for species such as mule deer, pronghorn antelope, pygmy rabbits, sage grouse, and bald eagles [22]. To mitigate impacts, wells were initially required to be 80 acres apart. Since then however, spacing has been reduced to 5 acres between some wells [26]. Ongoing efforts to mitigate impact have led many companies to use directional drilling. Directional drilling concentrates several wells in a single site to reduce the need for roads and reduces the number of pad sites. These efforts have resulted in 70% fewer roads and 100 fewer well pads [21].

Sublette County has certainly faced, and will continue to face, tradeoffs between a healthy outdoor amenity sector and energy development. The advent of natural gas development in Sublette County has brought some challenges, but it has also greatly lifted the county's economy and led to many positive economic outcomes. Sublette County continues to learn how to manage the tradeoffs in order to continue to see energy and amenities develop together, bolstering the county economy.

## 4. Sheridan County, Montana

Sheridan County is a small, rural community located in the northeastern corner of Montana. Sheridan County's economy is focused on oil and gas and agriculture, with a brief yearly economic boost during the hunting season. Flat and largely treeless, Sheridan County attracts few tourists. The majority of the land is private, with about 14% under the jurisdiction of the federal government or Native American Tribes [39]. The county's history demonstrates the vital role the oil and gas industry plays in rural communities, particularly where amenity development is not a viable economic option. The county population and employment trends closely follow the cyclical booms and busts of the local oil and gas industry [40].

Continued expansion of drilling in the Bakken Shale formation, which extends into Sheridan County, presents the single biggest potential for economic growth in the area. Very little of Sheridan County's land area is federally owned. Medicine Lake National Wildlife Refuge and Medicine Lake Wilderness are the exceptions, and both are located in the southeastern portion of the county.

### 4.1 Energy development

Oil was first discovered in Sheridan County in 1951, and the county experienced its first oil boom from the late 1950s into the early 1960s. As demand later declined, so did the county's production. Oil output in Sheridan County flattened again through the late 1970s and then peaked in 1985. After 1985 the area's oil industry entered a period of long decline that has continued until the present day. The county's negative population growth correlates with the drop in oil production. Population peaked around 1985 at about 5800 people, fell to a low of approximately 3200 around 2007, and has since recovered slightly; the county population is now about 3400 [39].

Oil production varied slightly between 2000 and 2007 and declined after 2008, though there was slight growth from 2011 to 2012. In 2011 Sheridan County produced nearly 1.3 million barrels of oil and in 2012 production increased to 1.4 million barrels [40]. This accounted for about 5% of total oil production in Montana in 2012 [40].

Along with oil, Sheridan County also produces natural gas. Gas production reached a high, during the decade shown, of 997.6 million cubic feet of gas in 2002. Sheridan County's gas production has trended downward and substantially declined after 2007, reaching 511.3 million cubic feet in 2012, representing only about 2.5% of total gas production in the state that year [40].

Sheridan County is geographically similar to the neighboring counties of Daniels and Roosevelt, but has historically produced more oil and gas than either of them. In the past few years, however, Roosevelt County has significantly increased its production of oil, surpassing Sheridan County. This change is due to activity in Roosevelt County in the Bakken Shale formation. Though Sheridan County is also geographically part of the formation, County Commissioner Bill Nyby reports that they have not yet begun energy extraction operations in the county Companies, however, have already begun purchasing land in the area in preparation for future development, and one company has acquired as much as 24,000 acres there [41]. With farming and trade in decline, future expansion of Bakken Shale oil and gas extraction into Sheridan County is the single largest potential source of economic growth for the county.

### 4.2 Amenity development

Sheridan County has limited amenity opportunities, though the county does have a few attractions. The county has the fifth largest population of white pelicans and 225 other bird species. Many of these bird species reside in Medicine Lake National Wildlife Refuge. The site is a sanctuary for duck and geese populations, and serves as a breeding habitat for the migrating waterfowl [42]. Administered by the USFWS, the refuge reported 16,000 visitors in 2004 [43]. The refuge's most popular attractions are the nature trails and observation platforms. Hunting and fishing is also prevalent on the land, and attracted 3000 visitors also in 2004 [43].

Brush Lake State Park, also known as "Oasis on the Prairie," is a spring-fed lake that became a state park in 2003 [44]. The lake is less than 300 acres, but is popular with locals for water sports [45].

Because Sheridan County is very rural, it does not boast the same visitation as other counties profiled in this report. It is expected the county will have a difficult time attracting the large number of tourists seen in Teton County, for example, due to the lack of internationally—or even nationally—known landmarks.

Though the tourism industry is limited, Sheridan County does have agricultural activities. There were 1.06 million acres of land in farms in the county in 2007—almost 98% of the county's total 1.09 million acres [46]. Three quarters of the land in the county is tillable land, with soil that is of glacier origin, which makes it ideal for grain production Sheridan County's agricultural sector produces mostly durum wheat, which is used in pastas and cereals, and also has significant lentil and dry edible peas production. Each year the county hosts a Farm Expo, which brings together farmers from Montana and Canada for seminars, a Farm and Ranch Appreciation Breakfast, and a bread fair for kids [47].

### 4.3 Economic indicators

U.S. Census Bureau data shows that the number of individuals employed in the agricultural sector has decreased significantly over time, from 2352 individuals in 1978 (a full 40% of county residents at the time) to only 648 individuals in 2005 (only 18% of residents that year) [39].

Sheridan County has seen significant growth in tax revenues from the petroleum industry. Nyby reported that revenues have increased significantly in the past 10 years, despite a decrease in gas production. In 2003 Sheridan County received just over $5 million in revenues from the petroleum industry, and by 2011 that number had increased to nearly $11 million. Between 2003 and 2011, Sheridan County received a total of $90 million in revenues from petroleum, $23 million of which was specifically allocated to county schools Tax revenues represent an important benefit that oil and gas development bring to Sheridan County. Future development of the Bakken Shale formation would likely increase these revenues even more, bringing added benefits to the local economy.

The oil and gas industry makes up a small but significant portion of employment in Sheridan County. In Sheridan County nearly 21% of employment is in this sector. That number is nearly three times the state average of 7.10%, and reflects the importance of extractive industries and agriculture within Sheridan County. Only 5.59% of the county's employment was in arts, entertainment, recreation, accommodation, and food services; that number is much lower than the state average of 10.57%, reflecting the county's limited amenity development.

Oil and gas production has a significant impact on workers the county in the form of higher average annual pay. Average annual pay in the upstream oil and gas sector is much higher than annual pay in agriculture or hospitality and recreation. Hospitality and recreation saw a pay increase of about $4000 from 2009 to 2011. In recent years, average annual pay in oil and gas has also moved upwards, increasing by $6500 from 2010 to 2011, while pay has decreased slightly in agriculture. In 2011 average annual pay for upstream oil and gas workers was about three times the average annual pay for hospitality and recreation [48].

### 4.4 Development strategies

Sheridan County has chosen a development path consistent with its resource endowments and has both energy and amenity development. The county participates in programs like the state-funded Reclamation and Development Grants Program (RDGP), a portion of which is funded by oil and gas taxes. The RDGP allows Montana communities, counties, universities, conservation districts, and others to apply for funding to complete projects that "indemnify the people of the state for the effects of mineral development on public resources" [49].

In Sheridan County, extractive industries have developed alongside the county's natural amenities, mainly its agricultural sector as Sheridan County's other amenity potential is limited. Some oil and gas development is occurring alongside amenity development (e.g. in the Medicine Lake National Wildlife Refuge).

With little opportunity to develop amenities and decreasing trade, oil and gas production is expected to become more prominent in the Sheridan County economy. Oil and gas production brings in millions of dollars in tax revenue each year. Although decreased production in the past has proved challenging to the county, Sheridan potentially could gain enormously from expanding development of extractive industries in the Bakken Shale formation.

## 5. Teton County, Wyoming

Located in the northwestern corner of Wyoming, Teton County was established as a small ranching community at the base of the majestic Teton Mountain Range. The area remained primarily ranching land until the creation of Teton National Park in 1929, when economic focus shifted from ranching to tourism and recreation. The county contains many protected public lands, including national parks, national forests, wilderness areas, and a wildlife refuge. Federal lands, which include Grand Teton National Park, Targhee National Forest, Teton National Forest, the National Elk Refuge, Jackson Lake, the Gros Ventre Wilderness, the Teton Wilderness, and over 40% of Yellowstone Park are located in the county. These public lands comprise 97% of the county, private lands make up the remaining 3% [50]. Because Teton County is overwhelmingly owned by the federal government, county officials have limited influence over what happens in their county and instead are subject to decisions at the federal level.

Natural recreation sites within Teton County attract more than 2.7 million visitors each year, fueling the area's tourism and amenity-based economy [51]. During the winter, local ski resorts attract tourists; however, the majority of visitors come to Teton County in the summer months. This seasonal cycle of tourism can be difficult for the county economy; this is an issue that faces many counties with single-focus economies, including counties that focus exclusively on oil and gas development. While not as predictable as seasonal cycles, the oil and gas sector also faces boom and bust periods. Teton County has no active oil and gas activity, which is not surprising based on its land composition.

### 5.1 Energy development

According to data from the Wyoming Oil and Gas Conservation Commission, there are no active oil and gas wells or visible potential for petroleum development in Teton County [23]. Additionally, even if gas and oil resources were found in Teton County, it could be difficult to access because 97% of Teton County consists of protected federal lands.

### 5.2 Amenity development

With Grand Teton National Park, John D. Rockefeller National Monument, and large portions of Yellowstone National Park all located within Teton County, there is a large seasonal influx of tourists. During the months of June, July, and August, Teton County receives the most visitors; these months are the most popular time to visit Teton County to take advantage of the many outdoor recreation opportunities, like hiking and camping, that the county offers [52].

Visitation to Grand Teton National Park increased almost every year from 1952 to 1970. After 1970 visitation was more variable and dropped significantly from 1983 to 1992. After 1992 visitation picked up and remained fairly constant with visitation dipping below 2.5 million only 5 years between 1992 and 2010 [51].

The Grand Teton National Park is located in central Teton County. The national park offers backcountry camping, rock climbing, and cross-country skiing. The truly adventurous can climb the granite summit of the Grand Teton that rises 13,770 feet above sea level [53]. Visitors can also hike, boat, fish, kayak, and photograph the mountain scenery. This national park is also home to over 300 species of birds, 6 species of game fish, and 60 mammal species [53]. Within this park is a portion of the Snake River offering world-class fishing, as well as 11 lakes that allow recreation, ranging from jet skiing to windsurfing [54]. In the winter the visitors can enjoy private Snowcat rentals, snowshoeing, backcountry and snowmobile tours, sleigh ride dinners, and skiing and snowboarding on the Grand Tetons [55].

In 1972 Congress created the John D. Rockefeller Jr. Memorial Parkway between Grand Teton National Park and Yellowstone National Park. Grand Teton National Park administers this parkway. The sloping hills at the end of the Teton Range characterize this parkway and provide "a natural link between the two national parks," as these slopes give way to the volcanic flows of Yellowstone [56].

Yellowstone National Park is one of America's most iconic national parks. Designated as a National Park in 1872, Yellowstone is considered by some to be a "living museum," and covers over 2.2 million acres in Wyoming, Montana, and Idaho [56]. The most famous sites inside the national park include Old Faithful, Lower Falls, and Yellowstone Lake. Visitors are cautioned to drive slowly and plan extra time to account for wildlife that often crosses the roads within the park [56]. Visitation to the national park has generally increased since 1946. In 2010 the park saw a record 3.6 million visitors [56].

Yellowstone offers activities outside of those normally offered within a park including pack trips, stagecoach rides, and old west cookouts. More traditional national park activities are also offered; visitors can hike, view wildlife, take horseback tours, fish, and boat. In the winter, when road conditions allow, visitors can cross-country ski and snowshoe. Visitors who want to stay within the park have lodging options that offer more amenities than a traditional campground, although that option is also available; within the park there are eight hotels or cabins [56].

Teton County also has the National Elk Refuge, which celebrated its centennial in 2012 [57]. Composed of almost 25,000 acres, this reserve has been designated to conserve the Jackson elk population after development in the late 1800s pushed the animals out of their traditional habitat into much more difficult terrain [57].

Jackson Hole, Wyoming, is a popular, year-round destination in Teton County. This area includes the Jackson Hole Mountain Resort with an average of 459 inches of snow each year [58]. The city of Jackson has over 20 art galleries, restaurants that have been featured on the Food Network, and is home to the Grand Teton Music Festival, during which live broadcasts from the Met Opera in Manhattan are shown to "complement the flow downslope" of the Tetons [59]. Overall, Teton County hosts almost every recreation activity available in the western United States, and Jackson Hole offers a small-town, yet urban vibe.

### 5.3 Economic indicators

Teton County's primary economic focus has been, and will continue to be, tourism encouraged by its abundant natural amenities. The county's vision is to "preserve and protect the area's ecosystem in order to ensure a healthy environment, community, and economy" [60]. This focus on tourism provides important jobs and revenue to the county, and also brings some challenges, such as low-wages and seasonality [61].

The unemployment rate spikes in Teton County during the winter months, reflecting the seasonal nature of the tourism industry. Sublette County's unemployment rate, also shown on the graph, is much more stable, reflecting its more balanced economy that does not rely so heavily on seasonal industries. When tourism hits its peak in July, with a visitor count of about 643,000, county employment also reaches its peak with almost 21,000 employees [48]. As visitors to the county increase, seasonal jobs are created; however, at the end of the season the visitor count decreases and the demand for seasonal jobs declines.

One notable aspect of the seasonal job growth and off-season decline is the attraction of non-resident employees to the area. In fact, seasonal jobs offered by Teton County attract nearly 5000 out-of-state employees [60]. Seasonal, non-resident employees tend to spend their wages outside of Teton County, mostly benefitting the communities where these employees live (though some do reside in the county during their working period), and Teton County is unable to capture the potential benefits these jobs create in the form of tax revenues. Aiming to increase both year-round occupancy and visitor spending to capture more benefits within the county, Teton County is working to attract more second home owners and retirees to their communities [60].

Recognizing the need for greater stability, the Teton County Planning Commission, in conjunction with Jackson County, included "[promoting] a stable and diverse economy" as one of its principles in the 2012 comprehensive county plan (the county plan focuses on the 3% of land in the county that is private). The commission is careful to note, however, that "tourism will continue to be the basis of our economy," and aims to create more stability and diversification by enhancing tourism, encouraging local entrepreneurial opportunities (particularly "green" opportunities), and promoting "light industry" [60]. The goal is to "develop the existing economy to be better, not necessarily bigger" [60].

The hospitality and recreation sector has grown for the majority of the decade. Employment began with about 5500 individuals in 2001 and grew to almost 7000 in 2008. After a decrease of over 500 employees in 2009 this sector grew slightly to 6600 employees in 2012 [48].

In 2010 one quarter of Teton County's civilian employees over the age of 16 were employed in the arts, entertainment, recreation, accommodation and food services sector; this is almost 16% higher than the state average. Teton County also has significant portions of its civilians employed in the construction; professional scientific, management, administrative, and waste management; and education services, health care, and social assistance sectors [48].

Although hospitality and recreation provides more jobs in Teton County than does agriculture, employees in hospitality and recreation earn lower wages than those working in agriculture. Over the decade, those employed in hospitality and recreation did see steadily increasing wages, from just over $17,000 in 2001 to just under $25,000 7 years later, though this data is reported in nominal dollars and has not been adjusted for inflation. Since 2008 wages have remained fairly static for this sector. Though limited data is available for the agriculture sector, average annual pay here appears to have been growing in recent years.

In 2012 Teton County collected almost $41 million in taxes from retail, trade, accommodation and food services sectors, nearly $11.7 million of which came from accommodation alone [32].

### 5.4 Development strategies

Teton County has developed a vibrant community with well-known amenities that attract millions of tourists each year. The Teton County Commission believes, however, that the county would benefit by diversifying the tourism industry that has grown out of what was once a small ranch community [60]. In order to maintain their community's roots and grow the economy, officials have developed a plan for growth that focuses on ecosystem stewardship, growth management, and quality of life [60]. Officials are using existing policy tools to protect wildlife habitats, natural skylines, and sustainability programs. Additionally, county officials work closely with towns to ensure that there is affordable housing and "year-round lifestyle-based tourism" that will create a more insulated economy [60]. Diversification of the economy would create jobs valuable to the local community [61]. Teton County demonstrates that county economic growth can occur in a way that is consistent with the community's character and resources.

## 6. Developing together energy and amenities

The factors that lead to economic growth at the county level are not always easy to identify or explain, though surely both energy and amenity resources can influence county growth. However, there are many other factors that can also influence growth, such as amenities in surrounding counties, the specifics of oil and gas development, and land-use policies. In examining the factors that affect county economic growth, several key findings emerge:

This study examines how counties balance energy extraction and development of amenities on their lands. It is important to note, however, that a county possesses only limited authority with respect to development issues; many dimensions of development lie outside of the county domain at the state or national levels.

Finding One: Counties tend to develop both energy extraction and amenity resources when possible.

Finding Two: In cases in which a county focuses exclusively on either energy or amenity development, it is usually because of constraints beyond the control of that county (e.g., a lack of natural amenities or land-use policy that prohibits energy exploration) and not because the county considers exclusivity the best option.

Finding Three: Energy extraction can directly advance the development of amenities.

Finding Four: The energy and amenity sectors can both be cyclical, although they tend to follow different cycles.

Finding Five: Energy extraction operations offer higher-paying jobs, while hospitality and recreation operations employ greater numbers of people. A county's economic well-being depends on having both high-paying jobs and a large number of jobs.

Across all our cases show consistent evidence that that energy and amenity development are not mutually exclusive. Further the evidence suggests the prominence of one industry over another is less a result of through planning and conscious choice but is more closely related to the geographic and resource endowment the county has. Further the cases we reviewed show that the development of one sector does not necessarily inherently limit growth in the other sector if a county has resource endowments in both areas.

Further because both energy and amenity resources provide value to a county, when counties have both resources they tend to develop both, and in a way that allows both sectors to grow. Further, energy development can directly promote the amenity sector by providing counties the funding necessary to develop and market available amenities. Together, these two sectors can comprise an integral part of a county's economy. They provide an employment base with diverse pay and employment levels, and they expand local revenue streams, which help furnish needed local resources like infrastructure and improved government services.

## Acknowledgements

I would like to acknowledge the collaboration of Dr. Randy T Simmons on earlier reports that this chapter is drawn from and to Kayla Dawn Harris that lead a team of student research assistants that were invaluable in helping gather the data and information on which this chapter is based. Those students included Nicholas Hilton, Jordan Carl Hunt, and Justin Larsen.

## Author details

Ryan M. Yonk[1,2]*

1 North Dakota State University, Fargo, North Dakota, United States of America

2 Rural Policy and Public Lands Institute, Utah, United States of America

*Address all correspondence to: ryan.yonk@ndsu.edu

## References

[1] Bureau of Land Management. A Long and Varied History. 2011. Retrieved from: http://www.blm.gov/wo/st/en/info/About_BLM/History.html

[2] Bureau of Land Mangement. Meeting the Challenge: Recreation on Public Lands. Retrieved from: http://www.blm.gov/pgdata/etc/medialib/blm/wo/Planning_and_Renewable_Resources/recreation_images/national_recreation/planning.Par.0634.File.dat/Rec%20trends%20&%20challenges%20-AORE%20-%2011-15%20web%20version.pdf

[3] United States Fish and Wildlife Service [USFWS]. Bitter Creek National Wildlife Refuge. 2012. Retrieved from: http://www.fws.gov/hoppermountain/BitterCreekNWR/BittercreekNWR.html

[4] Crandall M. Natural Resources and Amenities. Rural Communities Explorer. 2008. Retrieved from: http://oregonexplorer.info/rural/RuralIssues/NaturalResources

[5] Gerbremariam GH, Gebremedhin TG, Schaeffer PV, Jackson RW, Phipps TT. An empirical analysis of employment, migration, local public services, and regional income growth in appalachia. In: Presented at Northerneastern Agricultural and Resource Economic Association. Rehoboth Beach, Delaware; June 10-13, 2007. Retrieved from: http://www.rri.wvu.edu/pdffiles/wp2007-10.pdf

[6] Rudzitis G. Nonmetropolitan geography: Migration, sense of place, and the American west. Urban Geography. 1993;**14**(6):574-585

[7] Nelson PB. Quality of life, nontraditional income, and economic growth: New development opportunities for the rural west. Rural Development Perspectives. 1999;**14**(2):32-37

[8] Fuguitt GV, Beale CV. Recent trends and nonmetropolitan migration: Toward a new turnaround? Growth and Change. 1996;**27**:156-174

[9] Beyers WB, Lindalh DP. Lone eagles and high fliers in rural producer services. Rural Development Perspectives. 1996;**11**(3):2-10

[10] McGranahan DA, Wojan TR, Lambert DM. The rural growth trifecta: Outdoor amenities, creative class, and entrepreneurial context. Journal of Economic Geography. 2011;**11**(3):529-557

[11] Duffy-Deno KT. The effect of Federal Wilderness on County growth in the intermountain Western United States. Journal of Regional Science. 1998;**38**(1):109-136

[12] Deller SC, Tsung-Hsui ST, Marcouiller DW, English DBK. Role of amenities and quality of life in rural economic growth. American Journal of Agriculture and Economics. 2001;**83**(2):352-356

[13] Holmes P, Hecox W. Does wilderness impoverish rural areas? International Journal of Wilderness. 2002;**10**(3):34-39

[14] Krannich RS, Petrzelka P. Tourism and natural amenity development: Real opportunities? In: Brown DL, Swanson LE, Barton AW, editors. Challenges for Rural America in the Twenty First Century. University Park, PA: The Pennsylvania State University Press; 2004. pp. 190-202

[15] Yonk RM, Simmons RT, Steed B. Treasured Landscapes & Energy Resources. Logan Utah, USA:

The Center for Public Lands and Rural Economics; 2011

[16] Lorah P, Southwick R. Environmental protection, population change, and economic development in the rural Western United States. Population and Environment. 2003;**24**(3):255-272

[17] AmericanEnergyWorks.org. Strong Communities. 2012. Retrieved from: http://americanenergyworks.org/communities/wyoming

[18] AmericanEnergyWorks.org. Strong Communities. 2012. Retrieved from: http://americanenergyworks.org/communities/montana

[19] Ecosystem Research Group. Sublette County Commission (28 September 2009). Sublette County Socioeconomic Impact Study Phase II—Final Report. 2009. Retrieved from: http://www.sublettewyo.com/index.aspx?NID=309

[20] Pinedale Online. Community Profile, Pinedale Wyoming. 2009. Retrieved from: http://www.pinedaleonline.com/ComProfile.HTM

[21] Noble AC. The Jonah Field and Pinedale Anticline: A Natural-Gas Success Story. The Wyoming State Historical Society. 2010. Retrieved from: http://www.wyohistory.org/essays/jonah-field-and-pinedale-anticline-natural-gas-success-story

[22] Shell. Wyoming—Pinedale Anticline Project Area (PAPA). Retrieved from: http://www.shell.us/home/content/usa/aboutshell/projects_locations/wyoming/Sheridan

[23] Wyoming Oil and Gas Conservation Commission. County Reports. State of Wyoming. Retrieved from: http://wogcc.state.wy.us/

[24] U.S. Census Bureau. 2010 County Business Patterns: Geography Area Series, Sublette County Wyoming (CB1000A1). 2012. Retrieved from: http://factfinder2.census.gov/faces/tableservices/jsf/pages/productview.xhtml?src=bkmk

[25] Pinedale Travel & Tourism Commission. History and Heritage of Sublette. Pinedale Wy.: Pinedale Travel & Tourism; 2012

[26] Fuller A. Commentary: Drilling's Darker Side. CNN Money. 2008. Retrieved from: http://money.cnn.com/2008/10/27/commentary/drilling_wyoming_alexandra.fuller/index.htm

[27] Wyoming State Historical Society. Sublet County, Wyoming. WyoHistory.org. Retrieved from: http://www.wyohistory.org/encyclopedia/sublette-county-wyoming?page=2

[28] Sublette.com. Pinedale. Retrieved from: http://www.sublette.com/

[29] Jacquet J. Sublette County Socioeconomic Analysis. Social & Economic Impacts to Sublette County, WY from Natural Gas Development. 2007. Retrieved from: http://www.sublettewyo.com/index.aspx?NID=285

[30] USA.com. Sublette County Income and Careers. 2013. Retrieved from: http://www.usa.com/sublette-county-wy-income-and-careers.htm

[31] Jacquet J. Sublette County Commission, Sublette Community Partnership. Sublette County, Wyoming, Sales and Use Tax Report. 2006. Retrieved from: http://www.sublettewyo.com/index.aspx?NID=306

[32] Department of Administration and Information. Wyoming Sales, Use, and Lodging Tax Revenues Report. 2012. Retrieved from: http://eadiv.state.wy.us/s&utax/Report_FY12.pdf

[33] Bureau of Labor Statistics. Current Employment Statistics. 2012. Retrieved from: http://www.bls.gov/ces/

[34] Jacquet J. Sublette County Commission. The Sublette County Socioeconomic Analysis Advisory Committee. Sublette County Wage and Employment Study. 2006. Retrieved from: http://www.sublettewyo.com/DocumentCenter/Home/View/369

[35] Sublette County. Cost of Living. Retrieved from: http://www.sublettewyo.com/index.aspx?NID=282

[36] Earthjustice. Wyoming Citizens put EPA on Notice Over Ozone Pollution in Sublette County. Earthjustice. 2011. Retrieved from: http://earthjustice.org/news/press/2011/wyoming-citizens-put-epa-on-notice-over-ozone-pollution-in-sublette-county

[37] Sublette County WY, Board of Commissioners. Citizens Guide to Air Quality Management in Sublette County. Retrieved from: https://www.sublettewyo.com/DocumentCenter/View/433/AirQualityBooklet?bidId=

[38] Urbigkit C. Ozone mitigation efforts continue in sublette county, Wyoming. Casper Star Tribune. 2011. Retrieved from: https://trib.com/news/state-and-regional/ozone-mitigation-efforts-continue-in-sublette-county-wyoming/article_%20d1b0ff92-d3a0-5481-a9fc-e3ca505fbe12.html

[39] U.S. Census Bureau. Retrieved from: http://www.census.gov

[40] Montana Board of Oil and Gas Database. Retrieved from: http://bogc.dnrc.mt.gov/

[41] Kemmick E. The Bakken Boom. The Montanan. Retrieved from: www2.umt.edu/montanan/s12/The%20Bakken%20Boom.asp

[42] McKinney A. Medicine Lake National Wildlife Refuge. Montana Historical Society. 2004;**54**(1):78-80

[43] Caudill J, Henderson E. Banking on Nature 2004: The Economic Benefits to Local Communities of National Wildlife Refuge Visitation. U.S. Fish and Wildlife Service. 2005. Retrieved from: http://www.fws.gov/refuges/about/RefugeReports/

[44] Brush Lake State Park. Montana Fish, Wildlife & Parks. Retrieved from: http://fwp.mt.gov/mtoutdoors/HTML/articles/2005/BrushLake.htm

[45] Sheridan County Chamber of Commerce and Agriculture. Brush Lake State Park. Retrieved from: http://sheridancountychamber.org/

[46] USDA. 2007 Census of Agriculture. United State Department of Agriculture. 2007. Retrieved from: http://www.agcensus.usda.gov/Publications/2007/Online_Highlights/County_Profiles/Montana/cp30091.pdf

[47] State of Montana. Northeast Montana Farm Expo. Montana Official State Travel Site. 2013. Retrieved from: http://visitmt.com/listing/categories_NET/MoreInfo.aspx?IDRRecordID=14398&siteid=3

[48] Bureau of Labor Statistics. Quarterly Census of Employment and Wages: Teton County, Wyoming, Total Employment. 2012. Retrieved from: http://data.bls.gov/timeseries/ENU4201510510

[49] Stanley A. Governor's Executive Budget Fiscal Years 2014-2015. Department of Natural Resources and Conservation. 2013. Retrieved from: http://dnrc.mt.gov/AboutUs/Publications/2013/2014-2015RDGExecutiveBudget.pdf

[50] Board of County Commissioners. Learn about Teton County.

Retrieved from: http://www.tetonwyo.org/bcc/topics/learn-about-teton-county/251981/

[51] National Park Service. Visitor Count Chart, Year-by-Year, Dating Back to 1979. Recreation Visitors Grand Teton National Park. 2011. Retrieved from: https://irma.nps.gov/Stats/SSRSReports/Park%20Specific%20Reports/All%20Recreation%20Visitors%20By%20Month?Park=GRTE

[52] Town of Jackson. Comprehensive Plan: Chapter 5. 2002. Retrieved from: http://townofjackson.com:8307/compplan/Chapter5b.pdf

[53] Wyoming Tourism. Grand Teton National Park. 2013. Retrieved from: http://www.wyomingtourism.org/thingstodo/detail/Grand-Teton-National-Park/3135

[54] National Park Service. Boating and Floating. Grand Teton National Park. 2013. Retrieved from: http://www.nps.gov/grte/planyourvisit/boat.htm

[55] Grand Targhee Resort. Grand Targhee Winter Activities. Retrieved from: http://www.grandtarghee.com/winter/activities/index.php

[56] Wyoming Tourism. Yellowstone National Park. 2013. Retrieved from: http://www.wyomingtourism.org/thingstodo/detail/Yellowstone-National-Park/4796

[57] U.S. Fish and Wildlife Service. National Elk Refuge. 2013. Retrieved from: http://www.fws.gov/nationalelkrefuge/NERHistory.htm

[58] Jackson Hole. First Timers Guide. Retrieved from: http://www.jacksonhole.com/first-timers.html

[59] Jackson Hole. 36 Hours in Jackson Hole. Retrieved from: http://www.jacksonhole.com/36-hours-in-jackson-hole.html

[60] Teton County Planning Commission. Quality of Life: Common Value 3 of Community Character. CV-3-8. 2012. Retrieved from: http://www.tetonwyo.org/compplan/docs/2011/07/120406_JacksonTeton_Part4_CV-3_QualityofLife1.pdf

[61] Coupal R, Taylor D. Adding Value to Tourism: Exploring Ways to Increase Tourism's Impact on Local Economies. 2000. Retrieved from: http://wyocre.uwagec.org/Publications/ecotour-waea.pdf

Chapter 3

# Namibia's Triple Challenge and Its Economic Development

*Vito Bobek, Jellenz Moritz and Tatjana Horvat*


## Abstract

This chapter consists of two parts. In the first theoretical part, economic culture and economic performance are presented. Economic performance and development of market economy institutions depend on many factors. It became evident that economic and cultural factors play an important role. There is a lot of evidence that this role has been underconceptualized and analytically-experimentally underexploited. In the second empirical part, authors dive into the complex topic of Namibia's cultural changing process, combined with its economic development. Such development is only traceable if the historic cornerstones of the nation (e.g., colonization, genocide, apartheid, foreign administration, and independence) are taken under consideration. The emerging social and economic challenges, e.g., poverty, gender, and social inequalities as well as unemployment, will be monitored. To describe Namibia's economic development, several indices, for instance, *foreign direct investment*, *gross domestic product*, and *Hofstede six-dimension model*, will be applied. Furthermore, indices of Namibia's cultural development (*CDIS*) will be presented and analyzed. While demonstrating Namibia's significant cultural and economic aspects, perspectives in regard to the well-being of the next generations are incorporated.


**Keywords:** cultural development, economic development, FDI, GDP, Namibia's economy, sustainable economic development, unemployment

## 1. Introduction

Economic performance and development of market economy institutions depend on many factors. It became evident that economic and cultural factors play an important role. There is a lot of evidence that this role has been under-conceptualized and analytically-experimentally underexploited.

The sub-Saharan African country Namibia is a prime example of a country with diverse and extraordinary nature and culture but one that must overcome challenges. As a result of numerous drastic events in the past and the country's recent national independence, Namibia's government is facing several cultural and economic difficulties. Every 4–6 years a new *National Development Plan* (*NPD*) appears from the domestic government with different focuses. At this point of time, the fifth *NPD* has been introduced, describing the main goal in working together toward prosperity [1]. Similar goals have been recognized by the *World Bank* in 2019, stating that Namibia is facing three major long-term objectives: the combatting of inequality, unemployment, and poverty within the nation. These are formally known as the *triple challenge* [2].

## 2. Economic culture and economic success

The concept of economic culture is related to the concept of political culture which was consolidated by Almond and Verba [3] and others. Berger and Peter [4], in their book, focus on the theory of the economic culture of capitalism, exploring the social, political and cultural matrix, or context within which these particular economic processes work. In doing so, it does not presuppose a direct or indirect connection and does not presuppose that culture determines the economy or that economic factors determine culture. The concept of economic culture draws attention to the relationships that such an empirical study has to explore.

On the basis of the relevant economic knowledge, economic culture can be considered as a whole in the economy of the related knowledge, experience, perceptions, evaluations, norms, and styles of behavior of whole nations or certain groups of the population within a particular society [5], which affects the economically relevant decision-making and conduct of actors or groups of actors. Economic culture has constituent and regulatory elements [6]. Thus, the (often unconsciously) structure of economic perception of the world, as well as the values and norms that determine their motives and limitations of their behavior, is more accessible to everyday awareness [7]. According to Weiss's and Fershtman's economic culture, "it is by no means a static system of value fields that determine the maneuvering space of behavior and outline the directions of action that they make for meaningful" [8]. "Culture is therefore the one that directs the process of the evolution of a system" [9]. The orientation is carried out partially with the help of internationalization of value performances and, insofar as the direct guidance instruments are more abandoning, the "guiding function of cultural forms and value fields" is all the more important [5]. According to Jones "economic institutions do not exist in a vacuum but rather in a context of social and political structures, cultural patterns, and, indeed, structures of consciousness (values, ideas, belief systems). An economic culture then contains a number of elements linked together in an empirical totality. The question concerns the manner of linkage [10]. Boyd and Richerson perceive culture as "the transfer of knowledge, values and others to the behavior or behavior of relevant factors through teaching and imitation from one generation to the next" [11]. The Berger's concept of culture argues that "economic institutions do not exist in a vacuum but rather in a context of social and political structures, cultural patterns, and, indeed, structures of consciousness (values, ideas, belief systems). An economic culture then contains a number of elements linked together in an empirical totality. The question concerns the manner of linkage" [5]. Cultural factors have a holistic impact on the process of emergence and on the structure of flows and interconnection networks within a given formal framework and affect the recognition, guidance, and also the effectiveness of formal institutions. The conflicts between formal institutions that have emerged during the transition and between cultural factors that act as informal institutions form an essential part of the societal developmental dynamics [5].

### 2.1 Economic culture as a factor of transition

Economic institutions do not exist in a vacuum but in the context (matrix) of social and political structures, cultural patterns, and conscious structures (values, ideas, belief systems). Economic culture (in capitalism, in socialism, in Hinduism, or in any other society) contains a number of elements linked together. The question is in what way are they connected [4].

Transition to a modern market economy requires an integrated and well-rounded study of the specific features and factors of modern economic transformation. Undoubtedly, man is always the most important factor in the production and development of the economy. An important historical role of a democratic society is to free creative human resources from social and economic barriers and to enable people to work for their own benefit and profit. Motivation and interests are of primary importance in the creation of a modern market economy. Subjective social factors are a useful aspect of economic culture. This includes the economic policy, the quality of management, and the productivity of each individual and determines the functioning of socioeconomic laws. Economic culture is constantly changing people in society who work according to their level of economic knowledge, their managerial skills, and their view of the economy [12].

In a democratic society, economic culture represents economic relations and creative resources for the development of the economic life of social bodies, specialists, and entrepreneurs. They are all coordinated as the overall economic activity of people, where work practice and economic behavior play an important role in socioeconomic development. Economic culture is linked to the development of society and is crucial in ensuring a satisfactory life for people and for the development of a new quality of social life. The company is unified with economic culture, which operates not only through economic integration but also through the economic policy of the state. Democracy needs an industrial force of high quality. By people seeking new ways of satisfying their needs, economic culture is an objective need for a democratic society and becomes a coincidence for the country's economic policy. Economic culture is changing with social development. Today, an economic-cultural person must have economic knowledge, the ability to economize resources and draw attention to the quality and quantity of production, the ability to make decisions, and care for investment in time and resources. The main components of the economic culture are [12]:

- Economic knowledge
- Belief
- Experience
- Talent

Depending on these components, economic culture can be described as a way of creatively shaping the economic activity of people, based on deep economic and technological knowledge related to their problem and profession, sufficient scope of objective laws of socioeconomic development, and belief based on economic activity and experience [12].

Economic performance and the development of market economies are dependent on many factors. According to Elster et al. [13], Bulgaria and Slovakia faced major problems in adopting democratic institutions and market economy and understanding and internalizing their will in the 1990s, as their rapid and forced industrialization was in contrast to cultural and political modernization. Because of the traditional cultural implications of the Soviet type, the basic communist concepts and perceptions of the agrarian society (mostly under cover) can survive in the behavioral patterns, values, and worldviews of the communist era. The Soviet Communist regime served as a suitable host, which enabled the sustainability of many forms of traditional dominance of agrarian society also in industrial rather than simultaneously modernized society [14]. It is important that the legacy of the social and cultural capital of the past is able to adapt to the requirements of the present [13] in: [14]. It has become evident that economic-cultural factors also play an important role. There is a lot of evidence that this role has been under-conceptualized and analytically-experimentally underexploited. The project "Researching Transition Economic and Culturally" is based on four fundamental hypotheses [5]:

1. Success of economic transition in terms of a stable and economically viable change in the system depends on supporting economic and cultural factors.

2. Supportive economic-cultural factors occur in different transition countries or groups of countries of varying degrees. In some countries, the prevailing economic and cultural environment for transition is more aggressive than accelerating.

3. Further progress of transition to less successful countries depends on the extent to which the obvious conflicts between the dominant elements of the traditional economic culture and the democratic and market economy mechanisms supporting transition can be overcome.

4. Economic culture is a concept that should be taken into account both in the analysis of global societies and in the research of individual groups of actors.

In developing the appropriate conceptuality, it is possible to rely on an increasingly detailed conceptual apparatus, which is the result of an international cultural-oriented economic research. The reasons for the breakthrough of economic cognitive research are mutually accelerating factors of real change (Asian tigers, the collapse of global political blocs that hitherto covered cultural differences, different waves of transition) and the development of theory (the growth of the influence of the institutional economy, the evolutionary economy and economic sociology).

## 2.2 Economic theory: culture and economic success

Culture is a dynamic category; it changes over time. Changes are positions, values, norms, principles and customs, ideology, beliefs, behavior, etc. All of this is also linked to social structures, for example, in the economic system. Culture with its elements is the basis for the design and functioning of a social order and hence of economic regulation. It is understandable that social changes are changing with the changes in culture. On the other hand, we can expect that the change in economic regulation will affect the change of culture.

Economic activity of people is thus certainly among those that need to be judged from the point of view of good or bad. In the economy, people enter into urgent interrelationships, within which the basic existential issues are addressed, both at the individual and family level and at the level of the broader society as a whole. The socioeconomic order can only be effective if at the same time as the material goods increase, it also ensures the life of a human being to as many people as possible. In ethical issues in the economy, it is primarily because in material matters we are always looking for humanity [15].

The concept of culture is very wide, as it covers every part of personal life and has a direct impact on the patterns of life. Culture is a learned way of life within a given society. In essence, culture is a set of values and patterns of learned behaviors that are shaped as a result of living within a particular society.

This is enabled by the following processes:

- Cultural heritage as a way of transferring cultural values and norms from generation to generation (reproduction of cultural patterns)

- Upgrading culture based on the internal potential of cultural groups
- Borrowing from other cultures as a way of assuming certain elements of other cultures

Culture does not stand still but gradually changes.

In the broader sense, the economic system is defined as a set of mechanisms and institutions, laws, rules, traditions, and values that form a certain pattern of decision-making and the realization of economic decisions in the process of social reproduction and a certain pattern of behavior of economic operators [16].

Throughout history, each country has created an indicative concept of culture that has its own specific characteristics. In connection with these cultural characteristics, each country has also developed a specific economic arrangement. Therefore, we can not claim that the economic system is identical in all countries. Of course, this can not be true, as economic potentials and culture, as an important element of economic regulation, are different in different countries. This intertwining of economy and culture was largely neglected in older economic theories. Recent economic theorists, however, are trying to capture the cultural aspect of the economy in their theories.

An indirect link between culture and economy is possible through the role of the state as an institution and instance. In a dynamic market system with incomplete and diffuse information, culture is always the basis for competitive advantages in the realization of transactions.

North [17] states that the rules of the game in society are—or more formal—the constraints that people have built to create interactions. Consequently, they structure the incentives in political, social, or economic exchanges. Institutional changes shape a way of social development and are crucial to understanding historical change.

Institutions can not be seen, felt, touched, or measured—they are constructs of the human mind. However, neoclassical economists recognize their existence and are usually used (implicitly or explicitly) in their models as parameters [17]. In his work of the institution, institutional changes, and economic success, North [17] laid the foundations for the analysis of institutional changes on economic performance.

Keith Hudson [18], in his article in *The Economist*, asks what is crucial for the development—geography, institution, or politics. For many years, economists have emphasized the importance of good economic policy, and lately more emphasis is placed on long-stay institutions—political stability, property rights, the legal system, patterns of land ownership, etc. Other economists, on the contrary, emphasize geography, especially climate diseases, usability of certain technologies, agricultural opportunities, and access to the sea (influencing the extent of international integration). These explanatory factors do not necessarily have to be mutually exclusive[1].

Easterley and Levine [19] tested the importance of these groups of factors on a sample of 72 countries. The results of the survey are very impressive, as they have shown that institutional factors have a key effect on economic performance, while other factors are almost non-negligible.

Conceptual insights from contemporary social sciences show that the modern world is increasingly aware of the cultural condition of economic decisions. The decision-makers are not only economic but also cultural-national. The awareness of these complex relationships has not yet been sufficiently defined and researched. The Hofstede's six dimension model, where people's behavior conditions their values, is the cornerstone for the empirical model. In any case, we are aware that such an operational model has its own shortcomings, as are all mechanical methods [20].

[1] Rich economies usually combine appropriate policies, sound and stable institutions, and favorable geography. Many poor countries are poorly endowed with all three factors.

## 3. Introduction to empirical part: the case of Namibia

The sub-Saharan African country Namibia is a prime example of a country with diverse and extraordinary nature and culture but one that must overcome challenges. As a result of numerous drastic events in the past and the country's recent national independence, Namibia's government is facing several cultural and economic difficulties. Every 4–6 years a new *National Development Plan* (*NPD*) appears from the domestic government with different focuses. At this point of time, the fifth *NPD* has been introduced, describing the main goal in working together toward prosperity [1]. Similar goals are pursued also by the UNO: The Sustainable Development Goals are the blueprint to achieve a better and more sustainable future for all. They address the global challenges, including those related to poverty, inequality, climate, environmental degradation, prosperity, and peace and justice. The goals interconnect, and in order to leave no one behind, it is important that each goal and target by 2030 are achieved. Similar goals have been recognized also by the *World Bank* in 2019, stating that Namibia is facing three major long-term objectives: the combatting of inequality, unemployment, and poverty within the nation. These are formally known as the *triple challenge* [2].

### 3.1 Explanation

Before the in-depth explanation of the Namibian culture and economy, the reader finds a brief summary of the main indicators, in order to understand the significance of such, in the following sections.

#### *3.1.1 Culture for Development Indicator Suite (CDIS)*

As a project of the *United Nations Education, Scientific and Cultural Organization* (*UNESCO*), CDIS has been established in 2009 with the help of the Spanish government. With the contribution of more than 300 partners, the aim is to promote and to protect the diversity of cultural expressions globally. It is a multimethodological tool that measures and visualizes data in seven interrelated policy dimensions, including 22 indicators. Especially, the following dimensions that will be used in this chapter, in order to achieve fact-based assessments, are *economy, education, gender equality, social participation, and heritage.* This multidimensional instrument is only one project of the *UNESCO*, accessing international comparisons among nations and their facts of development. *Culture for Development Indicator Suite* gives an insight into the enrolment of culture in a nation's development. Additional results are indicating the potential of domestic sectors and exhibit obstacles hindering full potential. Namibia's government recognized the key factor of culture in its development process and introduced *CDIS* in November 2011 [21].

#### *3.1.2 Hofstede six-dimension model*

Between 1967 and 1973, the Dutch psychologist *Geert Hofstede* developed the origins of this model while conducting an international survey about national values for *International Business Machines* (*IBM*). He defined six dimensions that society needs in order to organize itself. A further purpose of *Hofstede's six dimension model* is to understand the contribution of national culture in habits and values in a professional environment. Global data manifest into six cultural dimensions, which enable comparisons among 76 countries, while Namibia is one of them. Especially the following three dimensions will be discussed within this chapter: *power distance, masculinity vs. femininity*, and *long-term orientation*. Those dimensions can be used most effectively for the clarification of cultural and economic correlations [22].

## 4. Namibian government facing "triple challenge"

### 4.1 Status quo of inequalities

Namibia is known worldwide as having tremendous inequality conditions, which can be traced back to their past. The nation's history still has an effect on their individual degree of trade, governance, and cultural factors [23].

These unequal conditions are affecting the 13 regions of the country in gender, education, health, wages, infrastructure, and a plethora of other aspects. When analyzing Hofstede's six dimension model, Namibia's ranking within the power distance dimension highlights these issues. It monitors to which extent power is distributed and how citizens of the analyzed country are satisfied with the distribution. Namibia currently reaches 65 out of 100, which indicates a hierarchical society with high inequalities [22].

#### *4.1.1 Societal segmentation*

The Republic of Namibia has witnessed turbulent historic times, including colonization by several foreign powers, genocide committed by the German's, and foreign administration by South Africa.

During the nineteenth century, Victorian Britain and Germany were the major players involved in the nation's colonialization [24]. In the early twentieth century, Namibia experienced the nation's first genocide. It was committed by the German general *Lothar von Trotha*, which killed more than 75,000 African primary residents and destroyed their tribal structures. Particularly the ethnic groups of Herero and Nama suffered the most from this event, which led to losses of approximately 80% (Herero) and 50% (Nama) in their tribal size [25, 26].

The previous influence of foreign policies in the twentieth century, e.g., the racial segregation formally known as apartheid, continues to impact the nation to this very day. Such events influenced the population in terms of behavior, structures, and their growth. However, these historic incidents have evoked societal inequalities [24, 27].

Although there is a lack of historical content from generation to generation, former leader of the ethnic group Nama has written controversially in his dagboek (*diary, English translation*): "*... no person, nor his money comes short in our way of living*" [24]. According to additional diary entries, it is liable that there have not been major inequalities in at least one of the ethnic groups before 1905 [24].

The national independence obtained in 1990 was an important first step out of several dependencies toward an emerging national and societal self-perception.

Nevertheless, Namibia suffered from a fragmented society in post-independent times: a gap between ethnic groups of the poor and rich arose. This created political and economic instability [28].

A new constitution was written with several different focuses, but the most intriguing was the empowerment of women and gender equality. It states that there should not be any discrimination because of sex [21].

The nation's second president, *Hifikepunye Pohamba*, also made these issues to one of his major duties in his period from 2005 to 2015, as well as several National Development Plans that followed [27].

According to data from the *World Population Review*, Namibia exhibits nine different ethnic groups. The largest ones are the Ovambo with 49.8%, followed by Kavango (9.3%), Herero (7.5%), Damara (7.5%), Whites (6.4%), Nama (4.8%), Caprivian (3.7%), San (2.9%), and Basters (2.5%). Whites are mainly consisting out of Portuguese, British, and German origin. The remaining 5.6% are assigned to a group of mixed races [29].

Currently, 65% of Namibia's population are living in communal areas owned by the government, which are covering only 40% of the nation. Such is attributable to the event of caging ethnic groups into rural areas in the mid-twentieth century, by the white population [27, 30].

Since their national independence, there has been a lot of resettlement within the nation. Unfortunately, inequalities are still present. An example is the distribution and access to information differentiate among inhabitants. Namibian society records high inequalities in information, information in technology such as TV and radio, and in financial facilities and services.

Furthermore, these issues also occur in terms of natural resources, e.g., water and fish stock [31]. According to the *World Population* Review, only 91% of Namibia's population has access to clean drinking water, while 65% is struggling to gain access to appropriate sanitation facilities [29].

One reason for these inequalities is the ongoing exclusive access to private farmlands by the wealthier population. In the long run, this will lead to even higher inequalities as well as challenges among demographics, environment, land distribution, and enjoyment of cultural rights [21, 28].

With a *Gini coefficient* of 61 out of 100—an indicator of a nation's distribution of income, economic inequality, and wealth distribution—it again gets determined Namibia is facing high inequalities [32]. The authors *Humavindu* and *Stage* strengthen this statement, by speaking distinctly about one of the highest unequal distributions of income on the continent of Africa. Typically, the rural areas are suffering from lower income, in comparison to cities [32].

A controversial impression of Namibia's society is indicated by *Hofstede's masculinity vs. femininity dimension*. Such provides information about the internal societal interaction. Namibia indicates with its result—40 out of 100—to be a rather feminine society. This is reflected in habits such as caring about each other, solidarity, and resolution of conflicts by negotiation. According to Hofstede, social status and inequalities should be of secondary importance which contradicts the situation in Namibia [22].

#### *4.1.2 Gender inequalities*

Another determining index is the *Gender Inequality Index* (*GII*), which measures gender-based inequalities out of the following three dimensions: reproductive health, empowerment, and economic development. The nation achieved position 115 out of 160, which confirms gender inequality as a major problem [33, 34].

*CDIS* is also observing gender inequality in one of their dimensions. According to their expendable result in the *Gender Equality Objective Outputs* indicator—0.84 out of 1—the governmental efforts are being reflected [21].

According to *Ferrant's* article "How do gender inequalities hinder development?," gender roles and gender inequalities emerge out of culture, religion, and agricultural practices [23].

##### *4.1.2.1 Gender roles*

Confirmable to the issue of gender inequality is the description of gender roles within the nation. There are minor differences in describing their functions among the nine different ethnic groups, but this is summarized as men enjoy higher status in Namibian society than women. When separating into core tasks and functions, men are known as the pillar for family and house. Their characterization is strong and tough and includes tasks, e.g., the protection of their families, responsibility for providing food and income, and livestock farming.

On the other hand, women are seen as physically weak and a dispensable tool for men. Women would not be able to survive without men. Interestingly, some of the ethnic groups are connecting women as the mother of the nation but still giving them a secondary legal status by describing them as a second-class citizen or as the property of men [31].

Women's suppression leads to governmental recognition. In Namibia's third *National Development Plan*, women are empowered to play a full cultural, social, and economic role. According to Ferrant, gender equality is leading to an increasing capita per income which results in long-term advantages for national economies [1, 23].

#### *4.1.2.2 Enrolment and wages*

These monitored gender roles are leading to the disqualification of women in society. This is visible in their limited access to assets, resources, technology, education, and employment.

Especially female-headed households are worse off. The usual case describes the eldest son as a decision-maker. However, these outcomes are also affecting the careers of female habitants. For instance, when applying for a profession, women have fewer chances to succeed when competing against man [31].

Alternatively, a household including male and female often leads to domestic abuse victims. As reported in the case study of *Angula*, the violence against women and children is still increasing in Namibia [31]. Additional evidence is given by the *Perception of Gender Indicator* of *CDIS*, stating that 38% of Namibian population thinks beating wives is fair enough when she, for instance, argues, burns the food, or denies sexual activity [21]. Outreaching, such behavior is leading to absenteeism of women, lower productivity, and collateral reduction in women's wages. Furthermore, it creates an inferiority cycle for women in Namibian society and economy [23].

### *4.1.3 Economic development and healthcare*

As mentioned above, gender inequalities do influence social and economic development. *Ferrant* confirms this statement by announcing that gender inequalities are internationally leading to a decrease of 3.4% in income per capita [23]. The empowerment and increasing wages of women are leading to a lower fertility rate and more consumption in nutrition, instead of alcohol and cigarettes [28]. That is also confirmed by growth literature, explaining that human and physical capital are the main drivers for economic growth [23].

Another example monitored in *Ferrant's* article describes the impact of an increased enrolment of women. If sub-Saharan African females have the same status than Western Europe's female, the mortality rate for children—less than 5 years—would decrease by 25% [23]. Namibia's current mortality rate for children under 5 years is 44.2 deaths per 1000 live births [35].

Additionally, according to studies from *Ainsworth*, *Fransen,* and *Over* in 1998, there is a positive correlation between gender inequality and health, especially AIDS/HIV. The HIV infection rate in cities with higher gender gaps increases stronger compared to low gender gap cities [36]. Latest results from *UNAIDS* are displaying Namibia's situation. There has been an estimated number of 200,000 people living with HIV and alarming 7400 new infections in the year of 2017. While the number of people living with HIV is slightly increasing, the infection rate in previous years has decreased [37].

#### *4.1.4 Education*

Often the foundation for economic and cultural inequalities emerges out of a weakened education sector. In the case of Namibia, a controversial but still similar situation is present.

In previous times, the Namibian population suffered from a low level of education and unskilled workers. The government recognized this issue and destined one-fourth of its annual budget for the national education system [28]. Likewise, education became part of their new constitution in post-independent times. It reports the access and right to education should be given to all citizens [21]. These various governmental efforts have been—partly—prosperous.

The second dimension of *CDIS, Education*, displays Namibia's adolescents—aged from 17 to 22—contributing in schooling by 8.4 years on average, while only 9% of them are showing less than 4 years of education [21]. The government succeeded partly because still the access and the contribution between male and female differ. Namibian women are still worse off in education than of their male counterparts [23].

*Ferrant* emphasizes that the level of corruption and nepotism is decreasing if the contribution of women in education increases. Women are simply less affected by such behavior compared to men [23]. Less corruption and nepotism will also influence the well-being of the next generations, the level and quality of human capital, and the nation's economic growth in a positive way, as already stated under Section 4 [38].

Even Namibia's high adolescence birth rate—75% out of 1000 women aged from 15 to 19 in 2016—is indicating a minor education status within the nation [32]. Such behavior influences participation in the labor market, as well as the health situation of adolescent Namibians [21].

Another example of *Klaasen*, *Gatti*, and *Dollar* is strengthening these statements. If a society has the same number of males and females participating in education but distributes scarce knowledge unequal, the outcome will represent more educated men that are less able than women. Furthermore, a gap in education leads to an unequal distribution of income and results in an even higher gender gap [38].

#### *4.1.5 Governmental recognition of inequalities*

There has already been recognition among several inequality issues by the Namibian government [31]. Working against them is their objective. But how is it possible to escape the vicious cycle of inequalities or at least to raise the equality standard?

Namibian governmental efforts are reflected in the contribution of several programs and by introducing new policies. Policies, for instance, to strengthen the perception of gender equalities, education, and culture and arts, have been designed [21]. The government of Namibia is also revising their *National Development Plans* every 4–6 years. A focus on crucial equality and cultural aspects has been made by the governmental third *National Development Plan* [1]. Namibia, with these actions, is trying to bridge the gap between postapartheid and post-independent times. It hopes to get the nation on a reliable track.

As indicated in *CDIS education* and *social participation* dimensions, further efforts should be made toward the thinking of Namibian citizens [1]. Due to the horrific events in former times, e.g., decades of occupation and genocide, the Namibian majority is not able to trust each other or to respect other cultures. Mostly there is low recognition of significant benefits emerging out of their multicultural society [1]. If changing these societal perspectives to preferable ones, the equality conditions will be favored in Namibia. Such will lead to greater achievement of sustainable cultural and economic development, as described in *Krugmann's* article [28].

### 4.2 Unemployment

The second out of the *Triple Three* governmental objectives deals with the diminishment of Namibia's unemployment rate [2]. Due to the fact that women and the young population are affected, it is interlinked to the previous topic of inequality.

According to data from *Trading Economics*, the unemployment rate in Namibia has increased from 27.9–34% in the years of 2014–2016. Current numbers monitor a minor decrease to 33.4% in 2018, which is equivalent to 364,411 unemployed persons. The youth unemployment rate of 46.1% in 2018 has experienced an all-time high [32]. Adolescents between the ages of 20 and 24 are majorly affected [39].

Compared to the previous numbers, the female unemployment rate is slightly lower. Latest data from 2018 monitor the female unemployment rate achieving 24.7% [2]. This is due to a high informal market within the nation [21].

Yet, women are not the only ones suffering in the Namibian labor market. Also, certain ethnic groups experience disadvantages in the job market due to historic events, cultural habits, and different values. For instance, members of the ethnic group San, which are mainly working in the service sector, are the first ones to be fired, because of their nomadic behavior. *Sylvain* describes them as decentralized workers in western clothing and justifies their manners with the statement: "*You can take the Bushmen out of the bush, but you can't take the bush out of the Bushman*" [30].

In addition, there is the presence of dealing with unemployment: Once Namibians are unemployed, their majority is seeking for assistance of families or friends, in order to get a new job.

An additional observation made by the *Namibian Labor Survey 2016* states that the majority of unemployed citizens stays without employment for at least 1 year. This indicates whether there is a low amount of available jobs, labor institutions need to improve, or inhabitants are indolent when it comes to finding new employment [39].

There are different reasons for the current situation of Namibia. First, it is explained by the historic labor movements. At the beginning of the twentieth century, Namibia was a cattle-based society, and wealth was equivalent to a high stock in cattle. However, all of these growing herds needed to be managed. This evoked a labor migration which resulted in a higher population and later in less labor due to changing professions [40].

Second, *the Culture for Development Indicator Suite* describes Namibia's tiny industry and the resulting low level of production as another reason for the present situation. The *World Bank* announces Namibians' major source of income as a third reason. The minority of Namibia's population is relying on income from employment, while the majority banks on subsidence farming, pensions, and grants [21].

One aim of the Namibian government is to promote the domestic labor market, especially for women. Their goal is to achieve a rate of 50% of female in decision-making positions, while, e.g., currently only 8% of them are working as regional councils. This rate can be traced back to the minor degree of access to the labor market, as well as the disadvantageous situation for women when competing against men [21].

The *Namibia Labour Force Survey 2016* states that the unemployment rate of a nation is directly linked to its economic growth. It is explained as follows: a decreasing unemployment rate, as it is hardly visible in Namibia, is a sign for economic growth. An increasing rate, as there are in the unemployment rates of women and youth, indicates an economy that is not able to absorb the people in working age [39]. Though to the slow but almost steady economic growth (described under Section 12) which results in job creation then, there is an improvement in sight [2].

Another correlation is being made between unemployment and poverty, which arose in post-independent times and will be discussed in the following section.

### 4.3 Poverty

The third aspect of Namibian governmental *triple challenge* is the fight against poverty. Poverty goes hand in hand with inequality and especially with unemployment and thereby arises the difficulty of monitoring the aspects of poverty isolated.

Namibia is reflecting poverty particularly in female-headed households, extended families, inhabitants with a low level of education, and farmworkers. When separating the occurrence of poverty into regions and economic sectors, it holds true for the rural communal land and the informal urban sector [2]. Nevertheless, which leverage yields out for Namibian inhabitants?

According to authors *Humavindu* and *Stage* and data from the *World Bank*, most of Namibians had to live with less than 2 USD per day in 2018 [2]. Even worse is the fact that the majority has to deal with an annual income of less than 100 USD [33, 34]. Plenty of inhabitants call upon urbanization, in the hope of better access to resources and professions, but mostly end up in worse conditions or the black market. Namibia's cities are currently recording an annual population growth of around 5–6% [28].

Wealth and income are distributed by far unequal, as already indicated with the *Gini coefficient* under Section 3. This also clarifies why the *World Bank* classified the nation in 2019 as an upper-middle-income nation while having tremendous poverty issues [2].

In terms of the *Human Development Index* (*HDI*), which focuses on people and their capabilities by analyzing data from three different dimensions—long and healthy life, being knowledgeable, and decent standard of living—Namibia ranked itself in position 129 out of 189 countries. This refers to a medium human development, which is surprisingly higher than the average in sub-Saharan Africa [33, 34].

Another indication strengthening the country's poverty is the small degree of domestic industry, as previously described. It causes minor economic development which results in negative outputs for domestic education, employment, and especially the nation's poverty.

Again, the contribution of history influences the current situation. Former drastic events, as already mentioned under Section 4, are responsible for the dominant degree of poverty in Namibia. Decades of suppression, exploitation, and slaughtering native population has long-lasting effects on their self-perception. Those effects are staying within the Namibian population and do not erase with their national independence or any other progressive event. It takes time to change the social and economic thinking toward favoring the nation and a self-decision-making concept. Namibian population is currently still suffering from former times. *CDIS* describes that such is especially visible in the gap of tolerating, trusting, and accepting other cultures [21].

Health and nutrition are also influencing the degree of poverty within Namibia. A constant nationwide supply leads to food security, agricultural production, and higher wages, which in return has a positive impact on the degree of poverty [28].

Furthermore, the "western economic" long-term thinking is missing. Namibia scored low in *Hofstede's long-term orientation dimension*—35 out of 100—which reflects a normative culture that thinks suspiciously among societal changes and that focuses on accomplishing quick results [22]. Namibian governmental efforts would be wasted if their inhabitants refuse to change. An example of the majorly nonexisting long-term thinking is described by *Sylvain*. In her article, she characterizes the San—besides their unfavorable economic situation—as spending all their wages on payday [30].

Efforts against poverty have been made by the Namibian government by doing it carefully and always in regard to the possible side effects, e.g., exploitation of natural resources. In compliance with *Krugmann's* article, the domestic government is working against poverty in direct and indirect ways. The direct way is tackling health, education, housing, pension, and resources, while the indirect form is dealing with topics as investment promotion and taxes [28]. Hence, Namibia was able to succeed by reducing the national poverty line from 69.3% to 17.4% in the years of 1993–2016, altogether in accordance with an upward trend and stability in their economy and politics [2].

## 5. Development of Namibia's economy

Besides the *Triple Three* challenge, sustainable economic growth is an additional objective that wants to be achieved by the Namibian government [28].

*Humavindu* and *Stage* are describing the current domestic economy as the combination of a modern market sector industry with farming while mainly focusing on sectors that have been successful in the past, e.g., the mining sector [33, 34]. Furthermore, the level of industrial activities remains low which represent an obstacle for sustainable economic growth. As one possible solution, the economic diversification of Namibia has been announced by *Krugmann* [28].

Additional assistance to achieve sustainable growth is generally given by the implementation of economic favoring policies. However, Namibia, as well as other emerging markets, is often confronted with institutional voids, which result in a lack of the governmental implementation process. One example is monitored by the*government* dimension of *CDIS*, describing issues in the implementation of Namibia's tax policies [21]. *Multinational enterprises* (*MNEs*) are able to recognize the favorable situation as comparative advantages while the local content is remaining low. The *Institute for Public Policy Research* (*IPPR*) describes the situation as an exploitation of Namibia. To a great extent, these are fundamental obstacles in order to achieve sustainable development [41].

### 5.1 Gross domestic product and trade

In accordance with the low level of industrial activities, Namibia has a relatively small economy that gets reflected in the nation's *Gross Domestic Product* (*GDP*). *The World Bank* indicates an increasing *GDP* of 14,522 billion USD in 2018, which is projected as a minor steady growing one [2].

Namibians have a high level of consumption of foreign goods, services, and activities. This has developed a domestic economy that is highly dependent on imports and exports [2]. Hence, Namibia's economy has reached a high degree of openness, which is visualized in the domestic *GDP*. More than 90% of it stems from imports and exports [33, 34]. The main imported goods are to the greatest extent represented in consumer goods, e.g., petroleum products, pharmaceuticals, plastic products, rubber, spare parts, textiles, and timber [42].

On the other hand, there are exported goods largely consisting of raw materials and semifinished goods, for instance, copper, cut diamonds, gemstones, granite, lead products, marble, uranium, and zinc. A large proportion of exported goods are represented in beef, which is mostly transferred to South Africa and the European Union [42].

The steady increasing economic growth of African emerging markets is favoring the economic situation of Namibia. Primarily responsible are their neighboring countries, such as Angola, Botswana, and South Africa [2].

### 5.2 Social accounting matrix

Defining economic key sectors is essential for any domestic economic growth. Key sectors represent the largest amount of independence among the rest of the economy. If investing in them, the probability of economic growth will be higher than investments into several non-key sectors [33, 34].

One possibility to highlight key sectors of any economy is the use of a *social accounting matrix* (*SAM*). The matrix merges data from all international and regional transactions, as well as transfers within the target economy. The most common sectors are resulting out of these data sets, defined as key sectors. In order to process a reliable output, a vast number of national data are needed [43]. Thus, the number of *SAMs* of emerging markets is slightly poor. Even if an emerging market succeeded in applying a *social accounting matrix*, their government often will not be able to encourage or invest in the defined key sectors.

Namibia achieved its first and last *SAM* in 2012, determining mining, mineral processing, and manufacturing as key sectors. According to the output, the nation is highly dependent on trade as already described in its domestic *GDP*. Such information is important for the improvement of Namibia's economy, in order to generate the highest possible output [33, 34].

Also relying on such information is the governmental policy-making process. Hence, the government is able to tailor policies to the needs of the domestic economy. Again, institutional voids may hinder such process, as described under Section 12.

### 5.3 Economic sectors

Apart from mining, other sectors of Namibia's economy are represented in mineral processing, governmental services, tourism, transport, logistics, agriculture, fishery, and manufacturing [33, 34].

The *High Commission of the Republic of Namibia* describes Namibia's mining sector as the fourth biggest nonfuel mining sector in Africa [42]. Accessing new technologies and including seabed operations enabled the sector to achieve an annual growth rate of 11% in 2018 [2]. Namibia's mineral resources include offshore oil, diamonds, lead, zinc, tin, silver, and tungsten. Additionally, the nation is globally known as the fifth biggest uranium producer [42].

The second-largest sector with the highest shares in *Namibia's gross domestic product* is tourism [42]. In 2015, it experienced a peak of 16.5% in domestic *GDP*, which decreased to a contribution of 13.8% in 2017 [35]. According to *Trading Economics*, the number of arrivals has reached almost 1.5 million in 2016 [32].

The agricultural sector of Namibia accomplished 6.85% of GDP in 2016, while more than 70% of their population is depending on farming [32–34]. Agriculture represents the main income of Namibia's population and includes, e.g., farming of cattle or crops. Nevertheless, there is still potential in the domestic agricultural sector which can be seen in the example of 2005 where Namibia still imported 50% of its cereals [42].

Due to Namibia's coastline of more than 1500 km, their fishery sector is also of high importance and represents one of the tenth largest globally. Main catches are hake and horse mackerel which are mostly exported to the neighboring countries, as well as the European Union [44].

### 5.4 Population

Namibia's economy is a rather small one compared to its dimensions. According to data from the *World Bank*, Namibia's population has increased to 2,448,255 million in 2018 [2]. It represents the second least populated country in the world—directly after Mongolia—with a population density of 3.13 people/km$^2$ [29].

The number of inhabitants is still increasing and indicates a relatively young population with high unemployment rates, as already mentioned under Section

14. The young population correlates with the national median age of 21.2 years, published by the *World Population Review* [29]. Complementarily to the described issues of unemployment and inequalities above is the fact that only 58.5% of women and 65.3% of man participated in the labor market in 2018 [33, 34].

### 5.5 Historical impact on Namibia's economy

In former times, the Namibian economy was not dependent on singular sectors. Missionaries that arrived in southern Africa during the nineteenth century, mostly due to the geographical and political importance of the trade network *Cape Colony*, described Namibian communities as multi-resource shepherds. Namibians in all its ethnics have been characterized as flexible and determined, with a wide range of interrelated economic activities [40].

Thus, at the end of the nineteenth century, most of Namibia's ethnic groups became part in a cattle-based society in which the number of cattle was a crucial sign of wealth. Consequentially, not everyone was able to grow stock organically, and raiding cattle among residents occurred. Some become wealthier, while others changed back to hunting and gathering society or suffered from starvation [40].

Additionally, trade also took place between Namibians and foreign powers. They have been trading cattle for horses, guns, ammunition, and several consumer goods, e.g., tobacco. As a result, a gun society emerged among those inhabitants who had the possibility to take part in trade. Due to repetitive years of raiding, gun owners were better off. Raiding was simply the most effective and common way to prosperity in former times [40].

In the late nineteenth century, Namibia became known as a nation rich in natural resources, e.g., uranium, vanadium, lithium, and tungsten but especially diamonds. Initially, ethnic tribes were able to gain advantages out of the economic situation by renting ox wagons to foreign missionaries [45].

The authors *Bollig*, *Schnegg*, and *Wotzka* are describing the phenomenon of ethnic groups establishing an intra- and inter-regional network of trade, where locals have been able to determine prices. At the beginning of the twentieth century, these golden economic ages were destroyed by colonial powers that occupied Namibia and forced its inhabitants to unfree labor and slavery [40].

The *League of Nations* in 1920 advocated for Namibia—at that time known as the protectorate of *South-West Africa*—by announcing South Africa as foreign administrator. Unfortunately, instead of administrating Namibia, South Africa made use of its power and exploited the nation. South Africa suppressed the Namibian economy, as well as their society until the national independence in the late twentieth century [27].

After all of its tumultuous history, Namibia continues facing economic and social disadvantages, for instance, the minor industry and inequalities among ethnicities.

### 5.6 Governmental efforts and foreign participation

Besides the *Triple Three* challenge and the aim of sustainable development, the Namibian government is trying to transform the country into an economic gateway of sub-Saharan Africa with several actions [46].

One of them is dealing with stimulating economic growth and employment. Thus, the government is trying to reach a broader scope internationally. The processes of redesigning and promotion of policies are also included, for instance, the *Green Scheme* program introduced in 2005. Such program is supporting the agricultural sector, in order to create more employment [42].

Additional economic weaknesses of Namibia are also pointed out by *CDIS*. According to *Culture for Development Indicator Suite*, the Namibian government should further work on the domestic level of education. Such results in higher gender equality and will lead to economic growth [21].

In order to achieve further development, *CDIS* also suggest investments to infrastructure, transportation, and *information and communication technology* (*ICT*). These suggestions have already been recognized and were part of Namibia's fourth *National Development Plan* during 2012/2013 and 2016/2017 [1, 21].

*Foreign direct investments* (*FDIs*) are another crucial component for the development of any economy [47, 48]. *The Global Economy* indicates significant economic success with a continuously annual *FDI* of approximately 5–6% of GDP [49].

Between the years of 1986 and 2017, Namibia achieved an average *FDI* rate of 4.21% in *GDP* [49]. According to latest data from the World Bank, the nation accomplished an amount of almost 220 million USD in *FDI* in 2018 [2].

The Namibian government tries to increase these numbers by several incentives which favor *MNEs* to invest. For instance, a no-tax policy for certain machinery and special amortization plans have been introduced [46].

Furthermore, Namibia joined several programs, institutions, and trade zones: *World Trade Organization* (*WTO*), *World Bank*, *International Monetary Fund* (*IMF*), *Foreign Investment Act*, *Doha Development Agenda*, *Export Processing Zone*, and *South African Customs Union* (*SACU*).

This should lead to higher profits from trade, an increasing number of *FDIs*, and a greater awareness of the country [42].

Namibia's *Ministry of Industrialization, Trade and SME Development* introduces further incentives. These incentives give Namibia access into the manufacturing markets of the USA, the EU, and other nations. They also promote foreign investments by allowing manufacturers to locate their operations wherever they want [46].

### 5.7 Sustainable development and economic diversification

On the one hand, the Namibian government tries to raise its reputation on the global trade market. *MNEs* should invest in the nation and stimulate the domestic industry toward sustainable development. This needs to be done carefully because the current degree of industrial action is low. *MNEs* have high influence and could also harm their economy or even worse exploit them [28].

On the other hand, the government of Namibia needs to pay attention to its already limited natural resources. According to *Krugmann*, those are land, water, and fish stock. Higher rates in *FDI* are often attached to an increasing consumption of resources. This especially holds true for investments in already high resource-consuming sectors, e.g., fishery [28].

Therefore, the Namibian government has to diversify its economy, in order to achieve sustainable development. *Krugmann* mentions that it is necessary to find the balance between economic, environmental, and social objectives [28].

Hence, plenty of challenges are arising. For instance, almost all of these factors are interlinked with each other. Isolating and influencing single ones are almost impossible.

The increasing number of Namibian citizens, which is equivalent to higher participation in their economy, is resulting in an upward trend in air and water pollution. This is leading to either exploitation of scarce resources or land contamination [28].

*Krugmann* emphasizes that access to limited resources should be efficient, as well as restricted. In terms of water, it would result in higher import rates of water-intensive goods, e.g., tomatoes. Regarding efficient usage, recycling, reusing, and waste reduction are viable solutions to tackle this issue. Namibia is in need of a governmental strategy toward reinvesting into natural resources [28].

Unemployment and inequalities, as indicated above under Section 8, are also obstacles for sustainable development. *Sylvain* describes that white settlers owned 65% of Namibia's land during colonial rule, while they have been only 8% of the nation's total population [30].

Even though governmental resettlement took place in post-independent times, the *UNESCO* describes that currently the unequal distribution of land still holds true to a certain degree [50]. The difficulty arising from such is the necessity of owning land in order to have access to resources and participate in agriculture.

As *Krugmann* states, achieving economic diversity and sustainable development in Namibia is possible if directly supporting the poor population. This includes the promotion of education, the entrepreneurial drive, the nation's employment options, and the agricultural sector. Additional governmental efforts in renewable resources and the creation of a dynamic industry and service sectors would boost this process [28].

## 6. Conclusion

Historic events are large-scale contributors in shaping the fragmented society and the slightly growing economy that Namibian is currently facing. Poor conditions majorly emerged out of former occurrences, as, e.g., colonization, genocide, apartheid, and foreign administration. Domestic residents have to deal with tremendous trust issues among different cultures and societies as well as with one of the highest inequalities worldwide.

The Namibian government evolved effective ways in order to tackle the appearing social and economic objectives. One of them is the repetitive process of designing a *National Development Plan* that gets replaced every 4–6 years. Thus, it is able to ensure performing flexible in their combat of occurring challenges.

According to the economic situation of Namibia, the country exhibits a minor degree of industrialization that leads to huge opportunities for *multinational enterprises* to stimulate the domestic economy. Simultaneously it causes threats in terms of exploitation through external interests.

Special attention needs to be paid toward the nation's already scarce natural resources, which are mainly represented in land, water, and fish stock. Finding the balance between the sustainable economic growth and the right degree of using natural resources will remain as a national objective.

Furthermore, Namibia is supposed to develop its own socioeconomic actions on a regional and international basis, in order to strengthen their self-esteem and the Namibian identity.

## Author details

Vito Bobek[1*], Jellenz Moritz[1] and Tatjana Horvat[2]

1 University of Applied Sciences FH Joanneum, Graz, Austria

2 University of Primorska, Koper, Slovenia

*Address all correspondence to: vito.bobek@fh-joanneum.at

## References

[1] Namibia NP. Republic of Namibia—Office of the President—National Planning Commission. 2019. Available from: https://www.npc.gov.na/?page_id=18

[2] Bank TW World Bank. 2019. Available from: https://data.worldbank.org/country/namibia

[3] Almond AG. In: Verba S, editor. The Civic Culture: Political Attitudes and Democracy in Five Nations. Boston: Little Brown; 1965

[4] Berger PL. The capitalist revolution: A fifty propositions about prosperity. In: Equality and Liberty. New York: Basic Books; 1986

[5] Hans-Herman H. Transformation zur Marktwirtschaft im Spannungsfeld von Politik und Gesellschaft. In: V Rusland—Fragmente einer postsowjetischen Kultur. Bremen: Forschungsstelle Osteuropa (Universität Bremen); 1999

[6] Paul DM. Culture and economy. In: The Handbook of Economic Sociology, Urednika Smelser in Swedberg. New York: Princeton University Press; 1994

[7] Stephan P. Kultur und evolutorische Ökonomik. In: Evolutorischer Ökonomik, Band 1. Marburg: Metropolis; 2005

[8] Fershtman C, Weiss Y. Social status, culture and economic performance. Economic Journal. 1993;**103**(419):946-959

[9] Inse C. Der Fall Japan—Kultur Als Triebkraft Wirtschaftlicher Entwicklung. Frankfurt/M: European University Studies; 1991

[10] Jones EL. Culture and its relationship to economic change. Journal of Institutional and Theoretical Economics. 1995;**151**:269-285

[11] Boyd R, Richerson PJ. Culture and the Evolutionary Process. Chicago: University of Chicago Press; 1985

[12] Botir V. The role of economic culture in social progress. Spiritual Values and Social Progress, Urednika Shermukhamedov in Levinskaya [Online]. 2000. Available from: http://www.crvp.org/book/Series03/IIIC-1/chapter_xii.htm

[13] Elster J, Offe C, Preuss UK. Institutional Design in Post-communist Societies: Rebuilding the Ship at Sea. Cambridge: Cambridge University Press; 1998

[14] Garsztecki S. Kulturkonzepte und Transformationsforschung: V. In: Kultur als Bestimmungsfaktor der Transformation im Osten Europas: Konzeptionelle Entwicklungen—empirische Befunde, Band 10. Bremen: Edition Temmen; 2001

[15] Kračun D. Uvod v Ekonomsko Teorijo 1. Maribor: Ekonomsko-poslovna fakulteta; 2000

[16] Žižmond E, Strašek S. Ekonomska Analiza in Politika. Maribor: Ekonomsko-poslovna fakulteta; 1999

[17] Douglas NC. Institucije, Institucionalne Spremembe in Gospodarska uspešnost. Ljubljana: Temeljna dela; 1998

[18] Hudson K. Roots of development: What matters most for development—Geography, institutions or policy? The Economist [Online]. 2002, 2002. Available from: http://www.economist.com

[19] Easterley W, Levine R. It's not factor accumulation: Stylized facts and growth

models. World Bank Economic Review [Online]. 2001;**2**:177-219. Available from: http://www.worldbank.org/research/growth/pdfiles/fact%20final.pdf

[20] Živko T. Empirična analiza vpliva ekonomske kulture na ekonomsko uspešnost držav(e)—Magistrsko Delo. Maribor: EPF; 2003

[21] UNESCO Diversity of Cultural Expressions. 2019. Available from: https://en.unesco.org/creativity/cdis

[22] Hofstede Insights. 2019. Available from: https://www.hofstede-insights.com/country-comparison/namibia/

[23] Ferrant G. How Do Gender Inequalities Hinder Development? Cross-Country Evidence. Annals of Economics and Statistics , No. 117/118, Special Issue on the Economics of Gender. 2015. pp. 313-352

[24] Chapman M. Making a literature: The case of Namibia. English in Africa. 1995;**22**(2):19-28

[25] Kössler R. Images of history and the nation: Namibia and Zimbabwe. South African Historical Journal. 2010;**62**(1):29-53

[26] Gascoigne AB. 2019History World. Available from: http://www.historyworld.net/wrldhis/PlainTextHistories.asp?historyid=ad32

[27] Planet, L. (2019, Lonely Planet. Available from: https://www.lonelyplanet.com/namibia/background/history/a/nar/1ee44733-6f42-43d1-8a7f-fa0c8282d095/355526

[28] Krugmann H. Fundamental Issues and the Threats to Sustainable Development in Namibia. Windhoek: Ministry of Environment and Tourism; 2001

[29] World Population Review. 2019. Avialable from: http://worldpopulationreview.com/countries/namibia-population/

[30] Sylvain R. Disorderly development: Globalization and the idea of "culture" in the Kalahari. American Ethnologist. 2005;**32**(3):354-370

[31] Angula M. Gender and Climate Change: Namibia Case Study. Cape Town: Heinrich Böll Foundation Southern Africa; 2010

[32] Trading Economics. 2019. Available form: https://tradingeconomics.com/namibia/indicators

[33] Humavindu MN, Stage J. Key Sectors of the Namibian Economy. Sundsvall: SpringerOpen; 2013

[34] United Nations Development Programme. 2019. Avialable from: http://hdr.undp.org/en

[35] Knoema. 2019. Available from: https://knoema.com/search?query=Namibia&pageIndex=&scope=&term=&correct=&source=Header

[36] Ainsworth M, Fransen L, Over M. Confronting AIDS: Evidence from the Developing World. Brussels: The European Commission; 1998

[37] UNAIDS. 2019. Available from: https://www.unaids.org/en/regionscountries/countries/namibia

[38] Dollar D, Fisman R, Gatti R. Are women really the "fairer" sex? Corruption and women in government. Journal of Economic Behavior & Organization, Elsevier. 2001;**46**(4):423-429

[39] Agency NS. The Namibia Labour Force Survey 2016 Report. Windhoek: Namibia Statistics Agency; 2017

[40] Bollig M, Schnegg M, Wotzka H-P. Pastoralism in Africa: Past, Present and Future. New York: Berghahn; 2013

[41] Institute for Public Policy Research (IPPR). 2019. Available from: https://ippr.org.na

[42] Namibia HC. Namibia High Commission London—Promoting Travel, Tourism, Trade & Investment. 2019. Available from: http://www.namibiahc.org.uk/economy.php

[43] Mainar-Causapé AJ, Ferrari E, McDonald S. Social Accounting Matrices: Basic Aspects and Main Steps for Estimation. Luxembourg: European Commission JRC Technical Reports; 2018

[44] Trust NF. Namibia Trade Directory. 2019. Available from: http://namibiatradedirectory.com/fishing/

[45] Online SA. South African History. 2019. Available from: https://www.sahistory.org.za/policy

[46] Republic of Namibia Ministry of Industrialisation, Trade and SME Development. 2019. Availble form: http://www.mti.gov.na/incentives.html

[47] Maček A, Ovin R. Does economic interventionism help strategic industries? Evidence from Europe. E+M: Ekonomie a Management. 2014;**17**(3):5-14

[48] Zvezdanović J, Maček A, Ovin R. Institutional setting as a determinant of FDI attraction—Example of Serbia. In: Petrović P, editor. International Thematic Proceedings Possibilities and Perspectives for Foreign Direct Investments in the Republic of Serbia. Belgrade: Institute of International Politics and Economics; 2013. pp. 17-41

[49] The Global Economy. 2019. Available from: https://www.theglobaleconomy.com/Namibia/Foreign_Direct_Investment/

[50] Unesco. 2019. Available from: https://en.unesco.org/creativity/sites/creativity/files/convention2005_basictext_en.pdf#page=15

Chapter 4

# Economic, Social, and Environmental Dimensions of Development in Sudan

*Elwasila Mohamed*


## Abstract

This chapter aims to investigate how social and environmental progress indicators lead economic indicators of development in Sudan. Economic indicators are represented by gross domestic product (GDP), investment, and unemployment. Social progress indicators are represented by life expectancy at birth standing for health and school enrollment for education. Environmental performance is indicated by access to safe drinking water and access to sanitation facilities. Trade as percentage of GDP is included to represent openness and outward of the economy. The study provides analytical links between these development dimensions and found empirical verification that social and environmental performance indicators cause economic growth rather than the other way around through dynamic econometric methods utilizing time series data over the period 1970–2017. Accordingly, the study provided recommendations and projections on enhancing social progress indicators toward 2030 Sustainable Development Goal (SDG) targets.


**Keywords:** economic growth, social progress, environmental performance, health, education, Sudan

## 1. Introduction

Development, however defined and measured, is something that has not been realized in low-income countries. From its narrow measurement through gross domestic product (GDP) to human development index (HDI) to a more comprehensive index of sustainable development, now development can be seen in low-income countries. Low-income levels have been associated with low achievements in all aspects of social and environmental progress in these countries. Even some levels of economic growth in terms of income per capita and social, political, and environmental indicators of progress are all lacking behind. That is, economic growth alone is not sufficient to advance societies and improve the quality of life of citizens. True success, and growth that is inclusive, requires achieving both economic and social progress (SPI, 2018) [3]. In short, economic progress should be accompanied with social and environmental progress. The measurement of economic development in terms of gross domestic product (GDP) was well established in the economic literature pioneered firstly by Simon Kuznets and developed into systems of national accounts adopted by the United Nation agencies since the 1960s. However, major criticisms have been raised against using GDP as a measure of economic and social welfare, particularly among scholars in the field on environmental economics. This literature has been arguing for modification of GDP to include resource depletion and environmental degradation associated with economic growth in a context of sustainable development. The World Bank has adopted and started measuring the so-called genuine savings indicator developed by Pearce and Atkinson [1] and the genuine progress indicator (GPI), as measures of sustainable development. Yet, a massive body of literature had been developing arguing that economic growth is the only way to protect the environment, in the context of the so-called environmental Kuznets curve. Since the early 1990s, the UN Development Programme has adopted and started measuring the human development index pioneered by Sen and Haq. The HDI encompasses measures of economic, health, and education and ranks countries in a scale of 100 points according to their achievements in these dimensions. All these measures have been developed in lines of calls sustainable development following the World Commission on Environment and Development Report in 1987 and the Agenda 21 adopted in Rio 1991. In 2000, the world nations adopted the Millennium Development Goals (MDGs). The agreed MDGs had to be achieved by 2015. Many low-income countries failed to achieve the targets, while the world nations went forward to adopt the Sustainable Development Goals (SDGs) to be achieved by 2030. In the light of their progress to achieve the MDGs, low-income countries are unlikely to move forward to make progress in achieving the SDGs in a matter of 10 years. However, SDGs remain a guide to economic, social, and environmental policies in all countries but particularly in low-income countries. Detailed discussions on these measures of development in the context of MDGs and SDGs can be found in Chapter 5 of the United Nation Global Sustainable Development Report [2].

## 2. Economic growth or social progress

The Social Progress Imperative has recently formed. This initiative defines social progress as the "capacity of a society to meet the basic human needs of its citizens, establish the building blocks that allow citizens and communities to enhance and sustain the quality of their lives, and create the conditions for all individuals to reach their full potential" [3]. The main feature of the Social Progress Index (SPI) is that it focuses exclusively on the aggregation of social and environmental output oriented measures. The Social Progress Index sets out to do so by asking three fundamental questions about a society. First of all, does everyone have the basic needs of survival: food, water, shelter, and safety? Secondly, does everyone have the building blocks of a better life: education, information, health, and a sustainable natural environment? And does everyone have the opportunity to improve his or her life, through rights, freedom of choice, tolerance and freedom from discrimination and freedom of mobility, and access to the world's most advanced knowledge? It measures these aspects of inclusion directly using only social and environmental indicators. By excluding traditional economic indicators from the model, it allows to better interrogate the relationship between social progress, and each of its 12 components, and economic growth, and in so doing more richly unpacking their relationships and identifying the true drivers of progress of the society in question. The SPI launched a global index in 2014, analyzing 132 countries using 52 indicators of social and environmental performance. In 2018, the SPI captures outcomes related to 16 of the 17 SDGs in a simple but rigorous framework designed for aggregation, making it an invaluable proxy measure of SDG performance. To translate this definition into a concrete measurement tool, some researchers constructed the Social Progress Index (SPI) [4]. They constructed a SPI and used it together with basic human needs and opportunity indictors and find that these social performance indictors strongly affect subjective well-being. Nevertheless, economics, with its all school of thought, has been playing a central role on these advances of definitions, measurements, and determinants of development. For Seligman [5], "economics is both the creature and the creator. It is the creature of the past; it is the creator of the future. Correctly conceived, adequately outlined, fearlessly developed, it is the prop of ethical upbuilding, it is the basis of social progress" (1903, p. 70). The development that took place in the West and the United States in particular was described as a transformation to industrial society with all of its economic, social, and political facts and facets. On this type of development and how it has been achieved, Seligman made six points which differentiate modern industrial society from all its predecessors. In today's less developing countries, these points differentiate success from failure to achieve development. The points are the practical exhaustion of free land, the predominance of industrial capital, the application of scientific methods, the existence of a competitive regime based on the newer conception of liberty, the spread of education and the birth of a distinct public opinion, and a true democratic spirit and the growth of a new idealism. Unless these points take place in today's less developing countries, it is unlikely that they be able to move forward for real socioeconomic development.

Economic growth or more widely some development achieved in low-income countries cannot be attributed to conventional factors of production such as physical capital and formal employment. It is rather an outcome of private investment, social households, and individual behaviors with the use of assets from the natural environment. We give some examples in justification of this argument. Private spending health has always been far larger than government spending on health in low-income countries, including Sudan. Even on primary education, household spending exceeds government spending although primary education is supposed to be free and universal. This can be indicated by a large number of school dropouts, where school-age children go to work in informal jobs so as to help their often poor families. In the political arena, political and personal rights are lacking behind, and individuals are left to themselves to find ways to exercise and express their views and voices. Social media have been playing a major role in providing information to the public replacing the official government media channels. This has typically taken place in Sudan since December 2018. Communications and organization of activities through social media have contributed strongly to massive demonstrations which succeeded in ousting the regime that ruled the country for almost three decades. Thus defective social and political fabrics in less developed countries cannot be disentangled from all types of economic and political corruption which have been the chronic illness in these countries in postcolonial periods. In such cases, it is by no means to expect that economic policies and pure economic factors contribute economic growth and development and social equity. Instead, social and environmental progresses achieved however small have to be attributed to the private and household's behaviors and initiatives and thus are the main contributors to economic growth. Furthermore, economic growth achieved through these channels is always skewed toward the rich who are not necessarily contributing a fair share to its achievement. This can be reflected by a wide and even increasing income gap between the rich and the poor in low-income countries. Also, economic growth can be expected really to resolve and revert environmental degradation in terms of massive resource depletion and accumulation of pollution. Thus, arguably it is not more than luxury to seek a verification of environmental Kuznets curve in low-income countries. Furthermore, environmental policies in these countries are usually lax and lacking behind. This in turn has been pushing low-income countries to trade environment for development and become pollution havens. It is a fact that trade in its export side has been intensive in primary products and natural resources, both renewable and nonrenewable. Even this pattern has been a major dragger to economic growth in the sense of the so-called resource curse hypothesis. These facts and accounts are our rationale to model GDP growth against social and environmental performance indicators, rather than the other way around.

## 3. Analytical framework: from social and environmental performance to economic performance

**Figure 1** shows a proposed analytical framework in which social and environmental indicators, together with investment and trade openness, are assumed to explain economic growth represented by the current gross domestic product (GDP). For a low-income country such as Sudan, social and environmental dimensions of development are more expected to lead economic dimension of development rather than economic leading to socio-environmental improvements. The framework also assumes that selected all economic, social, and environmental measures to affect economic development positively. In terms of causation, the analytical framework presumes that the causation runs from social and environmental performance to economic development as narrowly measured by GDP growth.

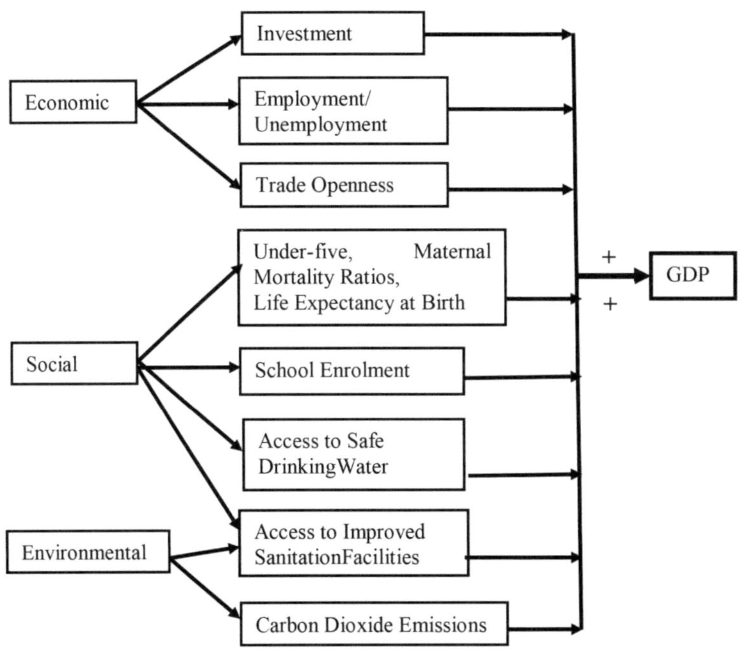


**Figure 1.**
*Economic, social, and environmental dimensions of development.*

## 4. Sudan: economic, social, and environmental dimensions of development

We used the framework set in **Figure 1** to explain how social and environmental indicators have affected development in its economic dimension as commonly measured by GDP. Variable selection is necessitated by availability of data, which is collected from the World Bank, World Development Indicators (WDI), and World

Bank 2018 [6] and complemented with other sources. The study variables are defined as follows:

Gross domestic product (GDP): GDP is the value of all goods and services produced in the economy expressed in current US dollars and stands for economic growth.

Domestic investment (INV): INV is measured by gross capital formation consisting of additions to the fixed assets of the economy plus net changes in the level of inventories. Fixed assets include land improvements (fences, ditches, drains, and so on); plant, machinery, and equipment purchases; and the construction of roads, railways, and the like, including schools, offices, hospitals, private residential dwellings, and commercial and industrial buildings. Inventories are stocks of goods held by firms to meet temporary or unexpected fluctuations in production or sales and work in progress.

Unemployment is represented by the total youth unemployment as percentage of total labor force ages (15–24), and it refers to the share of the labor force ages 15–24 without work but available for and seeking employment.

Life expectancy at birth indicates the number of years a newborn would live if prevailing patterns of mortality at the time of its birth were to stay the same throughout its life.

Average school enrollment (EDU): EDU is measured by net enrollment rate which is the ratio of children of official school age who are enrolled in school to the population of the corresponding official school age. The World Bank acknowledges that primary education provides children with basic reading, writing, and mathematics skills. These are basics for any progression to secondary and tertiary education.

Access to drinking water (ASW): Access to safe drinking water is measured by people using at least basic drinking water services (% of population). It encompasses both people using basic water services and those using safely managed water services. Basic drinking water services are defined as drinking water from an improved source, provided collection time is not more than 30 minutes for a round trip. Improved water sources include piped water, boreholes or tube wells, protected dug wells, protected springs, and packaged or delivered water.

Access to sanitation facilities (ASF): It is represented by people using safely managed sanitation services (% of population) defined as the percentage of people using improved sanitation facilities that are not shared with other households and where excreta are safely disposed of in situ or transported and treated off-site. Improved sanitation facilities include flush/pour flush to piped sewer systems, septic tanks, or pit latrines: ventilated improved pit latrines, compositing toilets, or pit latrines with slabs.

Access to electricity is measured by the average percentage of population with access to electricity.

Carbon dioxide emissions as defined by the World Bank are those stemming from the burning of fossil fuels and the manufacture of cement. They include carbon dioxide produced during consumption of solid, liquid, and gas fuels and gas flaring. $CO_2$ emissions are measured in metric tons per capita (CO2P).

Trade openness is measured as the sum of exports and imports of goods and services as percentage of gross domestic product.

## 5. Empirical analysis

### 5.1 Descriptive statistical analysis

**Table 1** presents the descriptive statistics of the study variables. From the Jarque-Bera (J-B) and associated prob. values, all variables look normally distributed expect education, access to drinking water, and access to electricity. The highest kurtosis is associated with GDP followed by access to drinking water and access to electricity. As for average rainfall, it has been reported that summer monthly precipitation over the Sahel is not normally distributed.

From the correlation matrix in **Table 2** noticeably, the GDP highly positively correlates with life expectancy at birth, education, access to drinking water, and access to electricity. Life expectancy and education both positively correlate with access to drinking water and access to electricity.

We conducted a graphical analysis of the study variables. **Figure 2** shows upward trend for current GDP, while **Figure 3** depicts erratic trend of investment. Also youth unemployment experiences high fluctuations as depicted in **Figure 4**. **Figure 5** indicates upward sloping life expectancy at birth over time. School enrolment shows upward trend with some small fluctuations as shown in **Figure 6**. Access to sanitation facilities runs through a period of upward trend and downward trend and more recently started to trend upward as depicted in **Figure 7**. Access to drinking water showed slow increase at the beginning of our time series but started to increase sharply after the year 2004 as shown in **Figure 8**. Access to electricity

| | GDP | INV | YUN | LE | EDU | ASF | ASW | ELC | CO2P | TOP |
|---|---|---|---|---|---|---|---|---|---|---|
| Mean | 2.60E+10 | 19.09 | 27.85 | 57.20 | 28.64 | 25.35 | 45.07 | 30.71 | 0.24 | 26.80 |
| Median | 1.24E+10 | 16.34 | 27.82 | 56.19 | 25.07 | 25.35 | 42.73 | 29.58 | 0.22 | 25.46 |
| Maximum | 1.17E+11 | 37.19 | 28.95 | 64.99 | 48.41 | 27.70 | 59.27 | 44.90 | 0.37 | 47.58 |
| Minimum | 2.44E+09 | 7.29 | 26.39 | 51.74 | 18.67 | 22.50 | 40.62 | 23.00 | 0.10 | 11.09 |
| Std. dev. | 2.91E+10 | 7.27 | 0.59 | 3.71 | 8.92 | 1.45 | 5.59 | 4.37 | 0.09 | 9.53 |
| Skewness | 1.60 | 0.67 | 0.03 | 0.51 | 0.93 | −0.15 | 1.52 | 0.87 | 0.28 | 0.19 |
| Kurtosis | 4.43 | 2.49 | 2.51 | 2.12 | 2.48 | 1.82 | 3.93 | 3.93 | 1.54 | 2.31 |
| J-B | 24.52 | 4.14 | 0.50 | 3.67 | 7.44 | 2.97 | 20.32 | 7.81 | 4.91 | 1.25 |
| Prob. | 0.000 | 0.126 | 0.780 | 0.160 | 0.024 | 0.226 | 0.000 | 0.020 | 0.086 | 0.535 |
| Obs. | 48 | 48 | 48 | 48 | 48 | 48 | 48 | 48 | 48 | 48 |

**Table 1.**
*Basic statistics.*

| | GDP | INV | YUN | LE | EDU | ASF | ASW | ELC | CO2P | TOP |
|---|---|---|---|---|---|---|---|---|---|---|
| GDP | 1.00 | | | | | | | | | |
| INV | −0.09 | 1.00 | | | | | | | | |
| YUN | −0.45 | 0.19 | 1.00 | | | | | | | |
| LE | 0.90 | 0.22 | −0.29 | 1.00 | | | | | | |
| EDU | 0.93 | 0.10 | −0.35 | 0.97 | 1.00 | | | | | |
| ASF | −0.44 | −0.06 | 0.31 | −0.48 | −0.54 | 1.00 | | | | |
| ASW | 0.98 | −0.06 | −0.39 | 0.91 | 0.95 | −0.45 | 1.00 | | | |
| ELC | 0.83 | 0.23 | −0.24 | 0.93 | 0.89 | −0.32 | 0.87 | 1.00 | | |
| CO2P | 0.63 | −0.26 | −0.54 | 0.44 | 0.60 | −0.67 | 0.62 | 0.36 | 1.00 | |
| TOP | 0.04 | 0.22 | −0.22 | 0.10 | 0.15 | −0.65 | 0.03 | −0.09 | 0.44 | 1.00 |

**Table 2.**
*Correlation matrix.*

*DOI: http://dx.doi.org/10.5772/intechopen.90752*

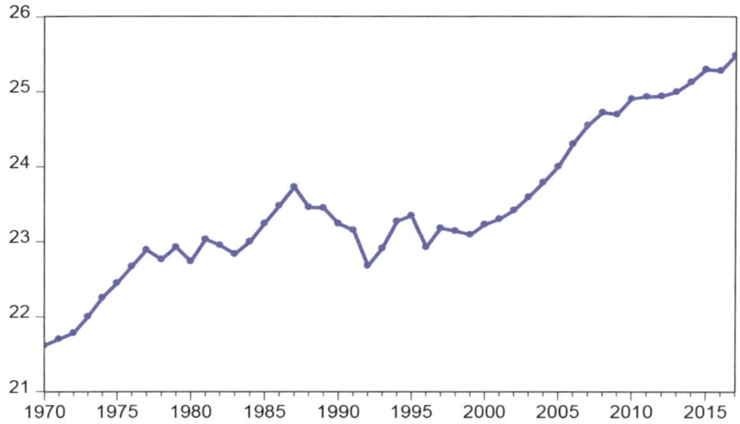


**Figure 2.**
*Log of GDP.*

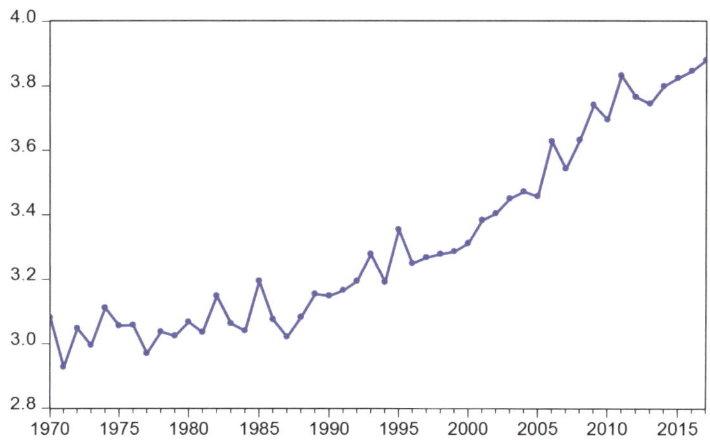


**Figure 3.**
*Log of investment.*

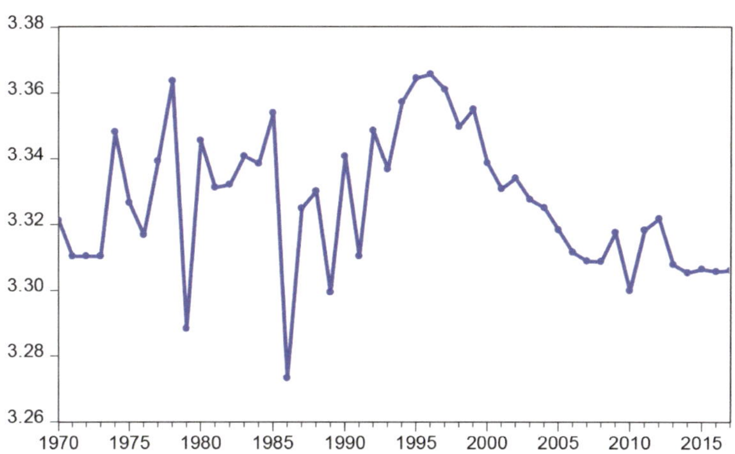


**Figure 4.**
*Log of youth unemployment.*

shows more erratic trend over time and only after 2002 started to show steady increase but with a drop in 2009 and a hike in 2014 as in **Figure 9**. Carbon dioxide emissions experienced a declining trend from 1974 until 1993 and then started to

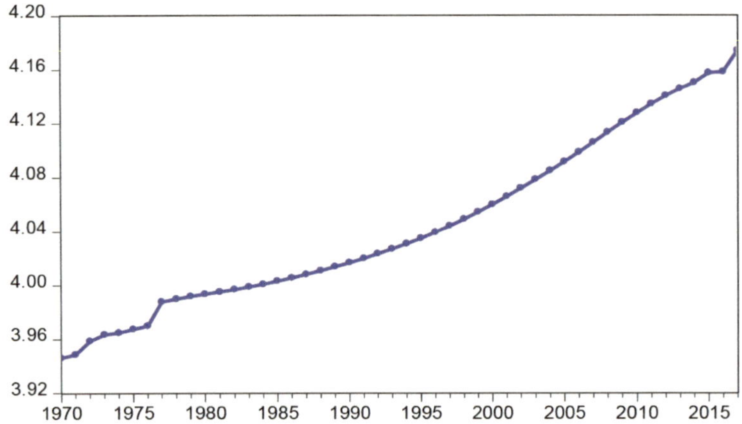


**Figure 5.**
*Log of life expectancy at birth.*

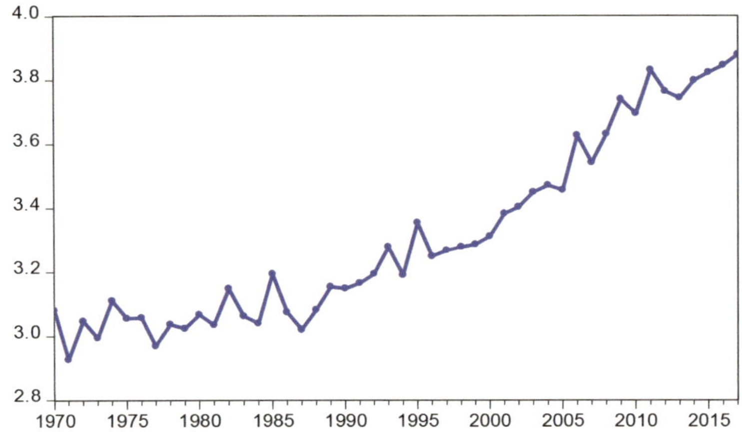


**Figure 6.**
*Log of primary school enrolment.*

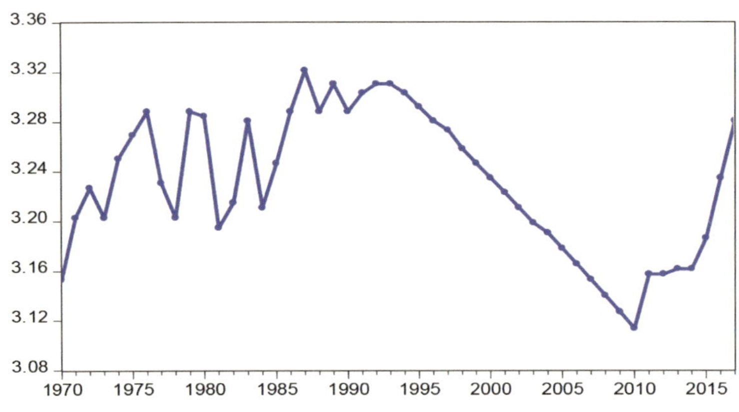


**Figure 7.**
*Log of access to sanitation facilities.*

increase over the rest of our time series frame as in **Figure 10**. Trade openness runs through relatively stable trend over the period 1970–1983, a massive decline from 1984 to 1993, an increase over the period 1994–2006, and then a decline over the rest of our time frameworks in **Figure 11**. These time trends of the economic, social, and environmental dimensions of development in Sudan reflect various episodes of war and environmental and climate change along generally failed macroeconomic policies to improve development with its multifacet and interacting dimensions.

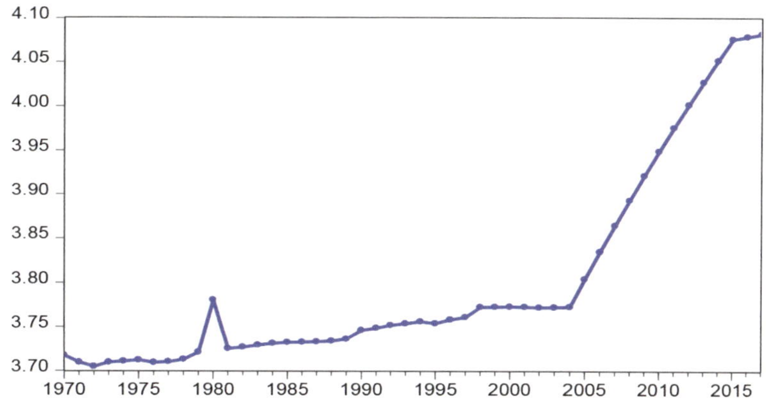


**Figure 8.**
*Log of access to drinking water.*

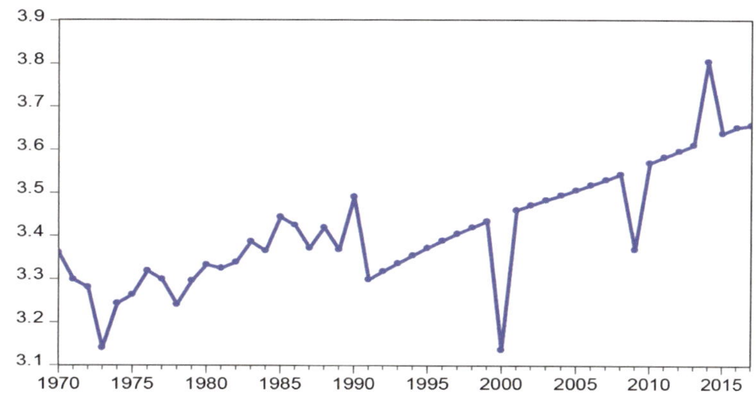


**Figure 9.**
*Log of access to electricity.*

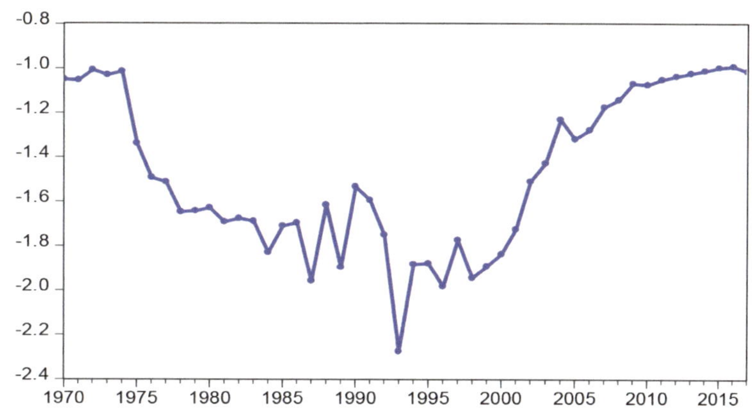


**Figure 10.**
*Log of carbon dioxide emissions per capita.*

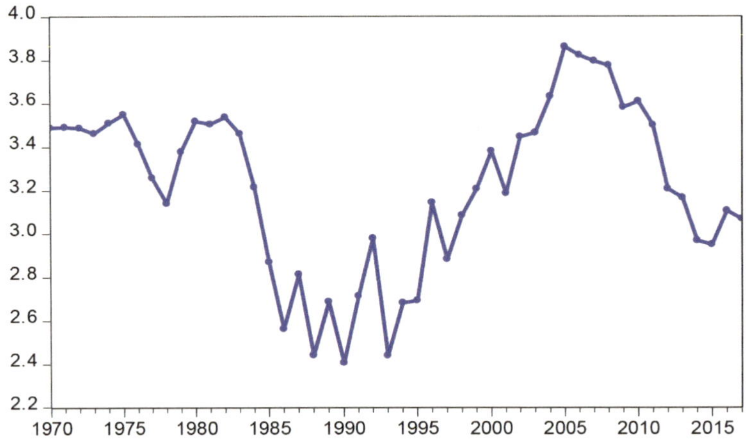


**Figure 11.**
*Log of trade openness.*

## 5.2 Empirical investigation

### *5.2.1 Econometric methods*

This study is empirical and quantitative, using statistical and econometric methods. Sound empirical studies on economic, social, and environmental dimensions of development need to be based on clear theoretical framework, rigorous methodology, and reliable data. Empirical quantitative studies using dynamic econometric methods on these relationships are rare, although empirical-quantitative research programs in all socioeconomic and environmental issues are usually more rigorous [7]. The study is very selective on variables included, which is necessitated by data availability and possible theoretical links. The study presumes that economic growth is affected by social and environmental progress indicators rather than the other way around. The study covers the period 1970–2017 with annual time series data on all of its variables. Economic growth represented by current GDP is treated as the dependent variable, and social and environmental indicators are the independent variables. Trade openness is included as a control variable and represents the exposure of Sudan economy to international shocks. A general log linear model to capture the complexity of economic, social, and environmental dimensions of development in Sudan is written as:

$$L(GDP) = \alpha + \beta_1 L(INV) + \beta_2 L(UNE) + \beta_3 L(LE) + \beta_4 L(EDU) + \beta_5 L(ASF) + \beta_6 L(ASW) + \beta_7 L(ELC) + \beta_8 L(CO2P) + \beta_9 L(TOP) + \beta_{10} DUM + \mu \quad (1)$$

where DUM stands for dummy that is 0 in 1978, 1997, and 2011 and 1 otherwise. These years are judged to represent breaks in Sudan economy as years of the first ever devaluation of the national currency, imposition of sanction on Sudan by the United States, and secession of South Sudan, respectively.

### *5.2.2 Stationary and cointegration of variables*

The first step is to use a preliminary statistic test to verify the stationarity for all variables. A time series is described as nonstationary if it has at least one of its moments (mean, variance, or covariance) as time independent.

However, a nonstationary series possessing a stochastic unit root can be differenced once to become stationary. Establishing stationarity of macroeconomic series is necessary for reliable econometric estimations and causality analysis tests and since most macroeconomic series are in fact not stationary. Stationary of time series included in this study is tested through the conventional augmented Dickey-Fuller (ADF) and Phillips-Perron (PP) unit root tests, complimented by Kwiatkowski-Phillips-Schmidt-Shin (KPSS [8]). The ADF test takes into account only the presence of autocorrelation in the series, but the PP test considers also the hypothesis of the presence of a heteroskedasticity dimension in the time series and Kwiatkowski-Phillips-Schmidt-Shin (KPSS [8]). In literature, tests designed following the null hypothesis that a series is I(1) have low power to reject the null. Therefore, KPSS is sometimes used along the widely used ADF and PP tests to have robust results. The findings from the ADF, PP, and KPSS tests are reported in **Table 3**. Investment and unemployment are found to be stationary at level I(0) and first difference I(1) while the first differencing makes all variables stationary.

Combined results from these three tests indicate all series are integrated to the order i.e., I(1) but some of them are stationary at level I(0), i.e., all series are I(0)/I (1). As a result, we choose to use the autoregressive distributed lag (ARDL) bound test for cointegration because one of its main advantages is that it does not impose a

| Variable | ADF | | PP | | KPSS | Order of integration |
|---|---|---|---|---|---|---|
| | Stat. | 5% cri. value | Stat. | 5% cri. value | Stat. | |
| L(GDP) | −0.380 | −2.925 | −0.400 | −2.925 | 0.799 | Nonstationary |
| *ΔL(GDP)* | *−6.349** | *−2.927* | *−6.349** | *−2.927* | *0.136** | *Stationary I(1)* |
| L(INV) | −3.048* | −2.925 | −2.897 | −2.925 | 0.450* | Stationary I(0) |
| *ΔL(INV)* | *−6.498** | *−2.928* | *−12.465** | *−2.927* | *0.500* | *Stationary I(1)* |
| L(YUN) | −2.555 | −2.927 | −5.338* | −2.925 | 0.201* | Stationary I(0) |
| *ΔL(YUN)* | *−8.931** | *−2.928* | *−16.341** | *−2.927* | *0.020** | *Stationary I(1)* |
| L(LE) | 2.102 | −2.931 | 2.679 | −2.925 | 0.891 | Nonstationary |
| *ΔL(LE)* | *−2.606* | *−2.929* | *−5.747** | *−2.927* | *0.632* | *Stationary I(1)* |
| L(EDU) | 0.025 | −2.928 | −0.282 | −2.925 | 0.788 | Nonstationary |
| *ΔL(EDU)* | *−10.722** | *−2.928* | *−11.275** | *−2.927* | *0.239** | *Stationary I(1)* |
| L(ASF) | −1.941 | −2.931 | −2.131 | −2.925 | 0.325* | Stationary I(0) |
| *ΔL(ASF)* | *−1.916* | *−2.931* | *−7.154** | *−2.927* | *0.131** | *Stationary I(1)* |
| L(ASW) | 2.643 | −2.925 | 2.487 | −2.925 | 0.707 | Stationary I(0) |
| *ΔL(ASW)* | *−3.243** | *−2.928* | *−5.924** | *−2.927* | *0.569* | *Stationary I(1)* |
| L(ELC) | 0.050 | −2.927 | −0.259 | −2.925 | 0.858 | Nonstationary |
| *ΔL(ELC)* | *−6.829** | *−2.927* | *−13.650** | *−2.927* | *0.319** | *Stationary I(1)* |
| L(CO2P) | −1.097 | −2.927 | −1.391 | −2.925 | 0.279* | Stationary I(0) |
| *Δ(CO2P)* | *−9.243** | *−2.927* | *−9.167** | *−2.927* | *0.254** | *Stationary I(1)* |
| L(TOP) | −1.920 | −2.925 | −1.888 | −2.925 | 0.133* | Stationary I(0) |
| *Δ L(TOP)* | *−8.488** | *−2.927* | *−8.370** | *−2.927* | *0.084** | *Stationary I(1)* |

*Note: The ADF and PP unit root tests employ null hypothesis with the series that has a unit root against the alternative of stationary. The null hypothesis for the KPSS assumes that the variable is stationary. KPSS critical value is 0.463.*
**indicates significance at 5% level.*

**Table 3.**
*Unit root test results.*

restrictive assumption that all variables should have the same integration order. Another advantage is that a dynamic error correction (EC) term can be derived from the ARDL through simple linear transformation. The error correction term shows the short-run dynamics with the long-run stable equilibrium without losing the long-run information.

### *5.2.3 ARDL model specification and estimation*

An autoregressive distributed lag model bound test advanced by Pesaran and Smith [9], Pesaran and Shin [10] and with the bound test of Pesaran et al. [11] is used to investigate cointegration and the short-run dynamics and long-run equilibrium of GDP as the dependent variable and social and environmental indicators as explanatory variables. An unrestricted ARDL model on the basis of Eq. (1) is specified as follows:

$$\begin{aligned}\Delta L(GDP)_t &= \alpha + \sum_{i=1}^{p} \beta_{1i} L(GDP)_{t-1} \\ &+ \sum_{i=0}^{p} \Delta\beta_{2i} L(INV)_{t-i} + \sum_{i=0}^{p} \beta_{3i} \Delta L(UNE)_{t-i} \\ &+ \sum_{i=0}^{p} \beta_{4i} \Delta L(LE)_{t-i} + \sum_{i=0}^{p} \beta_5 \Delta L(EDU)_{t-i} \\ &+ \sum_{i=0}^{p} \beta_6 \Delta L(ASF)_{t-i} + \sum_{i=0}^{p} \beta_7 \Delta L(ASW)_{t-i} \\ &+ \sum_{i=0}^{p} \beta_8 \Delta L(ELC)_{t-i} + \sum_{i=0}^{p} \beta_9 \Delta L(CO2P)_{t-i} \\ &+ \sum_{i=0}^{p} \beta_{10} \Delta L(TOP)_{t-i} + \beta_{10} L(GDP)_{t-1} + \beta_{11} L(INV)_{t-1} \\ &+ \beta_{12} L(UNE)_{t-1} + \beta_{13} L(LE)_{t-1} + \beta_{14} L(EDU)_{t-1} \\ &+ \beta_{15} L(ASF)_{t-1} + \beta_{16} L(ASW)_{t-1} + \beta_{17} L(ELC)_{t-1} \\ &+ \beta_{18} L(CO2P)_{t-1} + \beta_{19} L(TOP)_{t-1} + \beta_{20} DUM_t + EC_t + \mu_t\end{aligned} \tag{2}$$

All variables and abbreviations are as defined above. The parameter $p$ is the lag length, $\Delta$ is the difference operator, and EC is the ARDL error correction term. Eq. (2) can be estimated through the OLS to explore the long-run relationship of the model variables by performing an F-test statistics for the joint significance of the lagged-level variables. The null hypothesis of no cointegration (i.e., no long-run equilibrium relationship between the study variables) in Eq. (2) is: $H_0 : \beta_1 = \beta_2 = \beta_3 = \beta_4 = \beta_5 = \beta_6 = \beta_7 = \beta_8 + \beta_9 = \beta_{10} = 0$, against the alternative hypothesis of the existence of cointegration that: $H_1 : \beta_{11} \neq \beta_{12} \neq \beta_{13} \neq \beta_{14} \neq \beta_{15} \neq \beta_{16} \neq \beta_{17} \neq \beta_{18} \neq \beta_{19} \neq \beta_{20} \neq 0$.

The decision rule for the existence of cointegration in the bound testing approach according to Pesaran and Shin (1999) is two sets of critical values for the F-statistic: the lower bound where all variables are cointegrated of the order I(0) and the upper bound where all variables are cointegrated of the order I(1). If the F-statistic lies below the lower bound value, the conclusion is no cointegration, and if the F-statistic is found to be above the upper bound value, then cointegration exists, whereas if the F-statistic falls between the upper bound and the lower bound, then the test is inconclusive. The ARDL bound test is performed on Eq. (2), where each

| F-bound test | | Null hypothesis: no level relationship | | |
|---|---|---|---|---|
| **Test statistic** | **Value** | **Significance** | **I(0)** | **I(1)** |
| F-statistic | 7.47 | 10% | 1.8 | 2.8 |
| K | 9 | 5% | 2.04 | 2.08 |
| | | 2.5% | 2.24 | 3.35 |
| | | 1% | 2.5 | 3.68 |

**Table 4.**
*Bound test cointegration: GDP dependent variable.*

| Lag | LL | LR | FPE | AIC | SC | HQ |
|---|---|---|---|---|---|---|
| 0 | 467.371 | NA | 7.03e-22 | −20.328 | −19.926 | −20.178 |
| 1 | 791.748 | 490.169 | 3.63e-26 | −30.300 | −25.884* | −28.654 |
| 2 | 945.800 | *164.322*#* | 6.50e-27 | −32.702 | −24.271 | −29.560 |
| 3 | 1132.692 | 116.289 | 1.44e-27* | −36.564* | −24.118 | −31.924* |

**Indicates lag order selected by the criterion;*
*# at 5% level*
*LR, sequential modified LR test statistic (each test at 5% level); FPE, final prediction error; AIC, Akaike information criterion; SC, Schwarz information criterion; HQ, Hannan-Quinn information criterion.*

**Table 5.**
*VAR lag order selection criteria.*

variable is treated as dependent while all other variables are independent. The results show that there at least eight cointegrated forms as summarized in **Table 7**. Thus, the results of the bound test cointegration confirm the existence of a long-run equilibrium relationship between economic growth measured by GDP in relation to the set of social and environmental indicators and other covariates included as reported in **Table 4**.

We then turn to investigate how economic growth and social and environmental indicators interact in the short run and the long run. For this purpose, an ARDL to be estimated is chosen out of 39,366 models (2, 2, 0, 2, 0, 2, 2, 1, 0, 2) on the basis of criteria reported in **Table 5**.

The main ARDL results are summarized in **Table 6**.

The ARDL short-run dynamics and long-run equilibrium results are summarized in **Table 7**.

ARDL short-run dynamics and error correction (EC) results are summarized in **Table 8**.

The ARDL model shows that in the short run, investment has positive effect on GDP but with 1-year time lag. Life expectancy at birth has a negative effect on GDP with the highest elasticity coefficient of −16.45. Access to sanitation facilities exerts negative effect on GDP, while access to drinking water exerts positive effect on GDP although at 1-year time lag. Trade openness also has a negative effect on GDP. In the long run, GDP growth is positively and highly significantly affected by life expectancy at birth, access to sanitation facilities, and trade openness, respectively, while GDP is found to be negatively affected by youth unemployment followed by access to drinking water and investment. These long-run effects indicate that investments in physical capital and drinking water services have either been insufficient or ineffective in promoting economic growth in Sudan. Carbon dioxide emissions have no significant effect on economic growth in both the short and long run, although their coefficients are positive in two time frames.
Youth unemployment is the most hurting to economic growth in Sudan. The

coefficient of the error correction term estimated at −0.53 is highly significant confirming cointegration of the study variables and average speed of adjustment to equilibrium in the long run in response to the short-run shocks of the model variables. Results of the diagnostic tests show that the estimated ARDL suffers none of the conventional econometric problems associated with time series data. Thus, the estimated model is stable and robust and significantly captures the behavior of the association between economic growth and social and environmental progress indicators.

| Variable | Coefficient | Std. error | t-statistic | Prob.* |
|---|---|---|---|---|
| $L(GDP)_{t-1}$ | 0.69 | 0.123 | 5.620 | 0.000*** |
| $L(GDP)_{t-2}$ | −0.22 | 0.126 | −1.737 | 0.096* |
| L(INV) | −0.41 | 0.090 | −4.540 | 0.000*** |
| $L(INV)_{t-1}$ | 0.30 | 0.096 | 3.126 | 0.005*** |
| $L(INV)_{t-2}$ | −0.44 | 0.092 | −4.751 | 0.000*** |
| L(YUN) | −3.05 | 1.292 | −2.360 | 0.028** |
| L(LE) | 0.61 | 6.138 | 0.099 | 0.922 |
| $L(LE)_{t-1}$ | −6.81 | 10.036 | −0.679 | 0.504 |
| $L(LE)_{t-2}$ | 16.45 | 9.763 | 1.685 | 0.106* |
| L(ASE) | 0.28 | 0.430 | 0.650 | 0.523 |
| L(ASF) | 0.39 | 0.853 | 0.455 | 0.654 |
| $L(ASF)_{t-1}$ | 0.52 | 1.051 | 0.493 | 0.627 |
| $L(ASF)_{t-2}$ | 2.76 | 0.822 | 3.352 | 0.003*** |
| L(ASW) | −3.18 | 1.529 | −2.077 | 0.050** |
| $L(ASW)_{t-1}$ | 5.55 | 1.879 | 2.955 | 0.007*** |
| $L(ASW)_{t-2}$ | −3.91 | 1.461 | −2.676 | 0.014** |
| L(ELC) | 0.11 | 0.266 | 0.429 | 0.672 |
| $L(ELC)_{t-1}$ | 0.49 | 0.246 | 1.987 | 0.060* |
| L(CO2P) | 0.02 | 0.125 | 0.164 | 0.871 |
| L(TOP) | −0.03 | 0.115 | −0.269 | 0.791 |
| $L(TOP)_{t-1}$ | −0.04 | 0.135 | −0.284 | 0.779 |
| $L(TOP)_{t-2}$ | 0.49 | 0.128 | 3.832 | 0.001*** |
| DUM3 | 0.01 | 0.095 | 0.104 | 0.919 |
| C | −27.54 | 10.872 | −2.533 | 0.019** |
| R-squared = 0.994; adjusted R-squared = 0.988; SER = 0.102; SSR = 0.229; LL = 56.70; F-statistic = 167.22, P(0.000); AIC = −1.422; SC = −0.468; HQ = −1.064; DW = 2.15. | | | | |
| Diagnosis | Stat. | P. value | D.W. | |
| Normality | 0.04 | (0.979) | 2.15 | |
| Autocorrelation | 0.59 | (0.562) | 2.05 | |
| Heteroskedasticity | 0.32 | (0.996) | 2.36 | |
| Stability | 0.12 | (0.728) | 2.23 | |

****, **, and * indicate significance at 1%, 5%, and 10% level, respectively.*

**Table 6.**
*ARDL summary results.*

| Variable | Coefficient | Std. error | t-statistic | Prob. |
|---|---|---|---|---|
| L(INV) | −1.03 | 0.228 | −4.537 | 0.000*** |
| L(YUN) | −5.79 | 2.465 | −2.347 | 0.028** |
| L(LE) | 19.44 | 4.274 | 4.5480 | 0.000*** |
| L(EDU) | 0.53 | 0.842 | 0.629 | 0.536 |
| L(ASF) | 6.95 | 2.507 | 2.771 | 0.011** |
| L(ASW) | −2.91 | 1.471 | −1.978 | 0.061* |
| L(ELC) | 1.15 | 0.716 | 1.601 | 0.124 |
| L(CO2P) | 0.04 | 0.236 | 0.164 | 0.871 |
| L(TOP) | 0.80 | 0.257 | 3.114 | 0.005*** |
| C | −52.28 | 19.266 | −2.713 | 0.013*** |
| EC = L(GDP) − (−1.03 L(INV) − 5.79 L(YUN) + 19.44 L(LE) + 0.53 L(EDU) + 6.95 L(ASF) − 2.91 L(ASW) + 1.15 L(ELC) + 0.04 L(CO2P) + 0.80*L(TOP) − 52.28) | | | | |

****, **, and * indicate significance at 1%, 5%, and 10% level, respectively.*

**Table 7.**
*ARDL long-run form. Case 2: restricted constant and no trend.*

| Variable | Coefficient | Std. error | t-statistic | Prob. |
|---|---|---|---|---|
| $DL(GDP)_{t-1}$ | 0.22 | 0.077 | 2.816 | 0.010*** |
| DL(INV) | −0.41 | 0.052 | −7.776 | 0.000*** |
| $DL(INV)_{t-1}$ | 0.44 | 0.056 | 7.756 | 0.000*** |
| DL(LE) | 0.61 | 4.044 | 0.150 | 0.882 |
| $DL(LE)_{t-1}$ | −16.45 | 4.658 | −3.532 | 0.002*** |
| DL(ASF) | 0.39 | 0.437 | 0.888 | 0.384 |
| $DL(ASF)_{t-1}$ | −2.76 | 0.487 | −5.661 | 0.000*** |
| DL(ASW) | −3.18 | 0.940 | −3.379 | 0.003*** |
| $DL(ASW)_{t-1}$ | 3.91 | 0.909 | 4.302 | 0.000*** |
| DL(ELC) | 0.11 | 0.139 | 0.821 | 0.420 |
| DL(TOP) | −0.03 | 0.068 | −0.451 | 0.656 |
| $DL(TOP)_{t-1}$ | −0.49 | 0.072 | −6.819 | 0.000*** |
| DUM3 | 0.01 | 0.026 | 0.377 | 0.710 |
| $EC_{t-1}$ | −0.53 | 0.048 | −10.931 | 0.000*** |
| R-squared = 0.86; adjusted R-squared = 0.80; SER = 0.085; SSR = 0.229; LL = 56.70; AIC = −1.856; SC = −1.300; HQ = −1.648; DW = 2.15 | | | | |

*Note: Case 2—restricted constant and no trend;*
**** at 1% level.*

**Table 8.**
*ARDL short-run estimates.*

As evident from **Figures 12** and **13**, all plots of cumulative sum (CUSUM) and cumulative sum of squares (CUSUMSQ) statistics of the recursive residuals are well within the critical bounds, implying that the coefficients in the error correction model of the ARDL are stable.

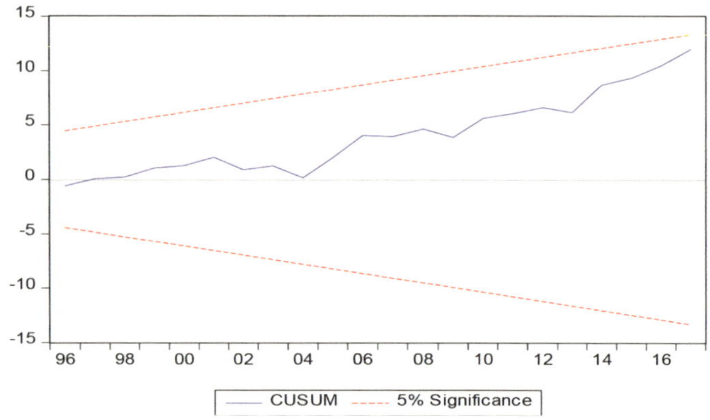


**Figure 12.**
*CUSUM of the residuals.*

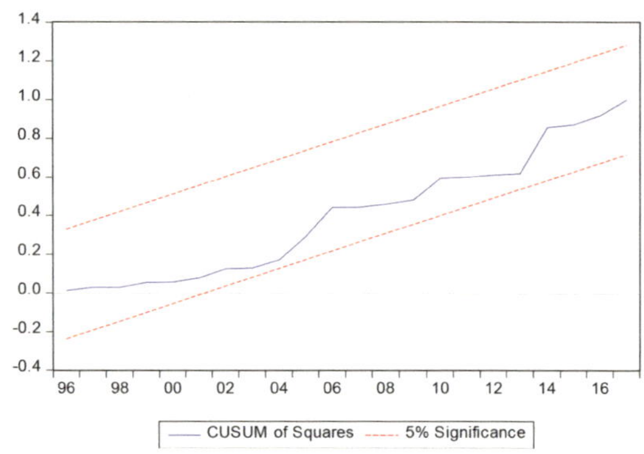


**Figure 13.**
*CUSUM of squares of the residuals.*

### *5.2.4 Johansen cointegration test*

In addition to the ARDL bound test approach, Johansen cointegration method is also employed at lag length of 2. The Johansen's cointegration test determines the number of cointegrating vectors of equations. It is based on the statistics of two different likelihood ratios (LR): the trace statistic and the maximum eigenvalue statistic. With the assumption of intercept only, the test shows the existence of nine cointegrating equations with the trace statistic and seven cointegrating equations with maximum eigenvalue, while with the assumption of intercept and trend, the test shows the existence of ten cointegrating equations using the trace statistic and five cointegrating equations when using the maximum eigenvalue as shown in **Table 9**. Thus, the test results show that a long-run equilibrium relationship exists among the variables of the study and also justifies the use of the ARDL bound test method to cointegration.

Thus both the ARDL and Johansen cointegration tests confirm the existence of a long-run equilibrium relationship which indicates that the social and environmental indicators, together with investment and trade openness, are simultaneously playing an important role in determining the GDP growth in Sudan.

### *5.2.5 Granger causality analysis*

Cointegration implies that causality exists between the series, but it does not indicate the direction of causality. Granger causality test enables to detect the

| $H_0$ | $H_1$ | Intercept only | | | | Intercept and trend | | | |
|---|---|---|---|---|---|---|---|---|---|
| | | Trace stat. | 0.05 cri. value | Max. eigenvalue stat. | 0.05 cri. value | Trace stat. | 0.05 cri. value | Max. eigenvalue stat. | 0.05 cri. value |
| r = 0 | r = 0 | 514.493* | 239.235 | 134.344* | 64.505 | 570.844* | 273.189 | 134.384* | 68.812 |
| r ≤ 1 | r = 1 | 380.149* | 197.371 | 101.701* | 58.434 | 436.460* | 228.298 | 106.157* | 62.752 |
| r ≤ 2 | r = 2 | 278.448* | 159.530 | 82.403* | 52.363 | 330.304* | 187.470 | 96.049* | 56.705 |
| r ≤ 3 | r = 3 | 196.046* | 125.615 | 50.966* | 46.231 | 234.254* | 150.559 | 53.479* | 50.600 |
| r ≤ 4 | r = 4 | 145.080* | 95.754 | 42.747* | 40.078 | 180.775* | 117.708 | 50.569* | 44.497 |
| r ≤ 5 | r = 5 | 102.333* | 69.819 | 36.978* | 33.877 | 130.206* | 88.804 | 37.727 | 38.331 |
| r ≤ 6 | r = 6 | 65.355* | 47.856 | 27.671 | 27.584 | 92.479* | 63.876 | 30.562 | 32.118 |
| r ≤ 7 | r = 7 | 37.684* | 29.797 | 20.444 | 21.132 | 61.917* | 42.915 | 27.665* | 25.823 |
| r ≤ 8 | r = 8 | 17.240* | 15.495 | 14.8780* | 14.265 | 34.252* | 25.872 | 19.378 | 19.387 |
| r ≤ 9 | r = 9 | 2.362 | 3.841 | 2.362 | 3.841 | 14.874* | 12.518 | 14.874* | 12.518 |

*Intercept only: Trace test indicates nine cointegrating equations; max. Eigenvalue test indicates seven cointegrating equations. Intercept and trend: Trace test indicates ten cointegrating equations; max. Eigenvalue test indicates five cointegrating equations;*
* *denotes rejection of the hypothesis at a 0.05 level.*

**Table 9.**
*Johansen cointegration results.*

direction of causality in which a series causes another series if the knowledge of the history of the first improves the prediction of the second. Therefore, consistent with the ARDL bound test and Johansen cointegration tests, the causal relationships among the economic, social, and environmental dimensions of development in Sudan is examined with lag length of 2. The Granger causality tests results are reported in **Table 10**. No causal relationship is found between investment and youth unemployment. Life expectancy at birth is found to cause GDP growth rather than the other way around. Also, education and access to sanitation facilities are found to cause GDP growth with no sign of feedback from these social and environmental indicators to GDP. A bidirectional relationship is found between access to drinking water and GDP growth. GDP is found to cause access to electricity rather than electricity causing GDP growth. GDP is also found to cause carbon dioxide emissions rather than the other way around. Trade openness is found to cause GDP growth with no sign of feedback from growth to trade openness as reported in **Table 10**. As for the causal relationships among the social and environmental indicators, we report the most notable and significant relationships. Education is found to cause investment. There exists a bidirectional relationship between access to sanitation facilities and investment. Both access to sanitation facilities and education are found to cause unemployment. Unemployment is found to cause access to drinking water. Both carbon dioxide emissions and trade openness are found to cause unemployment. Interestingly, a bidirectional causal relationship is found between life expectancy and education, which indicates the importance of investing simultaneously in both sectors. A unidirectional relationship is detected to run from life expectancy at birth to access to sanitation facilities, access to drinking water, access to electricity, and carbon dioxide emissions. Access to sanitation facilities is found to cause education, access to drinking water, and carbon dioxide emissions. Education is found to cause access to drinking water, access to electricity, and carbon dioxide emissions. A bidirectional relationship is detected between access to drinking water and access to sanitation facilities indicating the proximity

| $H_0$ | Obs. | F-statistic | Prob. | Decision | Direction of causality |
|---|---|---|---|---|---|
| $H_0$: L(INV) does not cause L(GDP) | 46 | 0.050 | 0.951 | Accept | None |
| $H_0$: L(GDP) does not cause L(INV) | 46 | 0.097 | 0.908 | Accept | None |
| $H_0$: L(YUN) does not cause L(GDP) | 46 | 0.284 | 0.754 | Accept | None |
| $H_0$: L(GDP) does not cause L(YUN) | 46 | 1.579 | 0.219 | Accept | None |
| $H_0$: L(LE) does not cause L(GDP) | 46 | 3.557 | 0.038 | Reject | LE to GDP |
| $H_0$: L(GDP) does not cause L(LE) | 46 | 1.122 | 0.335 | Accept | None |
| $H_0$: L(EDU) does not cause L(GDP) | 46 | 4.927 | 0.012 | Reject | EDU to GDP |
| $H_0$: L(GDP) does not cause L(EDU) | 46 | 0.268 | 0.766 | Accept | None |
| $H_0$: L(ASF) does not cause L(GDP) | 46 | 2.633 | 0.084 | Reject | ASF to GDP |
| $H_0$: L(GDP) does not cause L(ASF) | 46 | 0.111 | 0.895 | Accept | None |
| $H_0$: L(ASW) does not cause L(GDP) | 46 | 3.575 | 0.037 | Reject | ASW to GDP |
| $H_0$: L(GDP) does not cause L(ASW) | 46 | 5.142 | 0.010 | Reject | GDP to ASW |
| $H_0$: L(ELC) does not cause L(GDP) | 46 | 1.094 | 0.344 | Accept | None |
| $H_0$: L(GDP) does not cause L(ELC) | 46 | 9.590 | 0.000 | Reject | GDP to ELC |
| $H_0$: L(CO2P) does not cause L(GDP) | 46 | 1.501 | 0.235 | Accept | None |
| $H_0$: L(GDP) does not cause L(CO2P) | 46 | 4.860 | 0.013 | Reject | GDP to CO2P |
| $H_0$: L(TOP) does not cause L(GDP) | 46 | 6.196 | 0.005 | Reject | TOP to GDP |
| $H_0$: L(GDP) does not cause L(TOP) | 46 | 0.531 | 0.592 | Accept | None |
| $H_0$: Independent Variables | Obs. | F-Statistic | Prob. | Decision | Direction of causality |
| $H_0$: L(EDU) does not cause L(INV) | 46 | 3.243 | 0.050 | Reject | EDU to INV |
| $H_0$: L(ASF) does not cause L(INV) | 46 | 3.967 | 0.027 | Reject | ASF to INV |
| $H_0$: L(INV) does not cause L(ASF) | 46 | 4.141 | 0.023 | Reject | INV to ASF |
| $H_0$: L(EDU) does not cause L(YUN) | 46 | 2.457 | 0.098 | Accept | EDU to YUN |
| $H_0$: L(ASF) does not cause L(YUN) | 46 | 6.133 | 0.005 | Reject | ASF to YUN |
| $H_0$: L(YUN) does not cause L(ASW) | 46 | 5.478 | 0.008 | Reject | YUN to ASW |
| $H_0$: L(CO2P) does not cause L(YUN) | 46 | 4.850 | 0.013 | Reject | CO2P to YUN |
| $H_0$: L(TOP) does not cause L(YUN) | 46 | 3.244 | 0.049 | Reject | TOP to YUN |
| $H_0$: L(EDU) does not cause L(LE) | 46 | 2.628 | 0.084 | Reject | EDU to LE |
| $H_0$: L(LE) does not cause L(EDU) | 46 | 4.134 | 0.023 | Reject | LE to EDU |
| $H_0$: L(LE) does not cause L(ASF) | 46 | 4.282 | 0.021 | Reject | LE to ASF |
| $H_0$: L(LE) does not cause L(ASW) | 46 | 3.619 | 0.036 | Reject | LE to ASW |
| $H_0$: L(LE) does not cause L(ELC) | 46 | 11.616 | 0.000 | Reject | LE to ELC |
| $H_0$: L(LE) does not cause L(CO2P) | 46 | 3.370 | 0.044 | Reject | LE to CO2P |
| $H_0$: L(ASF) does not cause L(EDU) | 46 | 5.793 | 0.006 | Reject | ASF to EDU |
| $H_0$: L(EDU) does not cause L(ASW) | 46 | 4.372 | 0.019 | Reject | EDU to ASW |
| $H_0$: L(EDU) does not cause L(ELC) | 46 | 7.313 | 0.002 | Reject | EDU to ELC |
| $H_0$: L(EDU) does not cause L(CO2P) | 46 | 2.952 | 0.063 | Reject | EDU to CO2P |
| $H_0$: L(ASW) does not cause L(ASF) | 46 | 3.745 | 0.032 | Reject | ASW to ASF |
| $H_0$: L(ASF) does not cause L(ASW) | 46 | 5.227 | 0.010 | Reject | ASF to ASW |

| $H_0$ | Obs. | F-statistic | Prob. | Decision | Direction of causality |
|---|---|---|---|---|---|
| $H_0$: L(ASF) does not cause L(CO2P) | 46 | 6.213 | 0.004 | Reject | ASF to CO2P |
| $H_0$: L(TOP) does not cause L(ASF) | 46 | 5.610 | 0.007 | Reject | TOP to ASF |
| $H_0$: L(ASW) does not cause L(ELC) | 46 | 4.568 | 0.016 | Reject | ASW to ELC |

**Table 10.**
*Granger causality test results.*

| Year | UNE required increase | UMR SDG | MMR SDG | ASE SDG | ASW SDG | ASF SDG | ELC SDG |
|---|---|---|---|---|---|---|---|
| 2015 | 17.29 | 49.47 | 308.06 | 45.78 | 58.93 | 26.90 | 29.11 |
| 2016 | 17.27 | 48.09 | 231.05 | 46.81 | 59.09 | 26.60 | 29.61 |
| 2017 | 17.28 | 45.85 | 215.64 | 48.41 | 59.27 | 26.40 | 30.08 |
| 2018 | 17.15 | 43.62 | 200.24 | 52.40 | 60.33 | 28.95 | 32.86 |
| 2019 | 17.03 | 41.38 | 184.84 | 56.40 | 61.39 | 31.50 | 35.64 |
| 2020 | 16.91 | 39.14 | 169.43 | 60.39 | 62.45 | 34.05 | 38.42 |
| 2021 | 16.79 | 36.91 | 154.03 | 64.39 | 63.50 | 36.60 | 41.20 |
| 2022 | 16.67 | 34.67 | 138.63 | 68.38 | 64.56 | 39.15 | 43.98 |
| 2023 | 16.54 | 32.43 | 123.22 | 72.38 | 65.62 | 41.70 | 46.76 |
| 2024 | 16.42 | 30.20 | 107.82 | 76.37 | 66.67 | 44.25 | 49.54 |
| 2025 | 16.30 | 27.96 | 92.42 | 80.37 | 67.73 | 46.80 | 52.32 |
| 2026 | 16.18 | 25.72 | 77.02 | 84.36 | 68.79 | 49.35 | 55.10 |
| 2027 | 16.06 | 23.49 | 61.61 | 88.36 | 69.85 | 51.90 | 57.88 |
| 2028 | 15.93 | 21.25 | 46.21 | 92.35 | 70.90 | 54.45 | 60.66 |
| 2029 | 15.81 | 19.01 | 30.81 | 96.35 | 71.96 | 57.00 | 63.44 |
| 2030 | 15.69 | 16.78 | 15.40 | 100.34 | 73.02 | 59.55 | 66.22 |

**Table 11.**
*Projection of key socioeconomic indicators toward SDGs.*

of these variables to one another. Trade openness is found to cause access to sanitation facilities which might indicate the importance of imported goods to the improvement of sanitation facilities. Access to drinking water is found to cause access to electricity. Only significant causal relations between social and environmental dimensions of development are extracted and reported in **Table 10**.

In the light of our findings on the performance of Sudan on socioeconomic components of development, we make some projections for the period of 2015–2030. Projections are made according to the values of indicators in 2015 compared with that in 1990. We assume that the youth unemployment can be reduced to fluctuate around an average of 10%, and accordingly we projected the required job creation for youth in order to achieve this. Under five (UMR) and maternal mortality (MMR) ratios are projected according to the target of reduction by two third and 75%, respectively. Access to sanitation facilities, access to safe drinking water, and access to electricity are projected against full coverage of 100% of population. Projections are summarized in **Table 11**.

## 6. Conclusion

This study is a synthesis of arguments on economic, social, and environmental dimensions of development with empirical testing in the case of Sudan. The outcome of the study confirms that social and environmental indicators, together with investment, (un)employment, and trade openness, lead to economic growth measured by GDP and not the vice versa. That is, in whatsoever level of economic development achieved, the social progress indicators have been the main sources and not the factors of production as conventionally subtracted in physical capital and formal labor. This social factor-based economic development has also been backed with the use of natural environmental assets and amenities. Such findings have important policy implications for achieving development as an objective and on rethinking the real factor that has been leading to economic development in low-income countries such as Sudan, regardless of how small it has been. Although our findings are more on aggregate measures, they are in conformity with Hassan et al. [12], who found that social spending leads to an increase in GDP per capita and that an increase in primary education by 1% is associated with a growth by 0.8%, whereas health capital is found to have negative but insignificant effect. Accordingly we make the following general recommendations:

Spending on health and education has to be increased and be reverted in a social finance transition from a predominantly heavily burdened private and household sector to the government. Access to basic sanitation and drinking water facilities needs to be improved majorly, which contributes to health and education achievements. There is a need for planned gradual shifting of trade composition from export of environmental and primary products to high value added manufactured goods. On the other hand, there is an urgent need to regulate imports in favor of capital goods and equipments away from the imports of consumption goods particularly the luxurious ones. Efforts to adapt renewable energy sources should be enhanced, particularly in solar and wind energy which can be seen as the most possible investment for expansion access to modern energies in remote and rural areas of Sudan. These recommendations can be designed into operational polices and can be monitored in line with the guidelines provided by the OECD [13], in its *Policy Framework for Investment*.

## Author details

Elwasila Mohamed
Department of Economics, Faculty of Economic and Social Studies, University of Khartoum, Khartoum, Sudan

*Address all correspondence to: elwasila.sem@gmail.com

## References

[1] Pearce D, Atkinson G. Capital theory and the measurement of sustainable development: An indicator of "weak" sustainability. Ecological Economics. 1993;**8**(2):103-108

[2] United Nations. Prototype Global Sustainable Development Report. Chapter 5: Measuring Progress. 2014. Available from: https://sustainabledevelopment.un.org/content/documents/1454Prototype%20Global%20SD%20Report2.pdf

[3] Social Progress Imperative. 2018 Social Progress Index. Available from: www.socialimpertaive.org

[4] Fehder D, Porter M, Stern S. The empirics of social progress: The interplay between subjective well-being and societal performance. AEA Papers & Proceedings. 2018;**108**:477-482. Available from: https://www.aeaweb.org/articles?id=10.1257/pandp.20181036

[5] Seligman ERA. Economics and social progress. Publications of the American Economic Association. 1903;**4**(1):52-70

[6] World Bank. World Development Indicators. Available from: www.wordbank.org

[7] Ronald M, Bernauer T. Environmental research on international environmental policy: Designing quantitative case studies. Journal of Environment & Development. 1998;**7**(1):4-31

[8] Kwiatkowski D, Phillips PC, Schmidt P, Shin Y. Testing the null hypothesis of stationarity against the alternative of a unit root: How sure are we that economic time series have a unit root? Journal of Econometrics. 1992; **54**(1):159-178. DOI: 10.1016/0304-4076(92)90104-Y

[9] Pesaran MH, Smith RP. Structural analysis of cointegrating VARs. Journal of Economic Surveys. 1998;**12**(5): 471-505

[10] Pesaran MH, Shin Y. An autoregressive distributed lag modelling approach to cointegration analysis. In: Strom S, editor. Econometrics and Economic Theory in 20th Century: The Ragnar Frisch Centennial Symposium. Cambridge: Cambridge University Press; 1999

[11] Pesaran MH, Shin Y, Smith RJ. Bounds testing approaches to the analysis of level relationships. Journal of Applied Econometrics. 2001;**16**:289-326

[12] Hassan HM, Ali H, Mohamed A, Haleeb A. The effects of social spending on growth in Sudan. International Journal of Science and Research. 2015; **4**(5):52-59. Available from: www.ijsr.net

[13] OECD. Policy Framework for Investment: User's Toolkit, A publication of the Investment Division of the OECD Directorate for Financial and Enterprise Affairs. Benchmarking performance and measuring progress. 2012. Available from: http://www.oecd.org/investment/toolkit/measuringprogress/

Section 2

# Fiscal Policy and Economic Development

Chapter 5

# An Analysis of Drivers of International Investment Decisions in South Africa

*Itumeleng Pleasure Mongale and Livhuwani Baloyi*

## Abstract

The study investigated the drivers of international investment decisions in South Africa. As part of its investment drive, the government has embarked on a series of activities to lure investors. That been the case it appears that most of the empirical studies focused mainly on the relationship between investment and economic growth, hence very little seems to be known about the empirical evidence of other drivers of international investment decisions and their impact on the South African economy. The findings are envisaged to provide information and to add policy formulation to attract the much needed foreign investment. The autoregressive distribution lag approach was chosen to analyse the long and the short run relationships amongst the variables of interest and Granger Causality analysis was also employed to determine causal relationships between dependent variable and its regressors. The results indicated that a stronger statistical and economic basis for empirical error correction model was established by the presence of cointegration amongst the variables and all the regressors were found to have a positive effect in the stock of foreign direct investment. Empirical findings suggest that government should ensure stable macroeconomic policies and labour disputes that result into prolonged strike actions must be minimised.

**Keywords:** foreign direct investment, productivity, infrastructure investment, labour unrest, cointegration

## 1. Introduction

Most of the developing countries seek to maximise the benefits of foreign direct investments (FDI) to improve economy growth and to encourage foreign investment in both the public and private sectors. As a result, policymakers' direct resources at incentives aimed at attracting FDI flows because according to [1], FDI quality is also associated with positive and economically significant growth effects. The other perception is that FDI inflows will significantly improve technology and management practices as well as increase capital formation in a host country. As part of its investment drive, the South African government has embarked on a series of activities which include trips to Europe, Asia and across Africa to build an "investment book" to help plug a substantial shortfall of foreign and local direct investment. The purpose was to unlock a $100-billion investment plan to stimulate economic growth which was plummeted as a result of political and policy uncertainty which damaged both the investment and business confidences during the previous regime when the country's credit rating was slashed to junk by two of the top three agencies and economic growth slowed to a crawl [2, 3].

Such an initiative is anchored on the notion that foreign investment can enable the growth of businesses and creation of job opportunities that would not arise if reliant only on domestic investment. The idea is that the increase in foreign investment can have a spillover effect on the domestic firms, stimulates the economy and positively impacts the economic growth [4]. Therefore, attracting and encouraging FDI and domestic investments remain one of the priority goals of governments in most developing countries including South Africa.

Amongst the characteristics of globalisation is the unrestricted capital flow and access to world market. It has been established that the global FDI stocks have been on the increase (see [5, 6]). Many more African countries are becoming more open to FDI; however, it still remains low [7]. South Africa is amongst the top three countries within the sub-Saharan region which is taken as favourable destinations for FDI. That been the case, the country continues to promote FDI through its various investment promotion strategies. One such initiative is the Promotion and Protection of Investment Bill of 2013, which is the new effort to improve the quality of FDI flowing to South Africa.

The idea of the new administration to scour the globe for $100 billion in investment is that very same goal of attracting and increasing FDI into South Africa which was set in the past seems to be far from being realised because the government may not have done enough to promote it [8]. One of the reasons behind all these is that South Africa remains heavily dependent on foreign investment because of the lower domestic savings between 1994 and the first quarter of 1998 [9]. A total net inflow of capital of R57.4 billion, was realised between 1994 and the first quarter of 1998. However, since then, the long-term capital flows have slowed, and short-term capital has flowed out of the economy, contributing to the depression of the currency (Rand). In 2007, the National Treasury stated that policy reforms would raise investment growth rates, pulling in higher FDI [10].

Despite efforts to attract more FDI into South Africa and other African countries, the [11] global investment trend monitor reports that FDI flow to Africa dropped significantly (31%) in 2015 to an estimated US$38 billion from US$53.9 billion in 2014. This was a result of the largest decline seen by sub-Saharan Africa and Central and Southern Africa. For instance, in 2015, the flow to Mozambique dropped by 21% to US$4.9 billion but notably remains at an estimated US$3.8 billion; Nigeria recorded a reduction by 27% hit by drop in oil price to an estimated US $3.4 billion from US$4.7 billion. South Africa, with its more diversified economy and reputation as an investor-friendly business environment, achieved the highest FDI inflows in Africa during 2014 and 2013, although it should be noted that FDI inflows declined by 33% in 2014 from US$8.3 billion during 2013 to US$5.7 billion during 2014. In addition, South Africa has experienced low projected gross domestic product (GDP) growth rates in the past few years and often faces issues such as prolonged industrial actions, policy uncertainty relating to the mining industry and power shortages which make investors weary of the future of the economy.

The decline and relatively weak performance in FDI attraction happened during the period where the potential attractiveness of South Africa is regarded as high in comparison to other countries in the region and despite progress owing to investment potential in infrastructure [12]. Based on the Global Foreign Direct Investment Country Attractiveness (GFICA) Index, the country is ranked at position 45 out of 109 countries with a 50.5% GFICA index value. This puts it on the second position after Mauritius amongst its peers. The GFICA ranking history shows that it was ranked at number 48 in 2015, number 50 in 2016, number 44 in 2017 and number 45 in 2018 [13].

Furthermore, South Africa has experienced a decelerated growth for a longer time. This is attributed to several factors such as the declining global competitiveness, growing political instability and a weakened rule of law that in 2017 contributed to the country's investment-grade credit rating to be downgraded to junk status and denting the investor confidence. The government is thus confronted with the challenge of maintaining macroeconomic stability whilst facing a combination of rising public debt, inefficient state-owned enterprises and spending pressures [14]. The other school of thought argues that the weakened growth has been exacerbated by low commodity prices and the allegations of extreme corruption which contributed to political turmoil that helped to plunge the economy into recession in 2017. Furthermore, the situation was worsened by the fact that the economy slipped into a technical recession during the second quarter of 2018 where GDP shrank by 0.7% quarter on quarter (seasonally adjusted and annualised) after a revised 2.6% contraction in the first quarter of 2018 [14].

Just like any other developing country, South Africa is desperately in need of more investments in order to achieve some of its macroeconomic objectives. Even though several such studies such as [15–17] focused on several determinants of FDI, it appears that very little seems to be known about the drivers of international investment decisions in the South African context. Apart from contributing to policymaking and contribution to the existing body of knowledge, this study might benefit several stakeholders such as academia, government institutions and the policymakers.

As indicated by [18], South Africa, just like the rest of the world, is still in the formative stage of coming to grips with analytical challenges and policy quandaries associated with today's much more complicated realm of trade and investment. Bailey [19] also made suggestions for future research that stress a call for further contextualisation of the relationship. Moreover, this study is influenced by [20] who pointed out that there has been little investigation of FDI decision processes, most of which focused on strategic decision processes, although some research takes the neoclassical economic approach to microeconomic rational choice and behavioural FDI decision-making. Therefore, the purpose of this study was to investigate drivers of international investment decisions in South Africa. In order to achieve its objectives, several proxies for drivers of international investment decisions were used to determine the impact of investment drivers on FDI.

The chapter is planned as follows: Section 2 presents literature review, whilst research methodology and model are discussed in Section 3; the empirical results and discussions are presented in Section 4 and conclusion of the study summarised in the last section.

## 2. Literature review

The empirical literature produces divided views about the contribution of FDI in the host countries. Those who support the view that it has a positive impact on economic growth consider that there are different ways that produce positive contribution. Ndiaye and Xu [21] contended that FDI comes along with increased competition which will lead to increased productivity, efficiency and investment in human or physical capital. Such a competition can also lead to changes in the industrial structure through more competitive and more export-oriented activities.

Another advantage is the benefit the training, which may lead to increased workforce training and managerial skills and thirdly the connection, where foreign investments are often accompanied by technology transfer. Finally, there is a possibility for domestic firms to mimic advanced technologies used by foreign firms.

On the other hand, some scholars have questioned the role of FDI in the host country's economy. A study by [22] argued that the deterioration of external imbalances is one of the unfavourable effects of FDI inflows in developing countries. Other researchers such as [23, 24] postulated that the damaging and undesirable effects of FDI may be worsened if the technology transferred is inappropriate for developing countries and if FDI crowds out local investors. Others argued that its impact growth can be limited by the local conditions existing in the host developing countries such as the levels of human capital, financial development and institutional quality.

Despite the dichotomy about the contributions of FDI on the economy, its underlying drivers differ according to countries' locations. However, it is evident that a minimum set of factors must be present in the location for FDI to flow [17]. It could be assumed that investors would select an economy where profitability is expected to be high. However, in an extensive study on the factors influencing FDI, [16] posited that investors not only consider profitability when making investment decisions; other critical factors are taken into consideration such as availability of natural resources, institution environment, country risk, infrastructure availability, costs and the skills of workers. Empirical studies have tested various variables that can potentially attract or repel FDI. Such variables include market-driven variables such as rate of return and labour cost; structural variables, such as infrastructure development and political stability; and macroeconomic policies formulated to achieve economic growth, taxation and price stability.

A study by [25] found that FDI liberalisation is amongst the factors that affect FDI in Africa especially in the long term. Asiedu [26] argued that a good investment framework contributes to higher FDI for African countries. Hooda [15] studied the effects of FDI on the Indian economy between 1991 and 2008 using multiple regression models. The results indicated that the significant factors that determine FDI in developing countries are corporate taxes, labour costs, interest rates, stable political environment, exchange rates, infrastructural facilities and inflation.

As pointed out by [12], South Africa has many attractive assets for investors such as an important demography; a diversified, productive and advanced economy; abundant natural resources; a transparent legal system; and a certain political stability. In addition to the level of attractiveness, it is ranked number 82nd out of 190 economies in [27]'s Ease of Doing Business Score and Ease of Doing Business Ranking. However, as pointed out by [12], the country suffers from a high crime rate, increasing social unrest (strikes and demonstrations), high levels of corruption and structural issues in electricity supply and logistics.

## 3. Research methodology

The study employed the bound testing autoregressive distributed lag (ARDL) approach proposed by [28] to investigate drivers of international investment decisions in South Africa.

### 3.1 Data and model specification

This study used a quarterly time series data covering the period 2007–2017 obtained from the South African Reserve Bank and Quantec EasyData. FDI which a is net foreign direct investment as a percentage of GDP is a function of income levels (disposable income of households), labour productivity, infrastructure investment (measured by the gross fixed capital formation) interest rates (prime lending rates) and labour unrest.

Labour unrest was used as a dummy variable to capture the effects of labour unrests (strikes) which is a common phenomenon in the South African economy. For the period 2007–2011, the dummy variable will have a value of 0 which signifies the negligible incidents of labour unrest, and a value of 1 is used for the period between 2012 and 2017 due to the rise in the number of industrial actions. This is based on [29]'s report that a total of 99 strike incidents were recorded in 2012 as compared to 67 in 2011, 74 in 2010, 51 in 2009 and 57 in 2008. Working days lost amounted to about R3.3 million in 2012 (involving 241,391 employees) as compared to 2.8 million in 2011 (involving 203,138 employees). In terms of wages lost, R6.6 billion was lost in wages of striking workers during 2012.

The assumption is that foreign investors are sceptical to invest in nations where there is widespread industrial action. Santander Trade Portal [12] also noted that there were more concerns with the increased labour strikes in recent years because it is one of the points which rating agencies have warned could further lower South Africa's credit rating.

The functional form of the regression model is presented as follows:

$$FDI = f(IL, PL, InfInv, Intr, LU) \tag{1}$$

where *FDI*, foreign direct investment, *IL*, income levels; *PL*, productivity of labour; *InfInv*, infrastructure investment, *InfI*, interest rate; *LU*, labour unrests (dummy variable).

The decision to use FDI as a proxy for international investment decisions in Eq. (1) was based on [20]'s notion that the FDI decision-making process is influenced by the multinational enterprises' context in which decision-makers are situated, the type of a decision, and the investment project are situated.

Furthermore, Eq. (1) is expressed in a linear form with some of the variables being expressed as logarithms presented as follows:

$$InFDI_t = \alpha + \beta_1 InIL_t + \beta_2 InPL_t + \beta_3 InInfInv_t + \beta_4 Intr_t + \beta_5 LU_t + \varepsilon_t \tag{2}$$

where α is a constant, $\beta_1$ to $\beta_5$ are the coefficients to be estimated and $\varepsilon_t$ is the error term representing the influence of the omitted variables in the model.

The estimation technique followed a three-step modelling procedure, namely, testing for order of integration by means of unit root tests, the bounds cointegration test and Granger causality analysis. In addition, the model was taken through a battery of diagnostic and stability tests also known as stability testing to assist in deciding whether or not it has been correctly specified. The modelling procedure is as follows:

### 3.2 Unit root tests

The procedure was employed to examine the order of integration of variables which is a crucial step for setting up an econometric model and to do inference. The stationarity or otherwise of a series can strongly influence its behaviour and property. A time series data is stationary if it has a constant mean, constant variance and constant auto-variance for each given lag [30]. The unit root analysis was done by means of a commonly used augmented Dickey-Fuller (ADF) and, in addition, the Dickey-Fuller generalised least squares (DF-GLS) test applied as a confirmatory test. The DG-GLS test formulated by [31] is a modification of the ADF unit root test, and it transforms the time series such that the trend is removed. It involves a two-step process, in which the time series is estimated by generalised least squares in the first step before a normal Dickey-Fuller test is used to test for a unit root in the second step. This process improves the power of a regular ADF test when the autoregressive parameter is near one.

### 3.3 Cointegration analyses

The bound test analyses were done to model the long-run relationship between sets of variables. This procedure was preferred over the [32] cointegration procedure because it can be applied when series have different orders of integration. Following [28] the bound test procedure is applied by modelling the long-run equation as a general vector autoregressive (VAR) model of order $p$, in $Z_t$:

$$Z_t = c_0 + \beta_t + \sum_{i=1}^{p} \Phi_i z_{t-i} + \varepsilon_t t = 1, 2, 3, ...., T \tag{3}$$

with $c_0$ representing a (k + 1) vector of intercepts (drift) and $\beta$ denoting a (K + 1) vector of trend coefficients. From Eq. (3) [28] derived the following vector error correction model (VECM):

$$\Delta Z_t = c_0 + \beta_t + \Pi z_{t-1} + \sum_{i=1}^{p} \Gamma_i \Delta z_{t-1} + \varepsilon_t t = 1, 2, 3, ...., T \tag{4}$$

where the (k + 1) × (k + 1) are matrices.

$$\Pi = I_{k+1} + \sum_{t=1}^{p} \Psi_i \text{ and } \Gamma = -\sum_{j=i+1}^{p} i = 1, 2, 3, ..., p-1 \tag{5}$$

contain the long-run multipliers and short-run dynamic coefficients of VECM. $Z_t$ is the vector of variables $y_t$ and $x_t$. $Y_t$ is an I(1) dependent variable defined as FDI, and $x_t = \left[IL_t, PL_t, InflInv_t, Intr_t, LU_t\right]$ is a vector matrix of "forcing" I(0) and I(1).

In case we established a long-run relationship amongst the variables, the conditional VECM is specified as follows:

$$\Delta y_t = c_{yo} + \beta_t + \delta_{yy} y_{t-1} + \delta_{xx} x_{t-1} + \sum_{i=1}^{p=1} \lambda_i \Delta y_{t-1} + \sum_{i=0}^{p-1} \zeta_i \Delta X_{t-1} \varepsilon_{yt} \tag{6}$$

and the conditional VECM of the interest can be specified as:

$$\begin{aligned} \Delta InFDI_t &= c_0 + \delta_1 InFDI_{t-1} + \delta_2 InIL_{t-1} + \delta_3 InPL_{t-1} + \delta_4 InInfInv_{t-1} + \delta_5 Intr_{t-1} + \delta_6 LU_{t-1} \\ &+ \sum_{i=1}^{p} \phi_i \Delta InFDI_{t-i} + \sum_{j=1}^{q} \varpi_j \Delta InIL_{t-j} + \sum_{j=1}^{q} \varphi_j \Delta InPL_{t-j} + \sum_{m=1}^{q} \gamma_m \Delta InInfInv_{t-m} \\ &+ \sum_{o=1}^{q} \lambda_o \Delta Intr_{t-o} + \eta LU_t + \varepsilon_t \end{aligned} \tag{7}$$

where $\delta_1$ is the long-run multiplier, $c_0$ is the drift and $\varepsilon_t$ is the white noise error.

### 3.4 Causality testing

The purpose of this test is to examine the cause and effect relationship between variables. This investigates whether the direction of causality is from economic growth to credit extension, economic growth to household savings or household savings leading to credit extension and vice versa. Granger causality test can be described as the relationship between cause and effect. Basically, the term "causality" suggests a cause and effect relationship between two sets of variables, say, Y and X. Recent advances in graphical models and the logic of causation have given rise to new ways in which scientists analyse cause-effect relationships. Causality is tested amongst the variables that are found to be cointegrated [33]. In econometrics sense, causality is somewhat different to the concept in everyday use; it refers more to the ability of one variable to predict the other. The relationship between variables can be captured by a VAR model. The problem is to find an appropriate procedure that allows us to test and statistically detect the cause and effect relationship amongst the variables. [34] developed a relatively simple test that defined causality as follows: A variable is said to Granger-cause if it can be predicted with greater accuracy by using past values of the variable rather not using such past values, all other terms remaining unchanged.

The purpose of this test was to examine the cause and effect relationship between variables. Based on [33] the hypothesis is that variable $y_t$ Granger-causes $x_t$ if $x_t$ can be predicted by using past values of $y_t$, and it is expressed as follows:

$$y_t = a_1 + \sum_{i=1}^{n} \beta_i x_{t-1} + \sum_{j=1}^{m} \gamma_j y_{t-j} + e_{1t} \tag{8}$$

$$x_t = a_2 + \sum_{i-1}^{n} \theta_i x_{t-i} + \sum_{j=1}^{m} \delta_j y_{t-j} + e_{2t} \tag{9}$$

It is assumed that both $\varepsilon_{yt}$ and $\varepsilon_{xt}$ are uncorrelated white noise error terms. If the lagged $x$ term in Eq. (8) is statistically different from zero as a group, the lagged $y$ term is not statistically different from zero, then $x_t$ causes $y_t$. If the lagged $y$ term in Eq. (9) is statistically different from zero as a group, the lagged $x$ term is not statistically different from zero, then $y_t$ causes $x_t$. If both $x$ and $y$ terms are statistically different from zero, then there is two-way direction causality. If both $x$ and $y$ terms are not statistically different from zero, then $x_t$ is independent of $y_t$ [33].

### 3.5 Diagnostic and stability testing

Diagnostic testing was used to determine whether any of the assumptions of the classical normal linear regression model are violated, in other words to examine the goodness of fit of the model. The study engaged a battery of residual tests such as normality test, serial correlation, and heteroskedasticity.

As far as stability testing is concerned, the cumulative sum (CUSUM) and cumulative sum of squares (CUSUMSQ) tests for parameter stability were first introduced into the statistics and econometrics literatures by [35]. The test is based on the analysis of the scaled recursive residuals and has the significant advantage over the Chow tests for not requiring prior knowledge of the point at which the hypothesised structural break takes place [36]. In addition, the Ramsey's "regression specification test" (RESET) tests for misspecification of the functional form. This test helps to investigate the possibility that the dependent variable may be of a nonlinear form [37].

## 4. Empirical results and discussions

This section presents the results of all the empirical tests performed towards the investigation of drivers of international investment decisions in South Africa.

### 4.1 Unit root test results

The ADF and DG-GLS unit root tests were carried out at level and at first differences using intercept and intercept and trend. The results are presented in **Tables 1** and **2** as follows:

The unit root results in **Tables 1** and **2** indicate a mixture of I(0) and I(1) variables because FDI and income levels were found to be stationary at level, whilst all others became stationary at first difference.

| Variables at level | Model level | | Lag length | Variables at 1st difference | | Lag length | Order of integration |
|---|---|---|---|---|---|---|---|
| LFDI | Intercept | −6.909 (−2.937)** | 0 | *ΔInFDI* | −7.057 (−2.946)** | 3 | I(0) |
| | Trend & Intercept | −7.044 (−3.527)** | 0 | | −7.002 (−3.540)** | 3 | I(0) |
| LiL | Intercept | −1.120 (−2.943)** | 3 | *ΔInIL* | −30.037 (−2.943)** | 2 | I(1) |
| | Trend & Intercept | −8.035 (−3.527)** | 0 | | −10.155 (−3.529 ** | 0 | I(0) |
| LPL | Intercept | −1.082 (−2.937)** | 0 | *ΔInPL* | −4.786 (−2.939)** | 0 | I(1) |
| | Trend & Intercept | −2.231 (−3.527)** | 0 | | −4.024 (−3.540)** | 3 | I(1) |
| LInfInv | Intercept | −1.560 (−2.937)** | 1 | *ΔInInfInv* | −4.655 (−2.939)** | 1 | I(1) |
| | Trend & Intercept | −2.9379 (−3.527)** | 1 | | −4.680 (−3.530)** | 1 | I(1) |
| Intr | Intercept | −1.371 (−2.960)** | 9 | *ΔIntr* | −2.974 (−2.964)** | 9 | I(1) |
| | Trend & Intercept | −2.731 (−3.563)** | 9 | | −5.798 (−3.553)** | 6 | I(1) |
| LD | Intercept | −1.000 (−2.937)** | 0 | *ΔLU* | −6.245 (−2.939)** | 0 | I(1) |
| | Trend & Intercept | −1.973 (−3.527)** | 0 | | −6.161 (−3.530)** | 0 | I(1) |

**0.10 significance level.*
***0.05 significance level, Indicates critical value at 5% significance level.*
****0.01 significance level.*
*Notes: I(1) Indicates unit root at first difference being stationary.*
*I(0) Indicates unit root in level being stationary.*
*ΔIndicates changes in first difference.*

**Table 1.**
*ADF Unit root test results.*

| Variables at level | Model level | | Lag length | Variables at 1st difference | | Lag length | Order of integration |
|---|---|---|---|---|---|---|---|
| *InFDI* | Intercept | −6.999 (−1.949) | 0 | *ΔInFDI* | −10.790 (−1.949) | 0 | I(0) |
| | Trend & Intercept | −7.175 (−3.190) | 0 | | −6.587 (−3.190) | 3 | |
| *InIL* | Intercept | 2.786 (−1.950) | 3 | *ΔInIL* | −9.199 (−1.950) | 0 | I(0) |
| | Trend & Intercept | −7.576 (−3.190) | 0 | | −9.287 (−3.190) | 0 | |
| *InPL* | Intercept | −0.859 (−1.949) | 0 | *ΔInPL* | −4.704 (−1.950) | 0 | I(1) |
| | Trend & Intercept | −2.166 (−3.190) | 0 | | −4.820 (−3.190) | 0 | |
| *InfInv* | Intercept | −0.061 (−1.95) | 1 | *ΔInInfInv* | −3.288 (−1.950) | 0 | I(1) |
| | Trend & Intercept | −2.597 (−3.190) | 1 | | −3.339 (−3.190) | 0 | |
| *Intr* | Intercept | −1.965 (−1.951) | 5 | *ΔIntr* | −2.272 (−1.951) | 5 | I(1) |
| | Trend & Intercept | −2.178 (−3.190) | 5 | | −3.319 (−3.190) | 2 | |
| *LU* | Intercept | −0.661 (−1.949) | 0 | *ΔLU* | −6.294 (−1.950) | 0 | I(1) |
| | Trend & Intercept | −1.965 (−3.190) | 0 | | −6.321 (−3.190) | 0 | |

*Notes: The values in brackets are the t-statistics of corresponding estimated coefficients.*
*I(1) Indicates unit root at first difference being stationary.*
*I(0) Indicates unit root in level being stationary.*
*Δ Indicates changes at first difference.*

**Table 2.**
*DG-GLS unit root tests results [38, 43].*

## 4.2 Cointegration analysis results

Since the order of integration was found to be mixed and the fact that there was no I [2] variable, the bound test to cointegration was performed, and the results are presented in **Table 3**. Based on [28] significant levels for lower bound and upper bound are shown as follows:

Our results indicated that the calculated F-statistic of 9.10 is higher than the upper bound critical value 3.38 at the 5% level of significance. Thus, the null hypothesis of no cointegration is rejected, implying the presence of a long-run cointegration relationship amongst the variables. The next step was to examine the expected marginal impacts of the drivers of international investment decisions on international investment decisions in South Africa.

Our empirical evidence in **Table 4** reveals that the relationship between all the regressors and FDI is positive but not statistically significant with the exception of the dummy with the p-value of 0.0020 which means it is statistically significant.

| Test statistic | Value | K |
|---|---|---|
| F-statistic | 9.101 | 5 |
| **Critical value bounds** | | |
| **Significance (%)** | **I0 Bound** | **I1 Bound** |
| 10 | 2.26 | 3.35 |
| 5 | 2.62 | 3.79 |
| 2.5 | 2.96 | 4.18 |
| 1 | 3.41 | 4.68 |

**Table 3.**
*Bound test results.*

| Variable | Coefficient | Std. Error | t-Statistic | Prob. |
|---|---|---|---|---|
| IL | 0.254 | 7.948 | 0.032 | 0.975 |
| PL | 0.086 | 14.345 | 0.006 | 0.995 |
| LGFCF | 0.049 | 12.837 | 0.004 | 0.997 |
| INTR | 0.026 | 0.376 | 0.069 | 0.945 |
| DUMMY | 11.921 | 3.452 | 3.453 | 0.002 |
| C | 161.554 | 91.932 | 1.757 | 0.091 |
| R-squared | 0.733 | | | |
| Durbin-Watson stat | 2.192 | | | |
| F-statistic | 6.237 | | | |

**Table 4.**
*Estimated Long run results.*

Additionally, in **Table 4** the coefficient of determination ($R^2$) is 0.732920. The implication is that about 73% of variation in international investment decisions in South Africa is caused by variations in the explanatory variables. The Durbin-Watson statistics of 2.19 shows the absence of serial correlation.

The short-run relationship analysis results in **Table 5** show that cointegration is strongly confirmed given that the coefficient of the error correction term (−1.351344) has a negative sign. In line with [38], it shows that any deviation from the long-run equilibrium is corrected at the rate 135% for each period to return to the long-run equilibrium after a shock.

### 4.3 Causality test results

Since cointegration has been established, the study proceeded with Granger causality test, and the pairwise Granger causality test results are presented at the Appendix section. It was established that there was no causality between income level and FDI and between interest rate and FDI. Similarly, productivity of labour does not Granger-cause FDI; however, the null hypothesis of granger causality could not be rejected between FDI and labour unrests. A bidirectional causality between them was found. Likewise, Granger causality was established between productivity of labour and the labour unrest.

### 4.4 Diagnostic and stability test results

The results of both diagnostic and stability tests based on statistical estimations are presented in **Tables 6** and 7 and **Figure 1**, respectively.

The residuals are normally distributed, and there is no serial correlation. In the presence of heteroskedasticity, the null hypothesis is rejected (homoscedasticity), and the alternative is accepted.

The results of stability test are presented in **Table** 7 and **Figure 1**, respectively.

Based on the summary of results presented in **Table** 7, the null hypothesis of Ramsey RESET test shows that the model is correctly specified. In tandem with the Ramsey RESET test, the stability test results reveal that after incorporating the CUSUM and CUSUM of squares tests, ARDL model was found to be stable throughout the period of study.

| Variable | Coefficient | Std. Error | t-Statistic | Prob. |
|---|---|---|---|---|
| D(IL) | 0.343 | 10.739 | 0.032 | 0.974 |
| D(PL) | 0.121 | 32.574 | 0.004 | 0.997 |
| D(LGFCF) | 0.066 | 17.348 | 0.004 | 0.997 |
| D(INTR) | 0.035 | 0.509 | 0.069 | 0.945 |
| D(DUMMY) | 0.009 | 4.048 | 0.002 | 0.998 |
| D(DUMMY(-1)) | −0.313 | 4.864 | −0.064 | 0.949 |
| D(DUMMY(-2)) | −0.342 | 4.923 | −0.069 | 0.945 |
| D(DUMMY(-3)) | −13.909 | 4.181 | −3.327 | 0.002 |
| CointEq(-1) | −1.351 | 0.168 | −8.049 | 0.000 |
| *Cointeq = FDI−(0.254 × IL + 0.086 × PL + 0.049 × LGFCF + 0.026 × INTR + 11.921 × DUMMY + 161.555).* | | | | |

**Table 5.**
*Estimated short run analysis results.*

| Test | Null hypothesis | Test statistic | P-Value | Conclusion |
|---|---|---|---|---|
| Jarque-Bera | Residuals are normally distributed | 98.724 | 0.000 | We do not reject the $H_0$ because the P-value is greater than the LOS at 5%, hence the residuals are normally distributed. |
| Breusch Pargan-Godfrey | No serial correlation | 1.522 | 0.467 | We do not reject the reject $H_0$ because the P-value is greater than LOS at 5%, hence there is no serial correlation. |
| Arch | No heteroscedasticity | 0.031 | 0.859 | We do not reject $H_0$ as P- value is greater than LOS at 5%, hence there is no heteroscedasticity |

**Table 6.**
*Diagnostic tests results.*

| | Value | DF | Probability |
|---|---|---|---|
| t-statistic | 3.994 | 24 | 0.001 |
| F-statistic | 15.948 | (1, 24) | 0.001 |

**Table 7.**
*Ramsey RESET test results.*

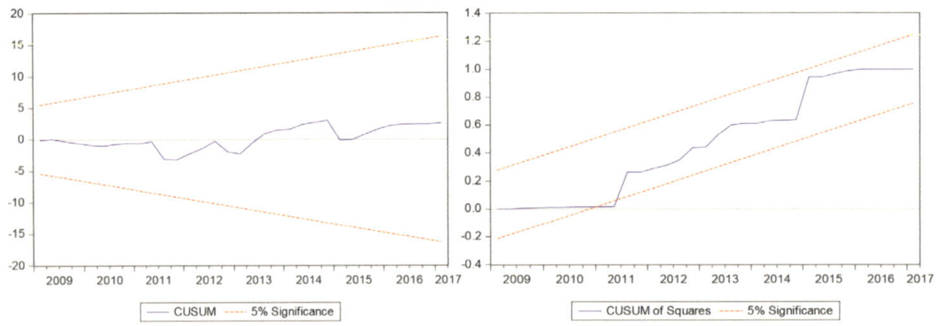


**Figure 1.**
*Stability test results.*

The plot of the cumulative sum of recursive residuals (CUSUM) and cumulative sum of squares recursive residuals (CUSUMQ) of the model presented in **Figure 1** indicates stability in the coefficients over the sample period as they fall within the critical bounds indicated by the 5% significance parameters.

## 5. Conclusions

The study investigated drivers of international investment decisions in South Africa by means of time series secondary data from the South African Reserve Bank and Quantec EasyData. The bound testing autoregressive distribution lag approach and the Granger causality analysis were employed to achieve the aim of the study.

The long-run analysis revealed that all the regressors have a positive relationship with FDI, but they were not statistically significant with the exception of the dummy with the p-value of 0.0020 which means it is statistically significant. Whilst the outcomes of this study about a positive association between FDI and some of the regressors like labour productivity, interest rates and infrastructural investment seem to be in line with studies such as [39–41], respectively, the findings of a positive relationship between FDI and labour unrest seem to be in inconsistent with [42] who found that labour unrest has a negative impact on FDI. The presence of cointegration was confirmed by the short-run analysis which also confirmed that any deviation from the long-run equilibrium is corrected to return to the long-run equilibrium after a shock. On the other hand, the pairwise Granger causality test results showed bidirectional causality between FDI and labour unrests.

Empirical findings suggest that government should ensure stable macroeconomic policies. Likewise, policies which promote increase in labour productivity should be encouraged, and labour disputes that result into prolonged strike actions must be minimised; hence consideration of modifying labour laws and regulations is submitted.

## Appendices and nomenclature

| Null Hypothesis | Obs | F-Statistic | Prob. |
|---|---|---|---|
| IL does not Granger Cause FDI | 39 | 1.019 | 0.371 |
| FDI does not Granger Cause IL | | 0.098 | 0.907 |
| PL does not Granger Cause FDI | 39 | 0.882 | 0.423 |

| | | | |
|---|---|---|---|
| FDI does not Granger Cause PL | | 1.3819 | 0.265 |
| InfInv does not Granger Cause FDI | 39 | 0.461 | 0.635 |
| FDI does not Granger Cause InfInv | | 0.256 | 0.776 |
| Intr does not Granger Cause FDI | 39 | 1.477 | 0.243 |
| FDI does not Granger Cause Intr | | 0.446 | 0.644 |
| LU does not Granger Cause FDI | 39 | 0.414 | 0.6645 |
| FDI does not Granger Cause LU | | 9.883 | 0.0004 |
| PL does not Granger Cause IL | 39 | 1.512 | 0.235 |
| IL does not Granger Cause PL | | 3.347 | 0.047 |
| InfInv does not Granger Cause IL | 39 | 0.918 | 0.409 |
| IL does not Granger Cause InfInv | | 0.513 | 0.603 |
| Intr does not Granger Cause IL | 39 | 0.597 | 0.556 |
| IL does not Granger Cause Intr | | 1.743 | 0.190 |
| LU does not Granger Cause IL | 39 | 1.923 | 0.162 |
| IL does not Granger Cause LU | | 2.543 | 0.094 |
| InfInv does not Granger Cause PL | 39 | 1.116 | 0.339 |
| PL does not Granger Cause InfInv | | 9.164 | 0.001 |
| Intr does not Granger Cause PL | 39 | 6.003 | 0.006 |
| PL does not Granger Cause Intr | | 3.472 | 0.043 |
| LU does not Granger Cause PL | 39 | 1.784 | 0.183 |
| PL does not Granger Cause LU | | 1.221 | 0.308 |
| Intr does not Granger Cause InfInv | 39 | 5.156 | 0.011 |
| InfInv does not Granger Cause Intr | | 1.114 | 0.339 |
| LU does not Granger Cause InfInv | 39 | 4.243 | 0.023 |
| InfInv does not Granger Cause LU | | 1.274 | 0.293 |
| LU does not Granger Cause Intr | 39 | 0.168 | 0.846 |
| Intr does not Granger Cause LU | | 1.563 | 0.224 |

## Author details

Itumeleng Pleasure Mongale* and Livhuwani Baloyi
Faculty of Management and Law, University of Limpopo, South Africa

*Address all correspondence to: itumeleng.mongale@ul.ac.za

## References

[1] Alfaro L, Charlton A. Growth and the Quality of Foreign Direct Investment: Is All FDI Equal. In: New Perspectives on Financial Globalization Research Department [Internet]. Washington: International Monetary Fund and Cornell University; 2007. Available from: http://www.china.org.cn/english/BAT/42600.htm [Accessed: 19 November 2018]

[2] Mhlanga T. Government, Business Gather to Unlock $100-Billion Investment for Ramaphosa New Dawn. Mail & Guardian. 2018]; Available from: https: //mg.co.za/article/2018-06-28-shaping-an-inclusive-and-sustainable-future-for-south-africans [Accessed: 19 November 2018]

[3] EWN. Ramaphosa Team to Seek $100bn Investment for South Africa. Eye Witness News [Internet]. 16 April 2018. Available from: https://www.reuters.com/article/us-safrica-ramaphosa-idUSKBN1HN2JR [Accessed: 19 November 2018]

[4] Chopra S, Kaur S. Analysis of FDI inflows and outflows in India. Journal of Advanced Management Science. 2014; **2**(4):326-332. Available from: http://www.joams.com/uploadfile/2014/0424/20140424052709217.pdf [Accessed: 19 November 2018]

[5] Waldkirch A, Ofosu A. Foreign presence, spillovers, and productivity: Evidence from Ghana. World Development. 2010;**38**(8, 26):1114. Available from: https://www.sciencedirect.com/science/article/pii/S0305750X10000100 [Accessed: 19 November 2018]

[6] Stiebale J, Reize F. The impact of FDI through mergers and acquisitions on innovation in target firms. International Journal of Industrial Organization. 2011; **29**(2):155-167. Available from: https://www.sciencedirect.com/science/article/pii/S0167718710000937 [Accessed: 19 November 2018]

[7] Agbloyor EK, Abor J, Adjasi CKD, Yawson A. Exploring the causality links between financial markets and foreign direct investment in Africa. Research in International Business and Finance. 2013;**28**(1):118-134 Available from: https://www.sciencedirect.com/science/article/pii/S0275531912000748 [Accessed: 19 November 2018]

[8] Barbour P. An Assessment of South Africa's Investment Incentive Regime with a Focus on the Manufacturing Sector [Internet]. London; 2005. Available from: https://www.academia.edu/4868929/An_Assessment_of_South_Africas_Investment_Incentive_Regime_with_a_Focus_on_the_Manufacturing_Sector [Accessed: 19 November 2018]

[9] Mahadea D, Simson R. The Challenge of Low Employment and Economic Growth in T South Africa: 1994-2008. South African Journal of Economic and Management Sciences. 2010;**13**:391-406. Available from: https://sajems.org/index.php/sajems/article/viewFile/92/11 [Accessed: 19 November 2018]

[10] Manuel TA. Economic Policy and South Africa's Growth Strategy [Internet]. Pretoria; 2007. Available from: http://www.treasury.gov.za/comm_media/speeches/2007/2007031901.pdf [Accessed: 19 November 2018]

[11] UNCTAD. Global Investment Prospects Assessment 2016–2018 [Internet]. New York; 2016. Available from: www.unctad.org/fdistatistics [Accessed: 19 November 2018]

[12] Santander Trade Portal. Foreign investment in South Africa: Santanderrtrade.com [Internet]. Santander Trade Portal. 2018. Available from: https://en.

portal.santandertrade.com/establish-overseas/south-africa/foreign-investment [Accessed: 19 November 2018]

[13] Ben JR. A Global Foreign Direct Invest Country Attractiveness Index [Internet]. 2018. Available from: http://www.fdiattractiveness.com/wp-content/uploads/2018/07/2018IndexReport.pdf [Accessed: 19 November 2018]

[14] The Heritage Foundation. Index of Economic Freedom: South Africa. The Heritage Foundation. 2018. pp. 2018-2021

[15] Hooda S. A Study of FDI and Indian Economy. Kurukshetra, Indian: Deemed University; 2011

[16] Ajayi SI. FDI and Economic development in Africa. In: ADB/AERC International Conference on Accelerating Africas Development Five Years into the Twenty-First Century [Internet]. Tunis; 2006. Available from: https://www.afdb.org/fileadmin/uploads/afdb/Documents/Knowledge/09484246-EN-FDI-AND-ECONOMIC-GROWTH.PDF [Accessed: 13 July 2019]

[17] Ngowi HP. Can Africa increase its global share of foreign direct investment (FDI)? West Africa Review. 2001;**2**(2):1-22. Available from: http://www.africaknowledgeproject.org/index.php/war/article/view/444 [Accessed: 13 April 2018]

[18] Moran TH. Foreword. In: Tavares-Lehmann AT, Toledano P, Johnson L, Sachs L, editors. Rethinking Investment Incentives. New York, USA: Columbia University Press; 2016. pp. VII-VIX. Available from: http://www.jstor.org/stable/10.7312/tava17298.3

[19] Bailey N. Exploring the relationship between institutional factors and FDI attractiveness: A meta-analytic review. International Business Review. 2018;**27**(1):139-148. Available from: http://linkinghub.elsevier.com/retrieve/pii/S0969593117303980 [Accessed: 2 May 2018]

[20] Chilton J, Philippe R, Millson B, Vakil T. The Business Expansion Decision Making Process for Multinational Enterprises Investing in Canada Clients [Internet]. 2013. Available from: https://dspace.library.uvic.ca/bitstream/handle/1828/4639/chilton_jenny_mpa_2013.pdf [Accessed: 12 July 2019]

[21] Ndiaye G, Xu H. Impact of foreign direct investment (FDI) on economic growth in WAEMU from 1990 to 2012. International Journal of Financial Research. 2016;7(4):33-44

[22] Guerin SS. The Relationship between Capital Flows and Current Account: Volatility and Causality [Internet]. SSRN. March 2012. Available from: http://www.ssrn.com/abstract=2018195 [Accessed: 13 July 2019]

[23] Ramirez MD. Is foreign direct investment beneficial for Mexico? An empirical analysis, 1960–2001. World Development [Internet]. 2006;**34**(5):802-817. Available from: https://www.sciencedirect.com/science/article/abs/pii/S0305750X06000234 [Accessed: 13 July 2019]

[24] Ram R, Zhang KH. Foreign direct investment and economic growth: Evidence from cross-country data for the 1990s. Economic Development and Cultural Change. 2002;**51**(1):205-215. DOI: 10.1086/345453

[25] Bende-Nabende A. Foreign direct investment determinants in Sub-Sahara Africa: A co-integration analysis. Economics Bulletin. 2002;**6**:1-19

[26] Asiedu E. Foreign direct Investment in Africa: The role of natural resources, market size, government Policy, institutions and political instability. World Economy. 2006;**29**(1):63-77.

Available from: http://www.ssrn.com/abstract=717361 [Accessed: 13 July 2019]

[27] World Bank. Ease of Doing Business Score and Ease of Doing Business Ranking [Internet]. New York; 2018. Available from: http://www.doingbusiness.org/content/dam/doingBusiness/media/Annual-Reports/English/DB19-Chapters/DB19-Score-and-DBRankings.pdf [Accessed: 23 October 2017]

[28] Pesaran MH, Shin Y, Smith RJ. Bounds testing approaches to the analysis of level relationships. Journal of Applied Econometrics. 2001;**16**(3): 289-326 Available from: http://doi.wiley.com [Accessed: 19 October 2017]

[29] Department of Labour. South Africa: Labour Industrial Action Report 2012 [Internet]. Pretoria; 2013. Available from: https://allafrica.com/stories/201309181024.html

[30] Casson M, Hashimzade N, editors. Large Databases in Economic History: Research Methods and Case Studies. 1st ed. Abingdon, UK: Routledge; 2013. Available from: https://www.routledge.com/Large-Databases-in-Economic-History-Research-Methods-and-Case-Studies/Casson-Hashimzade/p/book/9781138231474 [Accessed: 13 July 2019]

[31] Elliott G, Rothenberg TJ, Stock JHJ, Eliiot G, Rothernberg TJ, Stock JHJ. Efficient tests for an autoregressive unit root. Econometrica. 1996;**64**(4):813. Available from: http://www.jstor.org/stable/2171846?origin=crossref

[32] Johansen S, Juselius K. Maximum likelihood estimation and inference on co-integration. Oxford Bulletin of Economics and Statistics. 1990;**52**(2): 169-210. Available from: https://onlinelibrary.wiley.com [Accessed: 7 May 2019]

[33] Asteriou D, Stephen GH. Applied Econometrics: A Modern Approach using Eviews and Microfit. London, UK: Palgrave Macmillan; 2007. 421 p. Available from: https://books.google.co.za/books/about/Applied_Econometrics.html [Accessed: 30 October 2018]

[34] Granger CWJ. Investigating causal relations by econometric models and cross-spectral methods. Econometrica. 1969;**37**(3):424-438. Available from: https://www.jstor.org/stable/pdf/1912791.pdf

[35] Brown RL, Durbin J, Evans JM. Techniques for testing the constancy of regression relationships over time. Journal of the Royal Statistical Society. 1975;**37**(2):149-192

[36] Chow GC. Tests of equality between sets of coefficients in two linear regressions. Econometrica. 1969;**28**(3): 591-605

[37] Dougherty C. Introduction to Econometrics. 5th ed. Oxford: Oxford University Press; 2016. 590 p. Available from: https://global.oup.com/academic/product/introduction-to-econometrics-9780199676828?cc=us&lang=en [Accessed: 13 July 2019]

[38] Zafeiriou E, Azam M. CO2 emissions and economic performance in EU agriculture: Some evidence from Mediterranean countries. Ecological Indicators. 2017;**81**:104-114. Available from: https://linkinghub.elsevier.com/retrieve/pii/S1470160X17302947 [Accessed: 7 May 2019]

[39] Nahidi M. Investigation Effective Economic Factors on Foreign Direct Investment in IRAN, Under Stable and Non-Stable Conditions [Internet]. Islamic Azad University, Tehran Branch; 2010. Available from: https://scholar.google.co.za/scholar [Accessed: 13 July 2019]

[40] Uwubanmwen A, Mayowa AG. The determinants and impacts of foreign direct investment in Nigeria. International Journal of

Business & Management. 2012;**7**(24):
67-77

[41] Tampakoudis IA, Subeniotis DN, Kroustalis IG, Skouloudakis MI. Determinants of foreign direct investment in middle-income countries: New middle-income trap evidence. Mediterranean Journal of Social Sciences. 2017;**8**(1):58-70

[42] Krishna Prasanna P, Menon AS. Speed of information adjustment in Indian stock indices. IIMB Management Review. 2013;**23**(2013):150-159. Available from: https://ac.els-cdn.com/S0970389613000487/1-s2.0-S0970389613000487-main.pdf [Accessed: 6 March 2019]

[43] Alabdulrazag B, Alrajhi A. The validity of environmental kuznets curve hypotheis in the kingdom of saudi arabia: ARDL bounds testing approach to cointegration. International Review of Management and Business Research. 2016;**5**(4):1450-1464

Chapter 6

# Budget Deficit and the Federal Government Debt in Malaysia

*Mohamed Aslam and Raihan Jaafar*

## Abstract

In general, most countries in the world, particularly developing countries, are facing significant budget constraints, in which the collection of tax and nontax revenues is less than the government's total expenditure. Therefore, borrowing either from the local capital or international capital markets is made. Borrowing increases government debts. The budget deficits and the growth of the government debt are the major factors that determine the health of macroeconomics. There is a solid consensus among economists mainly on the effect of budget deficits on macroeconomics in terms of crowding out private investment, increasing interest rates, expanding money supply and escalating consumer price and in certain extent affect exchange rate. Government bonds issued to finance budget deficits are also in question as part of the net wealth of private sectors. On the other side, there is an agreement that the budget deficits financed by the issuance of bonds will crowd out private investment through increasing interest rate. This paper plans to investigate the impact of budget deficits on Malaysia's economy. Cointegration test and vector error correction models are used to examine the impact of budget deficits on certain macroeconomic variables.

**Keywords:** budget deficits, federal government debt, VECM, Malaysia

## 1. Introduction

In general, a persistent deficit in the government budgets would be a paramount issue to macroeconomic stability to any countries. Theory suggests that persistent and large budget deficits lead to a harmful effect on major macroeconomic fundamentals. In particular, massive budget deficits result in high interest rates as the government's demand for funds and this consequently conflicting with private sector demand for investment financing, thereby discouraging private investment expansion. The implications of high interest rates would affect severely residential construction, business investment in plant and equipment and consumer spending on durable goods by such a fiscal policy and along with non-accommodative monetary policy. Moreover, the budget deficits may affect interest rates via the channel of reduction in savings or deposits in the banking system.

Federal government debt relates to how much a country owes and is owed by a central government which acts as the liability of the nation. Changes in the government debt over time reflect the outcome of government deficits, for example when government spending exceeds its tax collections. When its tax collections are exceeded, it has a budget deficit, which it then finances by borrowing from the



IntechOpen

private sector or from foreign governments. In other words, budget deficit occurs when government spending exceeds its revenue; meanwhile, federal government debt is the accumulation of the deficits. Budget deficit and federal government debt are interrelated as they affect each other, for example deficit affects the debt by selling bonds. When the bonds are sold, it increases the money; this transaction is defined as public debt because these bonds are sold to the public. Another example is the way debt affects the deficit; in the long-run, debt that is owed by the federal government reduces tax revenues and increases the deficit further.

The budget deficits run by the government around the world particularly since 2008 which tackle the effect of global economic crisis had accelerated the growth of government debt and accumulated the debt which had reached critical level. As there is a continuous growth of debt, creditors may become concerned about the government's initiative to repay it. Over time, these creditors will expect higher interest payments to provide a greater return for their increased perceived risk as it is widely known that higher interest costs dampen economic growth. As interest rates rise, it becomes more expensive for a country to refinance its existing debt. The management of debt by way of service payment is the sum of the principal payments and interest actually paid in foreign currency, especially as foreign currency tends to affect exchange rates.

There has been a strong interest in the behaviour of public debt, particularly since the impact of Asian financial crisis and the global financial crisis. During those periods Malaysia budgets deficits financed by increasing debts, i.e., issuing of bonds. The issue of Malaysia's government debt became significant in the public interest especially after the dramatic increase of government debt in the year onwards of 2009. The government gross debt has climbed up from 41.2% of GDP in 2007 to 52.8% in 2009 and further increased to 54.5% in 2015. The large increase in government debt, especially during the recent years, might be related to the Vision 2020 in which it envisioned to make Malaysia as a developed and high-income country by the year 2020. The main objective of this research is to review the Malaysian federal government's debt and budget deficit during the period of 1985–2018.

## 2. Budget deficits and government debt

External markets have been the major factor influencing Malaysia's economic growth and development since the early 1900s. There were two sources of growth, foreign capital and major trade partners' commodity markets. The Malaysian economy grew rapidly with real GDP posting average annual growth rates of 6% during the period of 1956–2018. In 2009, the Malaysian economy contracted by 1.6% due to the world financial crisis that swept the US economy in late 2008. In 2010, the Malaysian economy bounced back to 7.2% and declined to 4.5% in 2018. In general, the country has grown rapidly by international standards. Its GDP growth averaged close to 6% from 1971 to 2018 (**Figure 1**). Within three decades from the 1970s to the 1990s, Malaysia's economy experienced an annual GDP growth of 6.0 and close to a 3.7 growth in per capita income. External markets have been the major factor influencing for economic growth. The impressive growth of the economy had accelerated demand for labour and reduced unemployment level. Since 1997 as shown in **Figures 1** and 2, the economy performance is much affected by external shocks. To tackle the economic mass, the government implemented budget deficits 4% of GDP constantly from 1998 to 2018. As shown in **Figure 2**, budget deficits declined from 1989 to 1997 but increased subsequently until today. Furthermore to stimulate further the economy, the interests reduced onward since 1998.

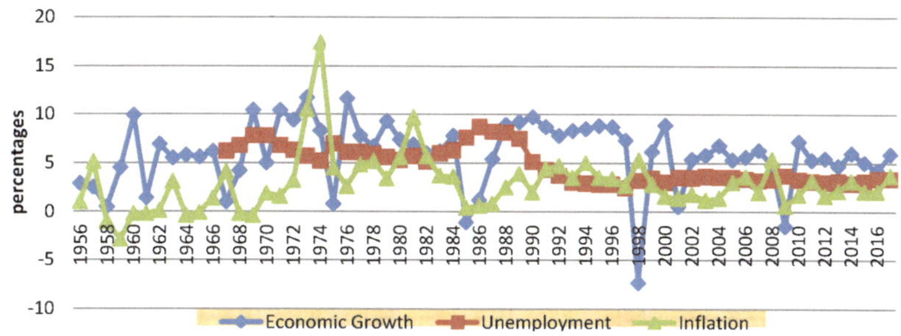


**Figure 1.**
*Malaysia: real economic growth rate, unemployment rate and inflation rate (%).*

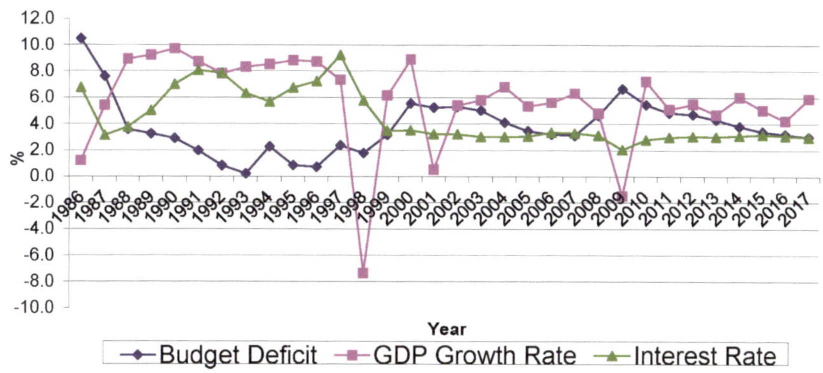


**Figure 2.**
*Malaysia: budget deficits, economic growth dan interest rate (%).*

However, both the traditional macroeconomic policies failed producing outstanding economic performance. The budget deficits implemented had increased the government debt thereafter.

In the 1990s, the Malaysian total outstanding government debt reached an all-time high of 80.7% and a record low of 31.8% in 1997. Malaysia's government debt to GDP averaged 50.2% from 1990 until 2018. Since the debt approaching to 55%, therefore, the government should control her spending before the debt affecting the government fiscal position. The government self-imposed debt ceiling has been raised multiple times from 40% in 2003 to 45% in 2008. In 2009 it rose to 55%, and currently the limit still stands at this figure. It seems that Malaysia federal government debt level has been increasing much faster than the GDP growth; the statutory borrowing ceiling has been raised by 15% of GDP within 6 years, 2009–2017. Malaysia has breached its own self-imposed debt limit. However, even though the ratio of debt to GDP approached the limit, the Ministry of Finance claims that the debt is still manageable. The high level of debt may limit the development and objective of Malaysia's economic transformation plan.

Uncertainties of the national debt service payment create discouragement, and ultimately, they form difficulties in the pursuit of economic reform [1]. The government spending must be paid by running the government in deficit and borrowing the money from the public or by raising today's taxes. However, if the government chooses to run in the budget deficit, the government must eventually raise their taxes to make interest payments in the future. In other words, the more spending made by the government, the higher the taxes will become; no matter if it is today or in the future.

In 2016 the World Bank downgraded GDP growth of Malaysia of 4.2% from the previous year, 2015, 4.4%. This is due to a weak global demand for manufactured exports and oil. When the demand for our crude oil is going down, the government revenue experiences a shortfall and fiscal deficit occurs. According to Foon [2], the Malaysian government will have a tough time lowering the deficit position caused by the shortfall in government revenue from crude oil. He added that the government set a limit for the budget deficit that year of 3.1%. But in the first half of 2016, the deficit rose to 5.6%.

Clearly, this is a very disturbing situation. What implications do large deficits have in store for our future as taxpayers? To determine the answers to the question, we must first determine whether or not federal borrowing drives up interest rates. If it does, we run a risk of crowding out private investment, thus leaving a smaller capital stock from which future tax collectors can draw to pay back the debt. There are many possible outcomes regarding the implication of budget deficit and federal government debt. Various economists predict that something detrimental will happen in the future based on the large deficits of the past, but a few also inform us not to worry so much about this matter.

## 2.1 Domestic loans

The federal government sector accounts are always in a state of deficit, except in 1960 and 1993–2018 (**Figures 2** and **3**). The deficit of the federal government was quite high in 1981, 1982 and 1986, where the deficit to GDP was 15.6, 16.7 and 10.5%, respectively. This deficit is due to the expansionary fiscal policy implemented from 1980 to 1987 to address the recession problem. In the early 1990s, the federal government deficit began to decline and has become excessive due to the government's public policies reducing spending and relaxing its role in the economy. At the same time, the government has encouraged large private sector participation in economic growth.

The federal government deficit can be said to be funded entirely by debt whether domestic or foreign borrowing or both. The size of the federal government debt as a percentage of GDP has increased from 29% in 1965 to 44% in 1980, 83% in 1990 and 53% in 1994. The highest increase was recorded in 1986 by 103%, in 1987 by 104% and in 1988 by 98%. The high debt ratio is largely related to the heavy industrial development program which was embarked in the early 1980s. The financing of various development programs in 1980s entirely by foreign borrowing. Most foreign loans made during this period were from the Japanese government (project loan) and Japanese financial institutions (market loans).

The structure of foreign loans is divided into two, namely project loans and market loans. Domestic borrowings are as attractive as borrowing sources come

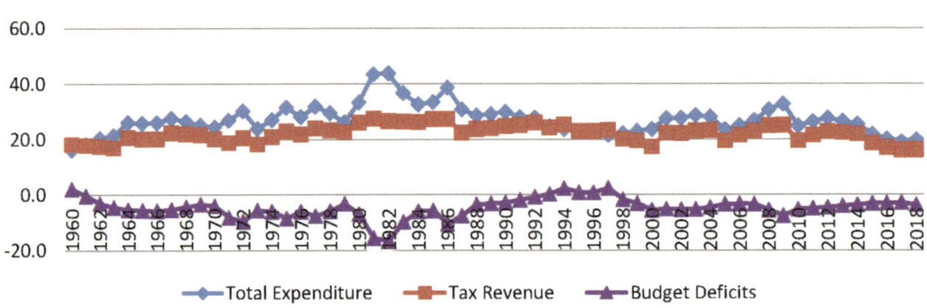


**Figure 3.**
*Malaysia: federal government budget and deficits (% of GDP).*

from noninflationary sources. However, foreign loans have risen as interest rates are lower than those offered locally.

Domestic borrowing is the main source of funding the federal government budget deficits. More than 60% of the federal government debt was from domestic borrowing. In 1965, the total domestic debt to total debt amounted to 82% (RM2134 million), the amount decreased to 79% (RM18.6 billions) in 1980, 74% (RM70 billions) in 1990 before it rose to 82% (RM78 billion) in 1995 and 97% (RM704 billion) in 2018. In terms of percentages to GDP, the amount of domestic debt was more than 50% in average from 1965 to 2018. The total domestic debt to GDP in 1965 was 24% and has increased to 35% in 1980, 61% in 1990 before declining to 35% in 2000 and increased to 50% in 2018 (**Table 1**).

Domestic borrowings are made through the sale of treasury bills, investment certificates, government guarantees and other credit instruments. Short-term loans are usually treasury bills, while long-term borrowings are usually a government guarantee letter. The government issued treasury bills with maturities of 3 months, 6 months and 12 months with interest rates ranging from 6.4 to 7.9%. This short-term loan is somewhat useful because the government's revenue is insufficient to meet the government obligations, i.e. the expenditure is more than the amount of revenue received. Generally, treasury bills are held by commercial banks and discount companies. This government debt papers are the main liquid assets in the banking systems. The central bank may influence the liquidity of these assets by buying or selling such bills through open market operation.

Government borrowing through by issuing treasury bills is around 6–23% of the total domestic borrowings. In the 1960s, the federal government debt in the form of treasury bills was more than 20%, dropped to 15% in the 1970s and about 6.8% from 1980 to 1995 and less than 10% from 1996 to 2018. In the future, borrowing

| Year | Federal govt. debt | | Domestic loan | | | External loan | | |
|---|---|---|---|---|---|---|---|---|
| | Total | % of GDP | Subtotal | % total debt | % of GDP | Subtotal | % total debt | % of GDP |
| 1965 | 2598 | 29 | 2134 | 82 | 24 | 464 | 18 | 5 |
| 1970 | 5028 | 40 | 4283 | 85 | 34 | 745 | 15 | 6 |
| 1975 | 11,387 | 51 | 8963 | 79 | 40 | 2424 | 22 | 10 |
| 1980 | 23,439 | 44 | 18,578 | 79 | 35 | 4861 | 21 | 9 |
| 1985 | 63,882 | 82 | 40,812 | 64 | 53 | 23,070 | 36 | 30 |
| 1990 | 94,713 | 83 | 69,987 | 74 | 61 | 24,726 | 26 | 22 |
| 1995 | 91,368 | 41 | 78,037 | 85 | 52 | 13,331 | 15 | 10 |
| 2000 | 12,560 | 37 | 10,680 | 85 | 35 | 1880 | 15 | 5 |
| 2005 | 22,870 | 44 | 19,870 | 87 | 35 | 3000 | 13 | 6 |
| 2010 | 408,178 | 53 | 390,724 | 99 | 38 | 13,786 | 10 | 9 |
| 2015 | 630,540 | 55 | 609,063 | 97 | 53 | 21,477 | 3 | 2 |
| 2016 | 648,475 | 53 | 624,822 | 96 | 51 | 23,653 | 4 | 2 |
| 2017 | 686,837 | 51 | 665,572 | 97 | 49 | 21,265 | 3 | 2 |
| 2018 | 725,241 | 52 | 704,101 | 97 | 50 | 21,140 | 3 | 2 |

*Source: Ministry of Finance, Economic Report [3–11], various issue 2.*

**Table 1.**
*Malaysia: composition federal government borrowing (RM' millions).*

by issuing treasury bills will become imperative, as the policy of deregulation or consolidation public debt with the reduction of government intervention will result in surplus budget. The surplus or government saving can be brought forward for later use.

The main domestic government medium-term and long-term loans are Malaysia government securities (MGS). MGS are usually issued on maturities of 2–3, 4–5, 6–9, 10–11, 12–15 and over 15 years with interest rates ranging from 8 to 8.5%. In the 1990s the government issued MGS with a fairly short maturity period to meet the needs of investors, but since 1998 the issuance of MGS in general is in medium and long terms. The total amount for MGS issued from 1980 to 2018 ranges from 70 to 80%.

Most of the MGS was held by the Employees' Provident Fund (EPF) Organisation, which holds more than 50%. In the early 1960s to 1970s, the MGS that held by EPF ranged from 60 to 70%. But in the late 1980s and early 1990s and in 2000s, the amount of holding dropped between 50 and 60%. The rest of the MGS were held by other financial institutions. In addition, investment certificates are also issued for additional funds. Generally, these investment certificates were issued to meet investors' demands and for OMO purpose rather than for financing budget deficits.

MGSs have become a major instrument in raising fund for the government. Since 1997, the federal government heavily relies on MGS for budget deficit financing. Based on **Figure 4**, the new government debt papers issued are substantial. The gap between the gross and net public fund raised was getting bigger. This also means that part of the budget deficits was financed by creating or printing new currency notes. Also part of the debt papers was monetized; therefore, money supply and currency in circulation increased sharply since 1999 (**Figure** 5).

## 2.2 External debt

In the case of Malaysia, relatively, external debt is regarded are not critical except during the period 1982–1990. During this period the percentage of external

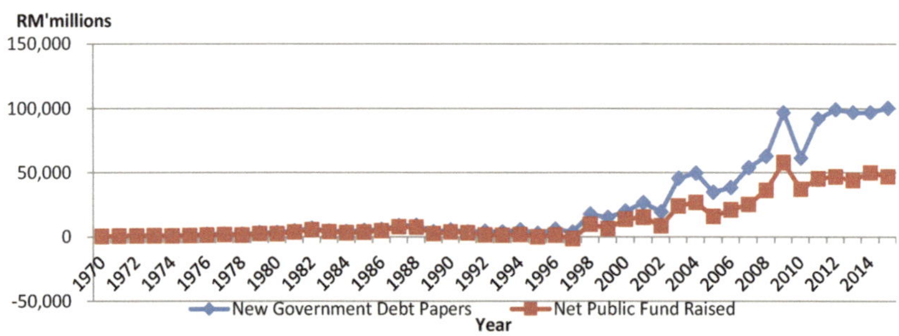


**Figure 4.**
*Malaysia: new government debt papers issued and net fund raised (RM' millions).*

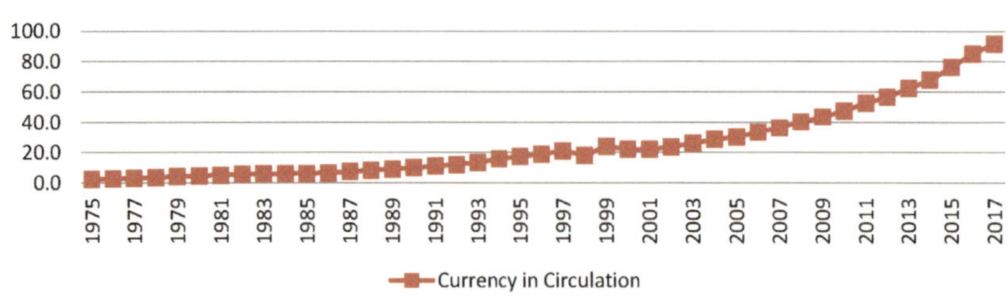


**Figure 5.**
*Malaysia: currency in circulation (RM' millions).*

debt has exceeded 30% of GDP (**Table 2**). Before the 1980s, foreign debt was between 5 and 11% of GDP. External debt has increased significantly in the 1980s, as domestic savings were inadequate at that time to cover federal government spending. The main purpose of the external borrowing during the period is (i) to overcome the economic downturn in the early 1980s, (ii) to finance heavy industrial development that was launched in the early 1980s, and (iii) to finance various mega infrastructure projects. The ratio of external debt to GDP since 1997 is lingering from 5 to 9% of GDP. However, the debt ratio of the total federal government debt from 1997 to 2018 is about 20%. As mentioned above for financing budget deficits, the government relies on domestic capital market.

External debt is divided into two, namely market loans and project loans. Market loans are loans where the government borrows from foreign financial institutions or foreign governments or borrows from foreigners by issuing government bonds. While project loans are loans made to finance major infrastructure projects, which are financed either from the World Bank, Asian Development Bank or from the foreign government.

Both forms of external debt above are important in government spending. The importance of both loans is similar except for the period before 1980 and from 2000 to 2005. During the period the government borrowed in large amount from overseas in the form of market loans to cover the government spending from 1980 to 1990 and to overcome economic recession. The total market borrowing from the total external debt was high in 1986 which was 36 and 30% of GDP.

The main sources of federal government external borrowing were the United States, Japan, and the World Bank. In the 1980s, the government borrowed in huge amount from Japan. However, the United States remains a major source of borrowing, but the volume of loans from the country has declined. External debt from the United States was in the form of market loans, while market loans from Japan were less. The project loans were mostly financed by the Japanese government as well as the World Bank. Japan was a major contributor to Malaysia's external debt and most of the debt for financing development projects, i.e. infrastructure.

The increase in federal government borrowing either from domestic or external capital markets has led to the increment of the amount of interest payments of the debt. The amount of interest payments of domestic debt from 1970 to 1995 was on average about 74% of the total interest payment. Interest payment on external debt was much lower, and this indicated that the government favours borrowing from domestic money or capital market because the cost of borrowing is cheaper than the external debt.

The main critical issue of external borrowing is linked to the fluctuations of exchange rate, in which the fluctuation had cost of government loans, particularly in terms of principal and interest payments. Since the Plaza Accord of 1985, the appreciation of Japanese yen against USD had increased the federal government debt burden, i.e. loan payment to Japanese government. The total interest payment of debt has increased from RM262 million in 1970 to RM1444 million in 1980 and RM7125 million in 1995 and RM20 billion in 2018. The total interest payment on domestic debt in 1970 was RM223 million, has increased to RM1070 million in 1980 and about RM6049 million in 1995 and in 2018 amounted to RM18 billion (**Table 2**). Interest payments on external debt have increased from RM11 million in 1980 to RM32 million in 1987 before it declined to RM16 million in 1995 and in 2018 about RM2 billion.

## 3. Literature review

Budget deficits can be viewed as the sum of structural and cyclical components. The cyclical component reflects the response of receipts and expenditures of the government to fluctuations in the business cycle, whereas the structural component is the result of discretionary fiscal policy [13]. De Leeuw and Holloway [14] stated that the structural component is an important indicator of the macroeconomic effects of fiscal policy. They argue that over the complete business cycle, the cyclical component has a tendency to negate its own effects; therefore, only the structural component is meaningful for long-run fiscal policy.

Eisner and Pieper [15] use an aggregate demand approach to determine the relationship between the federal deficit and the growth rate of GNP. They found that the coefficient on the deficit variable was positive and significant when the growth rate of GNP was regressed upon it. Kormendi [16] investigated the impact on consumption of government purchases, taxes, transfers, interest payments and the market value of government debt. His study was not limited to federal government activities as all his variables (where applicable) were the sum of the federal state and local governments. He found that the government purchases had a negative and significant impact on consumption. He also found that the government purchases were less than perfect substitutes for private consumption. Furthermore he discovered that the coefficient for the market value of government debt was negative and significant. This results a bit surprised as theory suggests that people view bonds as net wealth and would increase their consumption; therefore, yielding should be a positive sign.

Based on traditional view, Blinder and Solow [17] argue that a given level of government expenditures and a substitution of public debt for tax financing have a positive effect on aggregate demand. Their argument assumes that, through an increase in government bonds, there would be a perceived increase in the private sector wealth, resulting in an increase of current and future consumption at the expense of saving. Additionally, when private saving goes up by less than the debt issue, the real interest rate rises, and some form of crowding out of private investment will take place. Abderrezak [18] explains that, given the level of government expenditures, increases in government debt will stimulate consumption demand, which in turn provokes a rise in interest rates, and the latter will eventually crowd out some private investment expenditures. In other words, he suggested that even though the current deficits are expansionary, the anticipation of growing future deficits may well reduce economic activity in the future.

Most of the economists believe that current and expected government budget deficits will lead to higher interest rates. Penner [19] agreed on the conventional view that deficits/debts have a significant positive relationship with interest rates. According to the Ricardian equivalence theorem, higher future taxes, as implied by enlarged government debt, will cancel out the wealth effect that is credited by the conventional paradigm for increasing consumption at the expense of investment [18]. Blanchard [20] had analysed the relation between real interest rates, budget deficits and government debt. He argued that even if deficits are sustainable, they will still affect interest rates. Abderrezak also concludes that the short-term interest rate depends on the current level of debt but does not depend on the current level of deficits.

Blinder and Solow [17] describe how bond financed deficits increase competition for funds in credit markets and put upward pressure on interest rates. Accordingly, when the government issues new bonds to finance deficits, competition for funds increases interest rates to convince agents to hold more government bonds. That is, the price of bonds should decrease and interest rates should increase. The real interest rate is a common-sense idea because those lending funds are sensitive to the inflation rate expected over the period they lend the funds so that the return on the funds is sufficient to cover the deterioration in the value of money due to inflation [21]. The real interest rate is the nominal interest rate after subtracting expected inflation.

Hoelscher [22] examines the effects of the federal government borrowing on short-term interest rates in the case of the United States. His regressions test to see whether or not the level of federal borrowing is a statistically significant determinant of the 3-month treasury bill rate. He obtained very low t-statistics on the relevant variables and concluded that federal borrowing is not an important determinant of short-term interest rates. He also states that "to the extent that private expenditures are sensitive only to short-term rates, then Federal borrowing does not have financial crowding out effects". Meanwhile, de Leeuw and Holloway [14] found slightly different results. Their study covered 1955:1 to 1983:3 and regressed the interest rate on the deficit and a cyclically adjusted federal debt variable. They found the coefficient of the deficit variable to be insignificant and the coefficient of the debt variable to be both significant and positive. Barth et al. [23] found the coefficient of the federal debt variable to be positive and significant; therefore, this result supports the view that federal debt raises the interest rate through its impact on money demand.

The other method that would influence money demand is the purchase of government securities on the open market by the central banks. This activities by the central bank will result not only in an increase in net public financial assets but also in an increase in the reserves of the commercial banks and depository institutions as well as the amount of cash held by the public [24, 25]. This implies an increase in the monetary base which results in an overall increase in the money supply. Deficits financed in this fashion are said to be monetized or money financed. Wood [26] asserts if an increase in new money creation is used to finance part or all of a budget deficit, and, if necessary, a quantum of money is withdrawn from the economy via bond sales undertaken by the central bank, and then inflation would not increase, and a fiscal stimulus could be delivered in order to lift overall economic activity. Deravi et al. [27] prove that there is a relationship between government debt and interest rates via the demand for money. This relationship is examined through the wealth effect of government debt on money demand. They found evidence on government debt affecting the demand for money positively, implying that federal government debt is net wealth. Meanwhile, Giannaros and Kolluri [28] stated that the government budget deficit is not a determinant of money supply growth or of inflation (directly or indirectly). Friedman and Schwartz [29] explained, when interest rates are initially excessive, these lower interest rates may increase aggregate demand. When aggregate demand expands at a rate so fast that production and imports cannot satisfy the demand, then inflation develops.

Abizadeh and Yousefi [30] state that the influence of the foreign sector may or may not have a material effect on the deficits/debt-interest rate relationship, that is the deficit and debt do not have a significant positive relationship with interest rates. There is a large debate about the relationship between the budget deficit reduction and exchange rates. Greenspan [31] argued that deficit reduction could lead to currency appreciation, whereas Krugman [32] stressed that deficit reduction would lead to currency depreciation. Based on the debate over the relationship between deficit reduction and exchange rates, currency appreciation arises because the theory is ambiguous. Deficit reduction has sometimes been associated with stronger exchange rates, and sometimes it has been associated with weaker exchange rates. This difference in association commonly depends on certain factors or effects which tend to increase or decrease the exchange rates, such as the condition of the country or economy. To sort out the ambiguity on the budget deficits and the exchange rate relationship, Hakkio [33] states that deficit reduction through tax increases tends to weaken the exchange rate of countries with good records on inflation and debt. Whereas deficit reduction through spending cuts tends to strengthen the exchange rate of countries with poor records on inflation and debt.

### 3.1 Econometric models

To examine the effects of the debt on macroeconomy, we introduced few models which are explained below.

#### *3.1.1 Model 1: the federal government debt and interest rate*

$$IR = f\ (LBD, LGD, LMB, INF, LT) \tag{1}$$

where:

IR = the interest rate.
LBD = the budget deficit.
LGD = the government federal debt.
LMB = the monetary base.
INF = the inflation rate.
LT = the federal tax receipt.

The coefficient of the deficit term will be tested for crowding out. If the coefficient is found to be positive and significant, then crowding out is the case. If the term is statistically insignificant from zero, then neither crowding out nor crowding in is the case, but if it is negative and significant, then crowding in is the case. The coefficient of the debt variable can be positive and significant if we assume that the larger is the stock of publicly held government debt, the smaller is the supply of loanable funds available. The coefficient of the monetary base variable is assumed to be negative because as the monetary base grows so does the money supply. The coefficient of the inflationary expectations variable is assumed to be negative as the interest rate lowered; people are able to borrow money, and the consumer has more money to spend, causing the economy to grow and inflation to increase.

#### *3.1.2 Model 2: money demand model*

Ms is the money supply and measured by M1; *W* is variable for wealth and measured by federal government debt (bonds). For simplicity, we rewrite Model 1, as shown below:

$$LM1 = f\ (LGDP, IR, LGD, INF) \tag{2}$$

where LM1 = M1 money supply and LGDP = GDP.

The money supply is assumed to be positively related to income or GDP and inversely related to the opportunity cost of money which is measured by the interest rate. The wealth term, *W*, is partly measured by privately held government debt. The coefficient of the wealth variable (publicly held government debt) could have different signs depending upon which theory of government debt is assumed. If the sign is positive, then government debt is being treated as net wealth by the public, and the Ricardian theorem is disproved. If the coefficient is zero, then government debt is not being treated as net wealth, and one of the assumptions of the Ricardian theorem is verified. The expected inflation term is included as an explanatory variable in the money demand equation. A negative coefficient for the price expectations variable is assumed because if the public expects a higher inflation rate which will result in some erosion of the purchasing power of money, then rational consumers will lower their demand for money holdings.

#### *3.1.3 Model 3: investment and budget deficit*

Crowding out is a negative consequence of budget deficits in which higher interest rates lead to less private investment. The increase in the interest rate reduces the quantity of private investment demanded (crowding out private investment). The higher interest rate increases the demand for and reduces the supply of ringgit in the foreign exchange market. Below are the potential variables and their hypothesised signs of the selected variables.

Thus, investment model can be written as

$$LI = f\ (LBD, IR, GDP) \tag{3}$$

where LI = private investment.

The coefficient of budget deficit is expected to be negative, as well as interest rate, while the coefficient of GDP is expected to be positive. As the budget deficit increases, private investment will decline, because the rise in government borrowing will "crowd out' some of the funds that would otherwise have gone to the private sector.

#### *3.1.4 Model 4: inflation and budget deficit*

If monetary policy is accommodative to a budget deficit, money supply continues to rise for a long time. Aggregate demand increases as a result of this deficit financing, causing output to increase above the natural level of output. When prices rise for energy, food, commodities and other goods and services, the entire economy is affected. Rising prices, known as inflation, impact the cost of living, the cost of doing business, borrowing money, mortgages, corporate and government bond yields and every other facet of the economy. Therefore, there is a negative relationship between inflation and consumption. Budget deficit and money supply both have positive relationship with inflation. Below are the potential variables and their hypothesised signs of the selected variables.

Hence, the inflation model can be figured as follows:

$$INF = F\ (BD, LM1, CON) \tag{4}$$

where CON = the consumption.

Federal government debt data is collected from the Economic Planning Unit (EPU). Data such as GDP, budget deficits, M1 money supply, M2 money supply, money base and federal tax collection were extracted from the Asian Development Bank (ADB), while the data of inflation, investment, federal government debt and real interest rate are obtained from the World Bank.

## 4. Findings

For estimation this paper applies vector error correction model (VECM). The VECM method is a useful approach and able to provide an analytical estimate of the relationship among variables over short-run and long-run period, besides provides an evaluation of interaction among the variables.

Unit root testing will be conducted to determine the time series data whether consist nonstationarity. Most of the economic theory suggests that an existence of long-run relationships exist among the nonstationary time series variables. In both ADF and PP tests, the null hypothesis of the presence of a unit root in the time series is tested. The null hypothesis needs to be rejected either at the level form or at any level of differenced form for a variable to be stationary. The time series may, however, be stationary at the level, that is, I(0) or at the first difference, that is, I (1). The results will be summarised in **Tables 2** and **3**.

**Table 2** shows the results of ADF unit root test that include all the variables used in this study. The null hypothesis of the unit root can only be rejected if the probability is statistically significant at 1, 5 and 10% significant level. ADF test above portrays that all series are stationary at first difference. Hence, the results demonstrate that the variables are integrated at order I(1). This is supported by PP test that shows all the variables are at the stationary state, as can be seen below.

**Table 3** shows the PP unit root test results. The PP test uses the model similar to ADF test. The null hypothesis of the unit root can only be rejected if the probability is statistically significant at 1, 5 and 10% significant level. Like the ADF test, the null hypothesis of the presence of a unit root in the time series against the alternative hypothesis states that there is no unit root in the time series, or in other words, the time series is stationary. The results above indicate that all series are integrated at order I(1), which means all variables are stationary at first difference.

Therefore, the results of both ADF and PP unit root tests shown in **Tables 2** and **3** prove that the null hypotheses of the presence of a unit root in the time series are not rejected at the level, whereas test statistics of all the variables significantly reject the null hypotheses in favour of the alternative hypotheses of no unit root in the time series at the first difference. It can be inferred that all the time series variables are nonstationary at their level forms while they are stationary at their first difference forms.

The Johansen and Juselius [34] test and estimation strategy, which is maximum likelihood, makes it possible to estimate all cointegrating vectors when there are more than two variables. If there are three variables each with unit roots, there are at most two cointegrating vectors. Cointegration test will be used to determine the existence long-run relationship between the variables. JJ cointegration test is used in

| Variables | Level | | First difference | | Order of integration |
|---|---|---|---|---|---|
| | Constant | Constant and trend | Constant | Constant and trend | |
| IR | −0.536653 | 8.841934 | −0.077147*** | −0.429776*** | I(1) |
| LGD | −0.047514 | 0.715289 | 0.067136*** | 0.048809** | I(1) |
| LBD | 1.093009 | −1.230514 | 0.453952*** | 0.826004*** | I(1) |
| LMB | 0.336665 | 1.119646 | 0.111029*** | 0.155957*** | I(1) |
| INF | 1.899940 | 2.124994 | 0.144081*** | 0.794811*** | I(1) |
| LT | 0.218716 | 4.052012 | 0.098875*** | 0.161472*** | I(1) |
| LM1 | 0.268771 | 4.094348 | 0.150441*** | 0.186857*** | I(1) |
| LGDP | 4.755439 | 6.600148 | 0.159194*** | 1.195720*** | I(1) |
| LI | 3.324182 | 7.170082 | −0.072566*** | 0.056349*** | I(1) |
| LCON | 5.408854 | 0.739641 | 0.033803*** | −1.488369*** | I(1) |

*Notes: (i) ***, ** and * denote the rejection of null hypothesis at 1, 5 and 10% levels of significance, respectively. (ii) MacKinnon [12] one-sided P-values.*

**Table 2.**
*Augmented dickey-fuller (ADF) test for unit root.*

| Variables | Level | | First difference | | Order of integration |
|---|---|---|---|---|---|
| | Constant | Constant and trend | Constant | Constant and trend | |
| IR | 4.377255 | 9.596283 | −0.077147*** | −0.645455*** | I(1) |
| LGD | −0.043946 | 0.718857 | 0.070704*** | 0.052377** | I(1) |
| LBD | 1.216466 | −1.107057 | 0.577409*** | 0.949461*** | I(1) |
| LMB | 1.335435 | 2.118416 | 1.109799*** | 1.154727*** | I(1) |
| INF | 0.812287 | 1.037341 | −0.943572*** | −0.292842*** | I(1) |
| LT | 1.987622 | 5.820918 | 1.867781*** | 1.930378*** | I(1) |
| LM1 | 1.181116 | 5.006693 | 1.062786*** | 1.099202*** | I(1) |
| LGDP | 5.283645 | 7.128354 | 0.687400*** | 1.723926*** | I(1) |
| LI | 3.324182 | 7.170082 | −0.072566*** | 0.056349*** | I(1) |
| LCON | −0.113303 | −0.041706 | −0.897091*** | 0.094191*** | I(1) |

*Notes: (i) ***, ** and * denote the rejection of null hypothesis at 1, 5 and 10% levels of significance, respectively.*
*(ii) MacKinnon [12] one-sided P-values.*

**Table 3.**
*Phillips-Perron (PP) test for unit root.*

this study, mainly to seek whether the variables are bound by any relationships in the long-run. The result of JJ test for determining the existence of cointegration vectors will be presented in **Table 4** for two models of this study.

Based on the JJ cointegration tests above, the null hypothesis for all models has no cointegration vectors against the alternative hypothesis which indicated that one or more cointegrating vectors exist. Null hypothesis will be rejected if the analysis shows that there is cointegration among variables.

The results in **Table 4** confirm that cointegration exists for all models with regard to the federal government debt and budget deficits analysis. Model 1 exhibits that there are three cointegrating vectors among the variables in both trace statistics and Max-eigenvalue statistics tests. Meanwhile, Model 2 shows that trace statistics and Max-eigenvalue statistics are cointegrated at two cointegrating vectors among the variables. Models 3 and 4 both show that the test statistics and Max-eigenvalue statistics are cointegrated at two and one cointegrating vectors among the variables, respectively.

The trace test and the maximum eigenvalue test for all models reject the null hypothesis in favour of the alternative hypothesis if the critical value provided by JJ's table is exceeded by the test statistic found from the equation. Therefore, it can be inferred from Johansen-Juselius cointegration test results shown in **Table 4** that there exists at least one cointegrating vector between the variables that are certainly bound by a relationship in the long-run.

As Johansen-Juselius cointegration test results show the existence of long-run relationship of federal government debt and budget deficits; this implies that debt and deficit can be one of the effective instruments to explain the Malaysian economy in the long-term period. For example, each debt and deficit measure says something about public finances. Also, debt and deficit are subject to a binding fiscal rule or target. Debt and deficit encourage operations involving off-balance-sheet assets and liabilities. Overall, the Malaysian government should publish several measures of the debt and deficit in a form that clearly reveals their interrelationships.

| **Hypothesised no. of cointegrating equations (Ces).** | **Trace** | | **Maximum eigenvalue** | |
|---|---|---|---|---|
| | **Test statistic** | **Critical value (5%)** | **Max-eigen statistic** | **Critical value (5%)** |
| Model 1 | | | | |
| None | 143.2828* | 95.75366 | 51.52031* | 40.07757 |
| At most 1 | 91.76248* | 69.81889 | 34.9527* | 33.87687 |
| At most 2 | 56.80978* | 47.85613 | 27.83498* | 27.58434 |
| At most 3 | 28.9748 | 29.79707 | 14.2646 | 21.13162 |
| Model 2 | | | | |
| None | 100.1482* | 69.81889 | 38.71173* | 33.87687 |
| At most 1 | 61.43642* | 47.85613 | 33.53451* | 27.58434 |
| At most 2 | 27.90191 | 29.79707 | 17.96272 | 21.13162 |
| At most 3 | 9.939193 | 15.49471 | 9.83002 | 14.2646 |
| Model 3 | | | | |
| None | 84.82411* | 47.45613 | 49.37355* | 27.58434 |
| At most 1 | 35.44886* | 29.79707 | 21.90268* | 21.13162 |
| At most 2 | 13.54618 | 15.49471 | 10.60204 | 14.2646 |
| At most 3 | 2.944137 | 3.841466 | 2.944137 | 3.841466 |
| Model 4 | | | | |
| None | 39.89908* | 47.45613 | 20.89962* | 27.58434 |
| At most 1 | 18.99946 | 29.79707 | 11.48449 | 21.13162 |
| At most 2 | 7.514968 | 15.49471 | 7.069493 | 14.2646 |
| At most 3 | 0.445475 | 3.841466 | 3.841466 | 3.841466 |

**The rejection of null hypothesis of the presence of no cointegrating equations ($r = 0$) between the variables at 5% significance level in favour of the alternative hypothesis that there exists at least one cointegrating equation between the variables.*
*Notes: MacKinnon et al. [35] P-values.*

**Table 4.**
*Johansen-Juselius (JJ) cointegration test results.*

The test results made from Johansen-Juselius test clearly showed interest rate and money demand do have a long-run relationship in regard to debt and deficits. A study by Correia-Nunes and Stemitsiotis [36], over the long period, high real interest rates induced by large budget deficits have a negative impact on potential growth, shifting the economy to a low-level growth path and may therefore reduce future living standards. Meanwhile, Deravi et al. [27] proved that there is relationship between the wealth effect of government debt on money demand. In their study, they found that, over the long period, government debt is affecting the demand for money positively, implying that federal government debt is net wealth. Thus, the existence of cointegration relationships among the economic variables can be a good indication to the policymakers in their decision-making for the benefit of their countries.

## 5. Vector error correction model

The above Johansen-Juselius test informed that all four models have at least one cointegrating vectors which suggests the existence of error correction term (ECT) in these models under the VECM analysis (**Table 5**). The absolute value of ECT indicates the speed of adjustment from the short-run to the long-run equilibrium. The sign of ECT is expected to be negative.

In Model 1, ECT shows a negative and significant sign indicating that the interest rate adjusts to bring about the long-run equilibrium by closing 71% of the gap. In this analysis, it shows that government debt, budget deficit, money supply,

| **Model 1: [IR\|LGD, LBD, LMB, INF, LT]** | | | | | | |
|---|---|---|---|---|---|---|
| Variables | ΔIR | ΔLGD | ΔLBD | ΔLMB | ΔINF | ΔLT |
| Constant | 7.93* | 0.06* | −3.54 | 0.17 | 0.67 | 0.15 |
| | (2.02) | (1.00) | (−0.94) | (1.91) | (0.45) | (1.72) |
| ECT-1 | −0.71* | −0.04* | −1.14* | −1.09 | −1.62 | −0.59 |
| | (−0.51) | (−1.01) | (−0.76) | (−0.01) | (−0.16) | (−0.01) |
| *R*-squared | 0.95 | 0.96 | 0.91 | 0.82 | 0.73 | 0.69 |
| SE of regression | 3.92 | 0.07 | 3.75 | 0.09 | 1.47 | 0.09 |
| **Model 2: [LM1\|LGDP, IR, LGD, INF]** | | | | | | |
| Variables | ΔLM1 | ΔLGDP | ΔIR | ΔLGD | ΔINF | |
| Constant | 0.08* | 3.11* | 0.23 | 0.1* | 2.47 | |
| | (0.72) | (0.63) | (0.07) | (1.56) | (1.81) | |
| ECT-1 | −0.09* | −2.96 | −1.64 | −1.74* | −1.15 | |
| | (−0.13) | (−0.79) | (−1.15) | (−0.43) | (−2.67) | |
| *R*-squared | 0.74 | 0.88 | 0.70 | 0.91 | 0.65 | |
| SE of regression | 0.11 | 4.90 | 3.43 | 0.06 | 1.36 | |
| **Model 3: [LI\|LBD, IR, LGDP]** | | | | | | |
| Variables | ΔLI | ΔLBD | ΔIR | ΔLGDP | | |
| Constant | 0.04* | 0.19 | −0.08 | −1.11* | | |
| | (0.04) | (0.22) | (−0.12) | (−0.13) | | |
| ECT-1 | −0.67* | −0.53 | −1.99 | −1.08 | | |
| | (0.35) | (1.16) | (0.97) | (0.48) | | |
| *R*-squared | 0.88 | 0.84 | 0.9 | 0.76 | | |
| SE of regression | 0.81 | 0.87 | 0.67 | 0.79 | | |
| **Model 4: [INF\|LBD, LM1, LCON]** | | | | | | |
| Variables | ΔINF | ΔLBD | ΔLM1 | ΔLCON | | |
| Constant | 0.95* | 3.88* | 0.10 | −1.44* | | |
| | (0.92) | (1.5) | (1.46) | (−1.27) | | |
| ECT-1 | −0.14* | −0.05 | −0.63* | −5.59 | | |
| | (−2.07) | (2.53) | (−0.71) | (−1.28) | | |
| *R*-squared | 0.69 | 0.77 | 0.61 | 0.8 | | |
| SE of regression | 1.04 | 2.59 | 0.07 | 1.13 | | |

**The significance levels 5%.*
*Notes: (i) IR, LM1, I and INF are held dependent variables. (ii) t values are in parentheses. (iii) ECT = error correction term.*

**Table 5.**
*Summary results of vector error correction model.*

inflation, and tax revenue do have significant impact on interest rate whether in the short-run or long-run. Model 2 results illustrate the coefficient of ECT is negative and significant, indicating that the money demand adjusts to bring about the long-run equilibrium by closing 9% of the gap.

Based on the results of Model 3, the coefficient ECT shows that the investment will adjust to bring about the long-run equilibrium by closing 67% of the gap. The last model, which is Model 4, the negative and significant ECT tells the inflation will adjust to clear the disequilibrium to the long-run disequilibrium through 14% speed adjustment.

## 6. Discussion

The results of VECM suggest that there exists a short-run disequilibrium in all models and the error correction coefficient indicates the deviation of the adjusted percentage from equilibrium in the short-run. Therefore, VECM test testifies that there is a short-run and long-run relationship in all four models.

In view of the findings that the debt deficit exerts adverse impact on interest rate, it is imperative for the government to take account of policy responses that reduce deficit on its budget. The analysis depicts the budget deficit influencing the investment level in Malaysia. Government deficits crowd out private investments. In general fund for investment capital is scarce. Any government bonds issued to pay for a deficit are purchased with investment funds that might have otherwise gone towards private investment. If the government decides to raise taxes to finance a deficit, those additional taxes will further discourage private investment. Should the government decide to monetize the debt, the cost-of-living increases will also eat at savings and investment. According to Kato [37], a cut in future deficits must be followed by a decrease in public investment. Also Fatima et al. [38] stressed that there is the impact of government fiscal deficit on investment.

In addition, the VECM analysis exhibits that budget deficit has short-run and long-run relationship towards inflation in Malaysia. Solomon and De Wet [39] stated that due to the monetization of the budget deficit, significant inflationary effects are found for increases in the budget deficit. The budget deficit recorded for the remaining years was as a result of many factors that made the proposed expenditure to exceed the expected revenue. Inflation is one of the variables affected by budget deficit operation over the years in Malaysia. The government has continuously pursued an expansionary fiscal policy to improve economic growth and economic development. However, the major impact of the increase in budget deficit was felt in 1997, with high rate of inflation, which shows an evidence of a positive relationship between budget deficit and inflation in Malaysia, although other macroeconomic factors could have accounted for this. This scenario happened during the Asian financial crisis in the Malaysian market. Hondroyiannis and Papapetrou [40] show that in developing countries, there is evidence that there exists a positive relationship between budget deficit and inflation.

## 7. Conclusion

The VECM showed that the macroeconomic variables have an impact on dependent variables which are interest rate, money demand, investment and inflation, whether in the short-run and long-run as well. Based on VECM results, inflation plays a dominant role in determining the interest rate; GDP gives major impact on money demand; budget deficits effect the most on both investment and inflation level in Malaysia. This results in the economic impact of government debt and deficits on selected variables which leads one to accept the traditional view.

*DOI: http://dx.doi.org/10.5772/intechopen.91457*

Although different researchers have used different statistical techniques, economic variables and time periods, no conclusive results have appeared to prove or disprove either the Ricardian theorem or the crowding out hypothesis. The tests in this study have demonstrated an evidence on crowding out. Although the money demand model was not as convincing in its rejection of the Ricardian theorem as was the interest rate model acceptance of crowding out, at least it threw some doubt on the validity of the assumption that people do not treat government bonds as net wealth.

Another notable issue is the impact of budget deficits on balance of payments. The past 15 years have witnessed an increasing concern over Malaysia's trade position as the country fell into a net debtor nation in which imports level approached the exports. If a debt creation leads to an increase domestic interest rate, then this results in a net inflow of foreign capital, and this will increase demand for the Malaysian ringgit (RM) and thus an appreciation of the RM, and this certainly will reduce exports and will put a stress on GDP growth. When the ringgit is appreciated, Malaysia's goods for export become more expensive to consumers in other countries, and at the same time, the goods for import from other countries will become less expensive for domestic consumers. This situation would compound an already bad balance of trade position for Malaysia if indeed the debt creation has this effect. Thus, an empirical investigation into this apparent dilemma is critical to the understanding of Malaysia's current and future trade positions.

## Author details

Mohamed Aslam* and Raihan Jaafar
Faculty of Economics and Administration, University of Malaya, Kuala Lumpur, Malaysia

*Address all correspondence to: maslam@um.edu.my

## References

[1] Clements B, Bhattacharya R, Nguyen T. External debt, public investment, and growth in low income countries. IMF working paper No. WP/03/249. Washington, DC; 2003

[2] Foon HW. Will Malaysia's rating change? The Star Online. 2016 (Retrieved Oct 16, 2016, Kuala Lumpur, Malaysia)

[3] Ministry of Finance, Economic Reports 1975. Kuala Lumpur: Government Printer

[4] Ministry of Finance, Economic Reports 1985. Kuala Lumpur: Government Printer

[5] Ministry of Finance, Economic Reports 1990. Kuala Lumpur: Government Printer

[6] Ministry of Finance, Economic Reports 1995. Kuala Lumpur: Government Printer

[7] Ministry of Finance, Economic Reports 2000. Kuala Lumpur, Government Printer

[8] Ministry of Finance, Economic Reports 2005. Kuala Lumpur: Government Printer

[9] Ministry of Finance, Economic Reports 2010. Kuala Lumpur: Government Printer

[10] Ministry of Finance, Economic Reports 2015. Kuala Lumpur: Government Printer

[11] Ministry of Finance, Economic Reports 2018. Kuala Lumpur: Government Printer

[12] MacKinnon J. Numerical distribution functions for unit root and cointegration tests. Journal of Applied Econometrics. 1996;**11**(6):601-618

[13] Carlson KM. Federal fiscal policy since the employment act of 1946. Economic Review, (Federal Reserve Bank of St. louis). 1987:14-29

[14] de Leeuw F, Holloway TM. Cyclical adjustment of the federal budget and federal debt. Survey of Current Business. 1983;**63**(December):25-40

[15] Eisner R, Pieper PJ. A new view of the federal debt and budget deficits. American Economic Review. 1984;**74**: 11-29

[16] Kormendi RC. Government debt, government spending, and private sector behavior. The American Economic Review. 1983;**73**(5):994-1010

[17] Blinder AS, Solow RM. Does fiscal policy matter? Journal of Public Economics. 1973;**2**(4):319-337

[18] Abderrezak A. The impact of government budget deficits on interest rates, [PhD dissertation]. Kansas, USA: Kansas State University; 1987

[19] Penner RG. The Great Fiscal Experiment of the 1980s. Washington, DC: The Urban Institute Press; 1991

[20] Blanchard OJ. Current and anticipated deficits, interest rates, and economic activity. European Economic Review. 1984;**25**(1):7-27

[21] Makin JH, Tanzi V. Level and volatility of U.S. interest rates: Roles of expected inflation, real interest rates, and taxes. NBER Workiing Paper No. 1167, Washington, DC; 1983

[22] Hoelscher G. New evidence on deficits and interest rates. Journal of Money, Credit and Banking. 1986;**18**(1): 1-17

[23] Barth JR, Iden G, Russek FS. Federal borrowing and short-term interest rates:

Comment. Southern Economic Journal. 1985;**52**(2):554-559

[24] Barth JR, Morrell SO. 'A Primer on Budget Deficits', Federal Reserve Bank of Atlanta. Economic Review. 1982:6-17

[25] Burbidge J, Harrison AJ. An historical decomposition of the great depression to determine the role of money. Journal of Monetary Economics. 1985;**16**(1):45-54

[26] Wood R. Delivering economic stimulus, addressing rising public debt and avoiding inflation. Journal of Financial Economic Policy. 2012; **4**(1):4-24

[27] Deravi MK, Hegji CE, Moberly HD. Government debt and the demand for money: An extreme bound analysis. Economic Inquiry. 1990;**28**(2):390-401

[28] Giannaros DS, Kolluri BR. Deficit spending, money, and inflation: Some international empirical evidence. Journal of Macroeconomics. 1985;7(3): 401-417

[29] Friedman M, Schwartz A. A Monetary History of the United States, 1867–1960, Princeton University Press, New Jersey; 1963

[30] Abizadeh S, Yousefi M. Deficits and inflation: An open economy model of the United States. Applied Economics. 1998;**30**(10):1307-1316

[31] Greenspan A. Opening remarks. In: Budget Deficits and Debt: Issues and Options. A Symposium by the Federal Reserve Bank of Kansas City, August 31–September 2, Federal Reserve Bank of Kansas City, Kansas City, Missouri, USA. 1995

[32] Krugman P. Why higher savings may hit the dollar. Financial Times. 1995 (24 May, London, UK)

[33] Hakkio CS. The effects of budget deficit reduction on the exchange rate. Economic Review, (Third Quarter, Federal Reserve Bank of Kansas City). 1996:21-38

[34] Johansen S, Juselius K. Maximum likelihood estimation and inference on cointegration—With applications to the demand for money. Oxford Bulletin of Economics and Statistics. 1990;**52**(2): 169-210

[35] MacKinnon J, Haug A, Michelis L. Numerical distribution functions of likelihood ratio tests for cointegration. Journal of Applied Econometrics. 1999; **14**(5):563-577

[36] Correia-Nunes J, Stemitsiotis L. Budget deficit and interest rates: Is there a link? International evidence. Oxford Bulletin of Economics and Statistics. 1995;**57**(4):425-449

[37] Kato RR. Government deficit, public investment, and public capital in the transition to an aging Japan. Journal of the Japanese and International Economies. 2002;**16**(4):462-491

[38] Fatima G, Ahmed AM, Rehman WU. Fiscal deficit and economic growth: An analysis of Pakistan's economy. International Journal of Trade, Economics and Finance. 2011;**2**(6)

[39] Solomon M, De Wet DA. The effect of a budget deficit on inflation: the case of Tanzania. South African Journal of Economic and Management Sciences. 2004;7(1):100-116

[40] Hondroyiannis G, Papapetrou E. Are budget deficit inflationary? Applied Economics Letters. 1997;**4**(8):493-496

Chapter 7

# The Direction of Reforming the Tax System on the Basis of the Scientific Systemonomic Author's Model: Nalogonomy

*Irina A. Zhuravleva*

## Abstract

The article discusses the practical significance of the application of the Periodic System of Special Laws of Nalogonomy (PSSLN) on the basis of one of the laws, the law on "Manageability of Energy Information of Nalogonomy." The study was based on theoretical aspects and practical conclusions of the relationship and interdependence of indicators of the dynamics of gross domestic product, tax revenues to the budget system of the country, and the tax burden on the basis of the correlation-regression method. The philosophical principles of nalogonomy, which determine the hierarchy of the laws in the model of the evolutionary development of the tax system proposed by the author, are considered. The author focuses on the need to reorient the functioning of the tax system from the fiscal to stimulate economic development, to address social issues in society.The existing disproportion in the tax system manifests itself in its various forms and types as inconsistencies in its composition, content and dynamics, and elements, which causes uneven tax burdens on its various participants. At this stage of development of the state, the tax system needs a reorientation of interests, and then the result can surpass and drive the forecasts and expectations, both economic and social.

**Keywords:** taxes, tax system, nalogonomy, laws, systemonomy, tax system development, tax system evolution

## 1. Introduction

The tax system of any country is an important tool for adjusting the state of its socioeconomic sphere, investment activity, development of industries, and structural improvements in the economy due to the ability to influence the proportions of the distribution of national income. The effectiveness of the tax system depends on the construction of a functional-effective model of its development, both in economic (stimulating business development) value and in fiscal (withdrawing a portion of income to the budget system of the country). In this regard, it seems appropriate to study the imbalances of the existing tax system in order to identify problems of building a tax system.

The process of reforming the tax system of the country to a higher level of functioning has a constant tendency to improve, which has an important financial and economic importance and a relevant social component.

| Indicator | Year | | | | | |
|---|---|---|---|---|---|---|
| | 2012 | 2013 | 2014 | 2015 | 2016 | 2017 |
| The ease of paying taxes in the Russian Federation (rank/number of countries in the ranking) | 102/183 | 64/185 | 56/189 | 49/189 | 47/189 | 49/190 |
| Number of tax payments | 9 | 7 | 7 | 7 | 7 | 7 |
| Time spent on tax liabilities | 290 | 177 | 177 | 168 | 168 | 168 |
| Total tax rate (%) | 46.9 | 54.1 | 50.7 | 48.9 | 47 | 47.4 |

*Source: Compiled from the World Bank and PwC.*

**Table 1.**
*Indicators and positions of Russia.*

The tax system of the state is one of the control vectors in the structure of the country's economic system. The tax system is an integral part of the national economy, the effective functioning of which has a significant impact on its sustainability, especially in a recession, when the possibilities for using alternative taxes by the state to accumulate financial resources are limited. The current dilemma is sustainable development of the tax system, provided by the influence of the tax system on the development of the economy or through institutional economics in its potential. The considered scientific dilemma about the potential for the tax system to become more attractive to taxpayers and as progressive as possible at budget levels for the state is relevant.

At the present stage of development of the tax system, traditionally take into account the value of three indicators of its effective functioning:

- The number of tax payments
- The time spent by companies on the fulfillment of tax obligations
- Total tax rate.

**Table 1** shows selected indicators and positions of Russia in the ranking of Paying Taxes and Corruption Perception Index in 2012–2017.

Analyzing the indicators of **Table 1**, the tax system of the country can be characterized as a system that is in a consistent development, with a positive direction. But these data do not reflect the influence on the development of the economy. Studies of the potential and real impact of the tax system through tax regulation measures on the dynamics of economic growth are relevant today for the polemical discussion of modern economics.

## 2. Model of improvement of the tax system

### 2.1 Study of the periodic system of special Laws of Nalogonomy

This chapter invites the scientific community to consider the development of the tax system and its elements on the basis of a systematic approach, namely, the "Periodic System of Special Laws of Nalogonomy" (hereinafter referred to as PSSLN), compiled and opened by the author in 2017 [1].

It should be noted that in essence in the problem under consideration, the author applies. *The Systemonomic approach and the method*, since the tax system is the brainchild of systemonomy. "Systemonomy is a scientific tool for motivating the cosmic, spiritualized world outlook of humanity. The systemonomy is the next evolutionary step of comprehending the world system" [2].

The dilemma is relevant: the influence of the tax system on the development of the economy or institutional economy in its potential ensures the sustainable development of the tax system. By its general structure, construction principles, and the list, the Russian tax system basically corresponds to taxation systems operating in countries with market economies.

By M.V. Romanovsky and O.V. Vrubleva, the tax system is defined as "the totality of taxes, principles, forms and methods for their establishment, change and cancellation, payment and application of measures to pay them, tax control, as well as prosecution and liability for violation tax legislation"; V.G. Panskov adheres to a similar point of view, and he attaches great importance to the study of fundamental theoretical and practical problems of taxation, including the composition of payments included in the tax system and the status of customs duties [3].

L.I. Goncharenko gives the following definition of the concept of "tax system": it is a system of economic and legal relations implemented in the aggregate of taxes paid and levied in the state; rights and obligations (competencies) of state bodies of power and administration in the field of taxes; actions of a set of authorized (specialized) bodies in the tax sphere [4]. The scientific dilemma under consideration about the potential for the tax system to become more attractive for taxpayers and as progressive as possible at the budget levels for the state is relevant. Changes in tax legislation are aimed at increasing the efficiency of legal regulation of tax relations, are focused on "preventing any increase in the tax burden on the economy," and are also called on "to ensure the stability of the tax system and increase its attractiveness for investors," as indicated in the document "Basic directions of the tax policy of the Russian Federation for 2016 and for the planning period of 2017 and 2018." In a similar document, but already for the period 2020 and for the planning period 2021 and 2022, the goal was set to "create comfortable conditions for the voluntary and timely payment of taxes and other payments."

The indicators characterizing the efficiency of the tax authorities within the country include the following: level of tax collection in the territory; reduction in tax debt to the budget; the share of taxpayers with the ability to access via communication channels and the Internet; and a number of others. But the fact of influence on economic development does not reflect these data. Studies of the potential and real impact of the tax system through tax regulation on the dynamics of economic growth are relevant today for a polemic discussion of modern economic science. However, questions of a philosophical nature are not considered by the scientific community, and current issues of finding an effective model of the tax system in the country are not considered enough; they have a narrow focus on the elements of the system or its subsystem: towards either improving the quality of administration or increasing the tax burden by raising tax rates and the introduction of new payments in the second part of the tax code of the country, the change in budget redistribution of tax amounts (interest rates). For this period, there is no systematic, holistic approach to reforming the tax system.

We subject the taxation system to a comparative analysis with previously developed various systems. One of them is the General Theory of Systems (GTS) of academician Yu. A. Urmantsev (GTSU) [5]. This system is the most developed in the framework of GTSU and allows you to analyze the tax system in terms of system integrity. Systemological analysis involves the analysis of the presence of all components of the system, namely:

1. Goals

2. Elements

3. Unity of connections between elements

4. Composition

When studying taxes and the tax system, the systematic approach itself does not receive enough attention in the specialized literature [3].

Formed and entered into force on January 1, 1992, the Russian tax system was built on principles unconnected into a single whole, the most important of which were the following:

- Equal rights of all taxpayers, including the provision of tax benefits and protection of economic interests.

- Differentiation of rights to introduce and levy taxes between different levels of the government.

- Single taxation.

- Granting broad powers to executive authorities in interpreting the norms of tax laws and in establishing a number of tax elements, including tax rates and others [6].

To date, a substantial basis has been created to complete the formation of the country's tax system. Having gone a long way of reforming, the tax system has become more structured, a double interpretation of the concept of "tax law norm" has been eliminated, the latest information technologies are used in tax control measures, etc. Today we can talk about the stage of completion of the tax reform [6].

The tax system has its purpose and its elements. The purpose of the tax system is to mobilize tax revenues and other obligatory payments into the budget system. Elements of the tax system are shown in **Figure 1**.

However, we see that the two necessary components of the scientific concept of "system" according to GTSU are not formed. Namely:

- The composition of the rules of tax law does not have a clear systemic nature, which is expressed in the many explanations of the Ministry of Finance of the Russian Federation or the Federal Tax Service of the Russian Federation and the recommendations, changes, or amendments to the tax code of the Russian Federation, etc.

- The unity of the bonds of the elements is not determined by the ratios of their energy content through a single operator Ce (constant evolutionary step, Ce = 0.417897328) [7]. Ce shows the optimum amount of energy needed to form a new law. The modern tax system does not use this universal meter, which is confirmed by the lack of socioeconomic justification for the adoption of a law and amendments to the norms of tax law, and not all laws in the legal tax field carry a creative-creating motive.

So, the development of the tax system does not meet all the basic provisions of GTSU. This sets us the task of detecting the missing components for building the sphere of taxation as a system.

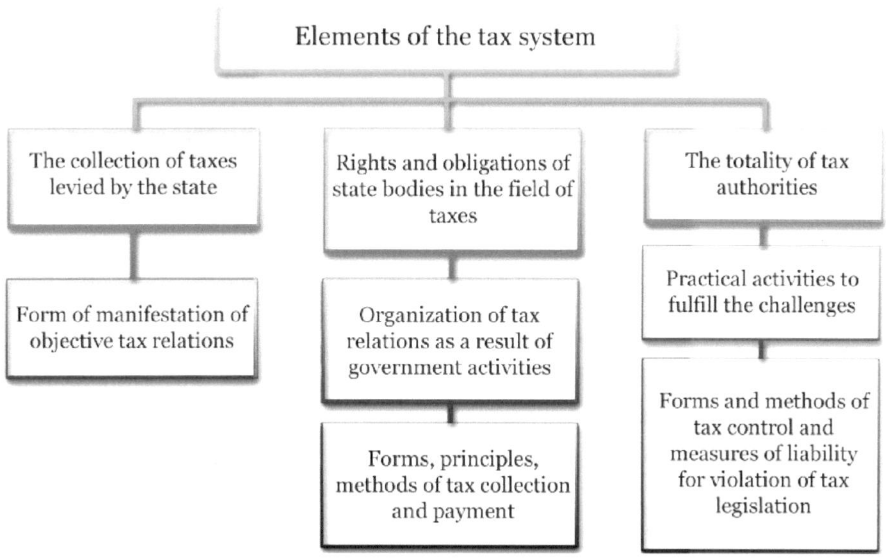


**Figure 1.**
*Elements of the tax system.*

At this stage of reforming the tax system, there is a tendency that the system is improving itself more in terms of tax administration, but not in terms of changing types of taxes, reforming tax bases, other elements of taxes, and the system as a whole. There is no systematic approach to achieving the tax system of its higher socioeconomic potential. The highest potential of the system is the integrated sum of all the capabilities of the system aimed at maximizing its self-disclosure and self-realization in achieving its mission [2]. The tax system, having both a fiscal function and a regulatory, distribution function, can and should perform a stimulating function at the present stage of economic development; perhaps this will be the system's entry into a new round of its evolutionary development.

The proposed author's model of nalogonomy was discovered relatively recently, in 2014. And at this stage, the author conducts a systemonomic analysis and develops a scientific evidence base for economic efficiency of the proposed model for improving the tax system.

Next, we look at the abstract evolution of the tax system in a positive way. Based on the analysis of **Table 2** "Table No. XVII" "Periodic System of Special Laws of Nalognomy" [8], compiled on the basis of "Periodic System of General Laws of the World," opened by academician N.V. Maslova in 2005, which, being a single interconnected system, are manifested in all phenomena, systems of the World: economic, social, scientific, financial, educational and others, are projected onto society, people and processes of cognition, shows the evolutionary path of development of the tax system according to the levels of being and a group of laws.

There are two system analyses to consider the identified problem.

The first is a systemological approach, which implies an analysis of the presence of all the components of the system, and in particular the tax system, and these are its goals, elements, the unity of relations between elements, and composition.

The second (the author proposes to consider it) is a systemonomic one, including the universal laws of the world, the general laws of cognition and comprehension of the world, the general laws of human society, the goal (the program of the purpose of the functioning of the system), elements of the system, and the unity of relations between elements of the system and composition of the system. The modern tax system is based on the first system analysis [9].

| Evolution principles | Levels of existence | Groups of special laws | | | | | | | |
|---|---|---|---|---|---|---|---|---|---|
| | | A<br>Before the tax period | B<br>Elements | C<br>Energy | D<br>Information | E<br>Self-organization | F<br>Evolution | G<br>System hierarchy | H<br>Highest Potential |
| Unity and infinity | Highest Potential 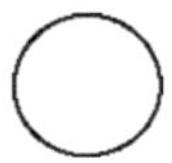 7. | Unity and infinity of the highest potential of precedence nalogonomy | Unity and infinity of the highest potential of the elements of nalogonomy | Unity and infinity of the highest potential of energy of nalogonomy | Unity and infinity of the highest potential of information of nalogonomy | Unity and infinity of the highest potential of self-organization of nalogonomy | Unity and infinity of the highest potential of evolution of nalogonomy | Unity and infinity of the highest potential of hierarchy of nalogonomy | Unity and infinity of the highest potential of nalogonomy |
| Structural and functional consistency | Hierarchy  6. | Structural and functional consistency of hierarchy of precedence of nalogonomy | Structural and functional consistency of hierarchy of elements of nalogonomy | Structural and functional consistency of hierarchy of energy of nalogonomy | Structural and functional consistency of hierarchy of energy of nalogonomy | Structural and functional consistency of hierarchy of self-organization of nalogonomy | Structural and functional consistency of hierarchy of evolution of nalogonomy | Structural and functional consistency of hierarchy of systems of nalogonomy | Structural and functional consistency of hierarchy of the highest potential of nalogonomy |
| Variability | Evolution  5. | Variability of evolution of precedence of nalogonomy | Variability of evolution of elements of nalogonomy | Variability of evolution of energy of nalogonomy | Variability of evolution of information of nalogonomy | Variability of evolution of self-organization of nalogonomy | Variability of evolution of nalogonomy | Variability of evolution of hierarchy of the system of nalogonomy | Variability of evolution of the highest potential of nalogonomy |
| Self-organization | Composition of the system 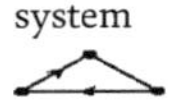 4. | Self-organization of composition of the system of precedence of nalogonomy | Self-organization of composition of the system of elements of nalogonomy | Self-organization of composition of the system of energy of nalogonomy | Self-organization of composition of the system of information of nalogonomy | Self-organization of composition of the system of self-organization of nalogonomy | Self-organization of composition of the system of evolution of nalogonomy | Self-organization of composition of the system of hierarchy of the systems of nalogonomy | Self-organization of composition of the system of the highest potential of nalogonomy |

DOI: http://dx.doi.org/10.5772/intechopen.91431

| Evolution principles | Levels of existence | Groups of special laws | | | | | | | |
|---|---|---|---|---|---|---|---|---|---|
| | | A<br>Before the tax period | B<br>Elements | C<br>Energy | D<br>Information | E<br>Self-organization | F<br>Evolution | G<br>System hierarchy | H<br>Highest Potential |
| Controllability | Information (energy information)<br>3. | Controllability of energy information of precedence of nalogonomy | Controllability of energy information of elements of nalogonomy | Controllability of energy information of energy of nalogonomy | Controllability of energy information of nalogonomy | Controllability of energy information of self-organization of nalogonomy | Controllability of energy information of evolution of nalogonomy | Controllability of energy information of hierarchy of systems of nalogonomy | Controllability of energy information of the highest potential of nalogonomy |
| Sufficiency | Energy<br>2. | Sufficiency of energy of precedence of nalogonomy | Sufficiency of energy of elements of nalogonomy | Sufficiency of energy of nalogonomy | Sufficiency of energy of information of nalogonomy | Sufficiency of energy of self-organization of nalogonomy | Sufficiency of energy of evolution of nalogonomy | Sufficiency of energy of hierarchy of systems of nalogonomy | Sufficiency of energy of the highest potential of nalogonomy |
| Necessity | Elements<br>1. | Necessity of elements of precedence of nalogonomy | Necessity of elements of nalogonomy | Necessity of elements of energy of nalogonomy | Necessity of elements of information of nalogonomy | Necessity of elements of self-organization of nalogonomy | Necessity of elements of evolution of nalogonomy | Necessity of elements of hierarchy of systems of nalogonomy | Necessity of elements of the highest potential of nalogonomy |
| Evolutionary - cyclic initiation | Precedence<br>0. | Evolutionary-cyclic initiation of precedence of nalogonomy | Evolutionary-cyclic initiation of precedence of elements of nalogonomy | Evolutionary-cyclic initiation of precedence of energy of nalogonomy | Evolutionary-cyclic initiation of precedence of information of nalogonomy | Evolutionary-cyclic initiation of precedence of self-organization of nalogonomy | Evolutionary-cyclic initiation of precedence of evolution of nalogonomy | Evolutionary-cyclic initiation of precedence of hierarchy of systems of nalogonomy | Evolutionary-cyclic initiation of precedence of the highest potential of nalogonomy |

**Table 2.**
*Table No. XVII: Periodic system of special Laws of Nalogonomy.*

The motivation of the author's proposal for the use of PSSLN is that, for the above reason, we cannot judge the quality of the evolution of the tax system in nature and society, in the worldview, and in the socioeconomic and financial orientation. This is the reason that does not allow the modern tax system to build harmonious relations between the state and taxpayers, the business community. The goal vector is not aimed at constructive comprehension of the universal laws of the world, human society, and knowledge/comprehension. Therefore, in the most general understanding of this situation, the existing tax system focuses only on fiscal policy, on the fragmentation of knowledge about the world, economic processes, and financial flows; there is no single core, the state axis of rotation, which has a creative-creative vector of direction. Shifting the tax burden on the final consumer (state citizens), increasing the basic VAT rate from 18 to 20%, introducing a tax on the self-employed population, increasing the tax base on property taxes for individuals (cadastral value of land, property), and a number of other economically unjustified fiscal measures lead to a serious imbalance in the country's economy: the profitability of citizens decreases, the purchasing power of the population decreases, the number of unemployed increases, stratification in society occurs, social insecurity is growing, and business confidence in the existing system of both public administration and taxation is falling.

For the aforementioned reason, the author offers a systematic model of the development of the tax system based on the systemonomic approach, which has the ability to determine the structure of the tax system, its orientation quality (social or fiscal), the role of the tax system in the socioeconomic evolution of the state. The considered periodic system of laws of nalogonomy is systemonomic and acts as the scientific basis, the basis and matrix for the implementation of systemonomic analysis. Before the publication of the periodic system of laws of nalogonomy, this innovative analytical approach was impossible, precisely because of the lack of a scientific basis for it.

The rationale for the systemonomy of the "Periodic System of Special Laws of Nalogonomy" is as follows.

The taxation process is a system. Upon closer examination, taxation mechanisms are based on the known or unknown universal laws of the world. In fact, in the process of comprehension, it is precisely the laws of the general that are studied through the knowledge of their particular manifestations. Thus, the construction of the tax system and its further development in the special financial or general sphere (socioeconomic) leads to the need to comprehend the relationship with other systems of laws. For example, the knowledge of economic laws as a system is in contact and cannot do without systems of financial laws, laws of mathematics, and statistics. The laws of taxation are impossible without the laws of knowledge both inside and outside the system itself.

The Periodic System of Special Laws of Nalogonomy is a holistic system, as it covers the entire system of laws and principles of construction and functioning of the tax system. Using separate laws in isolation from others is impractical, since such a one-sided judgment can lead to erroneous conclusions and dire consequences, which we can clearly see on the example of the destruction of the ecological system of our planet as a result of unilateral consumer approaches to solving socio-production and personal problems.

The author has already considered the concept of nalogonomy in a number of scientific works and is now preparing to publish a scientific article on noonomy as the main, fundamental system for the development of the tax system. Nalogonomy is a scientific system that studies the self-organizing structural and functional composition of primary elements of taxation in order to create, develop, and evolve a country's tax system [10].

Consider the concept of tax—this is a mandatory, individually gratuitous payment levied on organizations and individuals in the form of alienation of their money ownership, economic management, or operational management of funds in order to financially support the activities of the state and municipalities. The concept of nomology (Greek *Nomos,* law) is the study of laws. It considers the essence, definition, characteristics, applicability, and ability to work with natural laws. Earlier, we considered systemonomy as a science of building and functioning a system of laws, so it is necessary to consider a large-scale tax, since for calculating any tax, its elements, an administration system and a tax right field, and a number of other elements that create a taxation system are necessary.

The tax system also includes the principles of the establishment, introduction, and termination of local and regional taxes; the grounds and rules for the emergence, change, and termination of the duties of certain persons to pay taxes and fees; the procedure for the performance of these duties; rights and obligations of participants in relations arising in the taxation system (taxpayers, tax authorities, etc.); liability for violation of tax laws; forms, types, and methods of monitoring compliance with tax legislation; and information subsystem of the tax system (notices, tax service website, etc.) [11].

It is necessary to say that the derivative of the tax system, at the beginning of its formation, is a tax policy, and this is a system of measures undertaken by the state in the field of taxes and taxation on the basis of a combination of economic, financial, and legal measures of the state to form the country's tax system in order to ensure state needs [12].

The concept of "system" is "a whole made up of a number of interacting elements, each of which or their simple sum does not possess the whole complex of qualities that a system possesses, i.e. the system is emergent in relation to any of the elements that leave it, and therefore it is richer in the choice of means of evolutionary development" [13]. Nalogonomy in its scientific basis represents the science of the evolution of the tax system from the perspective of a scientific systematic approach.

For easier understanding it is necessary to mention that the levels of existence (stages of taxation system development) are a complex of increasingly complicating levels of existence in the material world (its energy base); in the periodic system of the laws, they are the following:

0 – Precedence.
I – Elements.
II – Energy.
III – Information.
IV – Structure of the system.
V – Evolutionary dynamics of the systems.
VI – Hierarchy.
VII – Highest potential system [13].

Philosophical principles of nalogonomy define and guide the hierarchy of the location of the laws in the periodic system of specific laws of nalogonomy, which were considered by the author in the article "Nalogonomy - the doctrine of the evolution of the tax system" [10].

These principles are as follows:

1. The principle of evolutionary-cyclic initiation.

2. Principle of necessity.

3. The principle is sufficient.

| **Evolutionary principles** | **Levels of being** | **Laws of nalogonomy elements** |
|---|---|---|
| Unity and infinity | 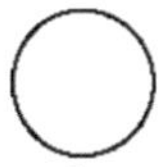 Higher potential 7 | A. The law of the embodiment of the highest potential elements of nalogonomy<br>B. The law of destination components (elements) of nalogonomy<br>C. The Law of Higher Potential for Nalogonomy Components |
| Structural and functional system |  Hierarchy 6 | A. The Law of the Hierarchy of Higher Potentials of the Components (Elements) of Nalogonomy<br>B. The Law of the Hierarchy of Destinations Higher Potentials of the Components (Elements) of Nalogonomy<br>C. The law of the hierarchy of components (elements) of nalogonomy |
| Variability |  Evolution 5 | A. The law of evolutionary-cosmic systemic complication of the components (elements) of nalogonomy<br>B. The law of the necessity of the emergent qualities of the components (elements) of nalogonomy<br>C. The law of dynamic variability of the components (elements) of nalogonomy<br>D. The law of conservation of evolutionarily mature structural-functional components (elements) of nalogonomy |
| Self-organization |  System composition 4 | A. The law of self-organization of the components (elements) of nalogonomy<br>B. The law of genetic potential of the components (elements) of nalogonomy<br>C. The law of individual choice of components (elements) of nalogonomy<br>D. The law of self-organization of the components (elements) of nalogonomy in the social system of society<br>E. The law of conformity of the components (elements) of nalogonomy to the evolutionary level of organization of the functioning of the tax system |
| Manageability Sufficiency |  Information (energy information) 3 | A. The law of energy information management components (elements) of nalogonomy<br>B. The law of genetic asymmetry of the components (elements) of nalogonomy<br>C. The law of choosing the direction of development of energy information of nalogonomy<br>D. The law of increasing nalogonomy potential<br>E. The law of wave resonances in nalogonomy |
| |  Energy 2 | A. The law of sufficiency of interaction of elements of nalogonomy<br>B. The law of interaction between the creative and stimulating energy of the components (elements) of nalogonomy (the taxpayer and the state) |
| Necessities |  Elements 1 | A. The law of the necessity of the elements of nalogonomy (the object of taxation, the base, the rates, the terms of payment, etc.) |
| Evolutionary-cyclic initiation |  Precedence 0 | A. The law of evolutionary-cyclic initiation of nalogonomy elements |

**Table 3.**
*Table D: Energy information laws of nalogonomy.*

4. Principle of control.

5. Principle of self-organization.

6. The principle of evolutionary variability.

7. The principle of structural and functional hierarchy.

In the article "The direction of improving the tax system in the structure of the economy on the basis of the Periodic System of Special Laws of Nalogonomy" [9], the author considered in detail the laws of the elements of nalogonomy and explicated these laws using a systematic approach that was applied relatively recently in the field of taxation. The legal regulation of the tax accounting system in the framework of the first and second parts of the tax code of the country is evidence of this scientific postulate.

From a scientific point of view, a methodical system can be understood as a set of techniques and methods aimed at disclosing the integrity of difficultly oriented objects and identifying the relationship between its components. The tax system and its legal field is the interconnection and interdependence of elements, components, provisions both within the system itself and in its external interaction with the authorities in the country and various ministries and departments.

It should be noted that in the proposed model for the development of the tax system, the basis of which is the PSSLN, it is advisable to consider groups of special laws located along the PSSLN diagonal. Further, the author suggests to theoretically consider how the group and the components of special laws of information of nalogonomy function.

Further, in **Table 4** "Information components of nalogonomy," the author reveals groups of laws, detailing the content of each, and establishes the rule of order for each law. Of the seven groups of laws, four will be considered. The scope of this scientific study does not allow to consider all 64 laws of the main and 154 groups of laws discovered by the author.

**Table 4** shows the explication of laws on the example of the detailed elaboration of four laws out of seven (see **Table 3**), giving an idea of the formation and development of the tax system in its proposed model as a doctrine of the evolution of the tax system. The following section will discuss the law "Manageability of Energy Information of Nalogonomy"—a cell in the PSSLN 3D consisting of the following laws:

a. The law of information management of nalogonomy

b. The law of energy informational bioresonances in the processes of nalogonomy

c. The law of synchronization of energy information in nalogonomy

d. The law of socioeconomic and financial determination of the choice of energy information of nalogonomy

From a scientific point of view, the fact that these laws act on the evolutionary path of development of the tax system is interesting. If we consider this law and a group of laws enlarged, then the laws reflect the influence of economic processes in society on the development of the tax system and its elements. Influence of information flows: intra-system (laws in the field of taxation, departmental letters,

| Code | General law and its content | | Order rule |
|---|---|---|---|
| D0 | Title | The law of the necessity of preceding the elements of energy information of nalogonomy | The rule of the structural-functional phase-cyclic transition of energy information of nalogonomy |
| | Content | The energy information of nalogonomy is preceded by the eight-phase evolution of each of its components:<br>• Targets and programs<br>• Elements<br>• Relations of their unity (wave, rhythmodynamic bioresonance processes of receiving, processing, archiving, transmitting, and information)<br>• Law composition<br>• The need to synchronize information of nalogonomy | |
| D1a | Title | The law of the necessary elements of information of nalogonomy | The rule of the structural composition of energy information of nalogonomy |
| | Content | The necessary elements of energy information of nalogonomy are:<br>• Their target programs of nalogonomy<br>• Subjects and objects of nalogonomy<br>• The relation of their unity, understanding, expressed by the synchronization of wave energy information resonances<br>• Law of the composition of nalogonomy, obeying which relations of unity of the law of synchronization of energy information are achieved | |
| D2a | Title | The law of sufficiency of genetic energy information of nalogonomy | The bioadminable energy rule of nalogonomy |
| | Content | Genetic energy information is sufficient to obtain adequate to nature, society, and the world of energy of nalogonomy | |
| D2b | Title | The law of sufficiency of asymmetric equilibrium energy information of nalogonomy | The rule of superiority of creative energy information overstimulating in nalogonomy |
| | Content | For the emergence and development of nalogonomy, enough interaction of socioeconomic and financial creative and stimulating asymmetrically balanced energy information | |
| D3a | Title | Information management law of nalogonomy | Management entity rule of nalogonomy |
| | Content | The development of nalogonomy is controlled by energy information: its presence or absence, sufficiency or deficiency, and quality and quantity | |
| D3b | Title | The law of energy information bioresonances in the processes of nalogonomy | The rule of energy information mechanisms of nalogonomy |
| | Content | Nalogonomy is carried out by means of energy information bioresonance processes of reception-processing-archiving-transmission of information signals (regardless of the forms: oral, written, | |

| Code | General law and its content | | Order rule |
|---|---|---|---|
| | | virtual, mediated by technical, artistic, religious means) | |
| D3c | title | The law of synchronization of energy information in nalogonomy | The rule of indication of bio-adequacy of communication in the process in nalogonomy |
| | Content | Nalogonomy arises and dynamically develops due to the process of wave synchronization of open biosocial systems, which is a method for indicating the bio-adequacy of the energy informational connection of all elements into the unified system of nalogonomy | |
| D3d | Title | The law of socioeconomic and financial determination of the choice of energy information of nalogonomy | The rule of structural-functional self-organization of nalogonomy |
| | Content | Nalogonomy selects, accepts, and transmits energy information, socioeconomic and financially deterministic and synchronized with the laws of the world | |
| D4a | Title | The law of self-organization of energy information of nalogonomy | Principle of information self-rule of nalogonomy |
| | Content | Nalogonomy arises and dynamically develops through self-organization of information and energy self-government: its languages, forms, dynamics, and goals | |
| D4b | Title | Biofeedback law (BFL) in nalogonomy | Self-indication rule in nalogonomy |
| | Content | Indication and control of the processes of nalogonomy by any of its participants is carried out by means of BFL—creating an individual image of nalogonomy, consistent with the goals, objectives, directions, dynamics, languages, and forms of the original and ideal information | |

**Table 4.**
*Information components of nalogonomy.*

instructions, orders, etc.) and external system (economic, geopolitical, social, etc.). Synchronization and synergy effect from the interaction and influence of tax law norms established in the state with economic processes. It reveals the dependence, direct and indirect, between the growth of GDP and the positive (negative) dynamics of tax revenues in the country's budget system. Some of these questions will be covered in the next section.

### 2.2 Practical application and scientific significance of the law "controllability of energy information of nalgonomy" of PSSLN

The tax system is of paramount importance in connection with the need to achieve a balanced development of the regions of the Russian Federation, addressing issues of social justice, leveling existing disparities, preserving the integrity and competitiveness of the state and its economic security, and solving tactical and strategic tasks. The tax system is the basis for the regulation of macroeconomic processes and the implementation of the financial and economic policy of the state. According to many researchers, taxes can change the investment activity of a business, solve social problems of the society, implement structural changes in the economy, and maintain the necessary pace of its development. Taxes from the means of raising state revenues were transformed into a regulator of the reproduction process, mediating the pace, conditions, and proportions of the economy. Many socioeconomic problems of the society are mediated by the state of the tax system.

The role of the tax system in the distribution of public goods and resources that activate certain forms of socioeconomic dynamics should be noted. These processes are important from the point of view of the basis of the formation of investment potential in the business environment and the formation of demand from individuals, which contributes to economic growth and quality of life.

Noting the essence of the tax system as a state institution, many scientists point to the need to harmonize the priorities of its development with the strategic guidelines of the state and society, which requires the improvement of its individual elements and the system as a whole.

Numerous studies of the economic situation in the country indicate that the current tax system of Russia is a factor hindering the activation of the potential of regional economies. Since 2019 the rate of value added tax was increased from 18 to 20%, which affects the inflationary process. In addition, excise taxes on excisable goods, in particular on alcohol and cigarettes, were increased by 10%. The most sensitive was the increase in fuel rates, since the movement of goods is provided by transportation, and thus, the higher the level of excise tax and the amount of value added tax, the higher the tax burden on final consumers of goods, since these are indirect taxes and their carrier is the same. In the formation of tax policy, the fiscal approach remains a priority, as a result of which the shadow (non-observed) economy grows.

In accordance with the studies of the current tax problems of the Russian federation, many scientists note the signs that the tax system should have: structuredness, subordination of a specific goal, integrity, interconnectedness of parts, and self-development. And in this regard, it is obvious that in the Russian practice of taxation, there are significant disproportions between the elements of the tax system, in compliance with the principles of taxation, in the mechanism of tax administration and interaction between public authorities in the field of taxes. In this place, it should be noted that the PSSLN model proposed by the author is based on the evolutionary principles of development: unity and infinity, structural and functional systemicity, variability, self-organization, controllability, sufficiency, necessity, and evolutionary-cyclic initiation. The proposed model allows us to state the dynamic development of the tax system; the adequacy of its current economic conditions and, in some cases, the tax system is ahead of schedule in terms of information technologies used in tax administration issues as compared with other sectoral areas. Tax law is a branch of law, but we can also say that the main financial component of the economy is in terms of paying citizens for services provided by the state.

The reality is that at this stage of development of the tax system in the country, there is an imbalance, as there is a discrepancy between the pace of development of parts of the system and economic realities, as a result of which there is no demand, not a part of the overall potential of the country's economic system and society as a whole. In addition, imbalances cause unproductive losses of capital and resources of economic systems. At the same time, any system assumes the presence of certain elements and interrelations between them, the essential benchmarks of which are integrity and balance.

The disproportions of the tax system manifest themselves in different forms and types of discrepancies in its composition, content, and dynamics and cause uneven pressures on its various elements and lead to an increase in the shadow economy and tax evasion.

The factors causing inconsistencies in the tax system hamper the legal receipt of tax revenues in the budgets of different levels and make the strategic goals of the development of the economy of the state and society unfulfilled. Scientists consider such conditions as volatility in tax legislation, uneven distribution of tax burden, inefficiency of the tax administration mechanism, inefficiency of tax benefits, etc.

It is impossible to say unequivocally that modern Russia has a system of maximum taxes, the result of which can be current in that, when the increase in the tax burden is not accompanied by an adequate increase in state revenues, therefore, the institutions need to be transformed into property, government, and a tax mechanism focused on economic growth and solution of social problems and reorientation of the fiscal function to the stimulating one. According to many scholars, the fiscal-oriented tax system in Russia has acquired a confiscatory character, the regulatory function is poorly implemented, and the stimulating one manifests itself in the provision of tax preferences for taxing a number of services, activities, scale of business, and others at different budget levels.

From the standpoint of forming the optimal development trajectory and the urgent need to transform the goals of the tax system of Russia along the lines of the idea of independence of territorial entities and minimizing the redistribution of financial resources, we will pay attention to the imbalances in the tax system that have been studied in numerous scientific and practical works in recent years. There is a dependence of the dynamics of the national economy on the level of the tax burden. A well-known factor is that an increase in the tax burden leads to a fall in the growth rate of GDP and vice versa. Reducing the tax burden, in their opinion, has a positive impact on business activity and contributes to increased investment activity. The data presented in **Table 5** reflects the level of tax burden in Russia for the period 2010–2017, which ranges from 30.8 to 34.50%. At the same time, an analysis of the level of tax burden on the economy, conducted for the BRICS countries and the Eurasian Economic Union, shows that this indicator in relation to Russia (according to the International Monetary Fund) mainly exceeds the BRICS countries and the Eurasian Economic Union for the period 2010–2017 ranges from 34.62 to 37.69%.

A comparative analysis of the dynamics of the tax burden in Russia and GDP and tax revenues of the consolidated budget of the Russian Federation in 2011–2017 was carried out, taking into account that the formation of tax revenues of the consolidated budget of the Russian Federation and GDP occurs in a certain institutional environment and the factor determining their volume and dynamics is the level of tax burden on the economy.

The author's correlation and regression analysis of the relationship between the dynamics of gross domestic product and the level of tax burden showed that the

| Indicator | 2011 | 2012 | 2013 | 2014 | 2015 | 2016 | 2017 |
|---|---|---|---|---|---|---|---|
| Tax burden, % of GDP | 34,50 | 32,49 | 31,80 | 31,89 | 32,3 | 31,1 | 30,8 |
| GDP dynamics at current prices, % | 4,3 | 3,7 | 1,8 | 0,7 | −2,8 | −0,2 | 1,5 |
| Tax revenues of the consolidated budget of the Russian Federation, billion rubles | 9715,2 | 10,954 | 11,321,6 | 12,606,4 | 13,720,1 | 14,386,3 | 17,197,2 |

*Compiled according to the Ministry of Finance of the Russian Federation.*

**Table 5.**
*Indicators of the dynamics of the level of tax burden and gross domestic product of the Russian Federation in 2011–2017.*

regression equation obtained for this sample characterizes the linear dependence of the dynamics of GDP on the level of tax burden. At the same time, the increase in the latter by 1% leads to an increase in GDP by an average of 0.6%. The value of the correlation coefficient rxy = 0.3 indicates that the level of tax burden does not significantly affect the dynamics of the gross domestic product and the closeness of the relationship between them is defined as weak. At the same time, the quality indicator of the regression equation R2 = 0.077 says that only in 7.8% of cases changes in the level of tax burden lead to a change in the dynamics of GDP. The remaining 92.2% of changes in GDP dynamics are explained by factors not taken into account in the model.

The results reflect the problem of an objective assessment of the real tax burden. The peculiarity of the modern Russian tax system is that there are many payments in it that are similar in their economic nature to taxes, but not related to those in tax legislation. As a result, the real tax burden is much higher than the figure declared by official statistics. In addition, the level of tax burden is determined by various methods, which has relevant consequences for an objective assessment of its impact on socially significant indicators.

The results of the correlation and regression analysis should also be linked to periods of financial crisis, price conditions of GDP formation, level of tax administration, etc., although, in fact, the inflation factor works. Although there is an increase in tax resources, the budget deficit is increasing at the same time due to the growth of expenses subject to inflation to a greater degree.

Correlation and regression analysis of the relationship between the dynamics of tax revenues of the consolidated budget of the Russian Federation and the level of tax burden for the period 2011–2017 showed that between the level of tax burden and tax revenues of the consolidated budget of the Russian Federation, there is a linear inverse correlation, and an increase in tax burden of 1% leads to a drop in tax revenues of the consolidated budget of the Russian Federation by 1056.7 billion rubles. The value of the correlation coefficient rxy = −0,42 indicates that the level of tax burden affects the amount of tax revenues of the consolidated budget of the Russian Federation and the relationship between them is defined as inverse and moderate. At the same time, the quality indicator of the regression equation R2 = 0.176 says that in 17.58% of cases, changes in the level of tax burden lead to a change in the volume of tax revenues of the consolidated budget of the Russian Federation. The remaining 82.42% of changes in tax revenues of the consolidated budget of the Russian Federation are explained by factors not taken into account in the model and indicate the complex structure and mechanism for the formation of tax revenues of the consolidated budget of the Russian Federation.

Based on the methodology, the Ministry of Finance estimated the fiscal burden of 26 large companies from various industries—fuel and energy, transportation, information and communication, mining, the auto industry, and energy. It turned out to be the highest in the fuel and energy complex—from 67% for Novatek to 83% for Rosneft. The lowest is the load in the automotive industry, while AvtoVAZ has 0% at all. In the practice of determining the tax burden, there are four to five methods for determining the tax burden; the methodology of the Ministry of Finance of Russia is generally accepted. Below, in **Table 6**, the calculation of the tax burden on a small business using a simplified tax system is given.

The next drawback of the tax system of the Russian Federation, which needs to be improved, is a manifestation of the uneven distribution of the tax burden among payer categories. The tax mechanism should be built with a focus on achieving social equilibrium in the society, and for modern Russia it is the social function of taxes that is important. Coordination of requests of different social strata of society is connected with the provision of a certain optimal combination of their interests and balance in incomes.

| The name of indicators | Values of indicators by year | | | | | Deviations of 2016 to 2013 | |
|---|---|---|---|---|---|---|---|
| | 2012 | 2013 | 2014 | 2015 | 2016 | Absolute. | Relative., % |
| A | 1 | 2 | 3 | 4 | 5 | 6 | 7 |
| The amount of income received by taxpayers with the object of taxation "income minus expenses" (billion rubles) | No data | 5622 | 3769 | 4261 | 4865 | −757 | 86,54 |
| The amount of tax payable for the tax period (million rubles), from income reduced by the amount of expenses | 29,977 | 32,606 | 35,541 | 39,908 | 47,032 | 14,426 | 144,24 |
| The amount of the minimum tax payable for the tax period (million rubles) | 14,142 | 15,441 | 17,050 | 19,553 | 22,584 | 7143 | 146,26 |
| Total value of taxes at the object "income minus expenses" | 44,119 | 48,047 | 52,591 | 59,461 | 69,616 | 21,569 | 144,89 |
| The tax burden, % | — | 0,85 | 1,40 | 1,40 | 1,43 | 0,58 | 168,24 |
| The amount of income received by taxpayers with the object of taxation "income" (billion rubles) | 2020 | 2170 | 2293 | 2389 | 2596 | 426 | 119,63 |
| The amount of tax payable for the tax period from income (million rubles) | 76,082 | 81,875 | 86,837 | 89, 963 | 97,612 | 15,737 | 119,22 |
| The tax burden, % | 3,76 | 3,77 | 3,79 | 3,77 | 3,76 | — | 100,00 |

*Compiled by the author.*

**Table 6.**
*Calculation of the tax burden on a single tax in the application of the simplified taxation system for organizations for 2012–2016.*

The idea of justice for Russian society is especially important, but in the 1990s this system collapsed. At present, this is a system consisting of two main subsystems: the subsystems of socially significant public goods provided by the state (reproduced through the mechanism of the tax system) and separately the tax system within itself which must carry elements of justice.

Analysis of the data on the distribution of the tax burden on personal income tax among various groups of citizens in the context of individual countries gave the following results, reflected in **Table 7**.

| Country | The share of taxes paid by 1% of the least secure taxpayers | Share of taxes paid by 10% of the least secured taxpayers | Share of taxes paid by 50% of the least secure taxpayers | The proportion of taxes paid by 1% of the most secured taxpayers |
|---|---|---|---|---|
| Russia | 0, | 1,7 | 21,4 | 5,1 |
| USA | 0,0 | 0,1 | 8,2 | 34,0 |
| United Kingdom | 0,0 | 0,6 | 11,2 | 26,5 |

**Table 7.**
*Distribution of tax burden on personal income tax among different groups of citizens in the context of individual countries, %.*

## 3. Conclusions

The above main problems and contradictions in the tax system required to consider the levels and criteria of direction and development and principles from the position of systemonomy and apply the methodology of systemonomy to create a systemonomic model of the tax system, presented in the form of a "Periodic System of Special Laws of Nalogonomy."

The systemonomy approach makes it possible to determine the presence of the necessary structural components of the tax system, its development trajectory, directions, targets, the existing involutionary vector of tax system development, and the evolutionary vector congruent by the general law of the world as well as to predict the stages and phases and compare them with the universal laws of the world, general laws of human society, and the laws of socioeconomic development of the state.

The goal of the research is to show the practical significance of the application of the periodic law of systemonomy to create a systemonomic model of nalogonomy, showing the stages and criteria for the development of all levels of the tax system, congruently with the universal law of the world. The object of the research was the methodology of the scientific and practical direction of the congruence of the tax system and economic processes in society. The subject of research is the systemonomic model of development of the tax system based on the analysis of a number of problems of the interdependence of the economy and elements of the taxation system. The hypothesis of the research was based on the following: The methodology of the scientific and practical direction of the taxonomy of the tax system will ensure a holistic study and development of all aspects and elements of the tax system, congruently with the universal law of the world, if the criteria for its evolutionary development correspond to the systemonomic model in the form of hierarchically organized systematization of special laws of nalogonomy.

The Periodic System of Special Laws introduced by the systemonomic method of nalogonomy is of scientific theoretical, epistemological, methodological, and practical importance for solving the problems of finding an integrative model of the tax system in the process of a new scientific direction in the field of taxation—nalogonomy.

I focus my attention on the practical meaning of the PSSLN, which is that the systemic and systemonomic approach allows us to predict the stages, phases, and congruent evolutionary changes in all structures of the tax system and the state as a whole and also to compare them with the universal laws of the world, thus systematically solving the issues of such a complex interbranch, interbudgetary, and intergovernmental phenomenon as the tax system.

The tax system should ensure the implementation of not only direct functions (fiscal, regulatory, etc.) but also functions such as stimulating, aimed at the realization of public interests, such as social cohesion, public confidence in the state, and the realization of the idea of justice. The evolutionary principles of the model proposed by the author will contribute to the improvement of the tax system.

The tax system should be focused on creating a mechanism to meet the challenges of developing the economy, attracting investment, improving the social and cultural standard of living of people, and other tasks, possibly intergovernmental, foreign policy. The effectiveness of such a mechanism is formed, taking into account the optimal model of nalogonomy proposed by the author.

Instability of the tax system today is the main problem of tax reform, but it is justified by international events and unpredictability. There are both objective and subjective reasons for it. The world is developing as a whole: in its production technology, payment systems, transmission of information, and economic interaction between countries. The full range of geopolitical factors influence the need for evolution of the tax system and, above all, structural and organizational evolution, with more democratic relations between the State and the taxpayer, becoming open and not burdensome [14]. As never before, nalogonomy is provided with the opportunity to achieve its highest potential. Perhaps in the future, on the basis of dialectical development of nalogonomy, the world will witness the creation of a tax-free space, self-sufficient in its economic potential.

## Author details

Irina A. Zhuravleva
Department of Tax Policy and Customs Tariff Regulation, Financial University under the Government of the Russian Federation, Member of the Russian Academy of Natural Sciences, Member of International Fiscal Association, Corresponding Member of the Ararat International Academy of Sciences, Moscow, Russia

*Address all correspondence to: sia.mir67@mail.ru

## References


[1] Zhuravleva IA. Nalogonomy - the doctrine of the evolution of the tax system/V-VI systemonomic readings. Collection of Articles, Reports, Research Papers; 2017. pp. 141-145

[2] Maslova NV. Periodic System of the Universal Laws of the World-M; 2005. p. 184

[3] Tax Reforms. Theory and Practice, under the editorship of Mayburov IA, Yu B. Ivanov. Moscow; 2015. p. 72

[4] Goncharenko LI, editor. Taxes and Tax System of the Russian Federation. Moscow: Yurayt; 2014. p. 69

[5] Urmantsev YA. The Symmetry of Nature and the Nature of Symmetry; 1974

[6] Panskov VG. Taxes and Taxation: Theory and Practice. Yurayt; 2019. p. 186

[7] Astafiev BA. Fundamentals of the Universe. White Alves; 2002. p. 320

[8] Zhuravleva IA. The philosophical foundations of a systemonomic model of the laws of nalogonomy: Theoretical principles, methodological foundations, structural consistency. Monography, "Tradition"; 2019. p. 67

[9] Zhuravleva IA. The direction of improving the tax system in the structure of the economy on the basis of the Periodic System of Special Laws of Nalogonomy/VII-VIII systemonomic readings. Collection of Articles, Reports, Research Papers; 2018–2019. pp. 112-119

[10] Zhuravleva IA. Nalogonomy, a model of the dialectic of the controlled development of the tax system. Global Economy in the XXI Century: Dialectics of Confrontation and Solidarity; 2018. pp. 141-151

[11] Galyautdinov RR. The tax system of Russia: concept, structure and levels of taxes. Website of the Teacher of Economics. 2015. Available from: http://galyautdinov.ru/post/nalogovaya-sistema-rossii [Accessed: 13 October 2019]

[12] Tax policy. Theory and practice: A textbook for undergraduates studying in the specialty "Finance and Credit", "Accounting, Analysis, Audit", "World Economy"[Mayburov et al, Zhuravleva IA] under the editorship of I.A. Mayburov. M: UNITY-DANA; 2017. 519 p

[13] Maslova NV. Systemonomy Scientific Publication. M.: NANO, KANON; 2015. p. 207

[14] Zhuravleva IA. Nalogonomy - model of the dialectic of the controlled development of tax system. The monograph was made the financial support of the Russian Foundation for Basic Research, project No 18-010-00877 A. The Problems of the Configuration of The Global Economy The XXI Century: The Ideal of The Socio-Economic Progress and The Possible Interpretations. London; LSP, P-480. 2018. pp. 377-389

Chapter 8

# The Financing of Spanish Colonial Commerce in America: The *Almojarifazgo* and the Port of Veracruz

*Emiliano Gil-Blanco*

> *La serie de almojarifazgo percibido en Veracruz sobre los movimientos de los navíos con España y América permanece casi constante. Nada hace pensar en una modificación radical de la eficacia de las obligaciones fiscales.*
>
> *(Chaunu [1], p. 542)*

## Abstract

The *Hacienda Real* during the colony taxed the commerce with several tariffs, the most important being the *avería* and the *almojarifazgo*. The latter would do so directly on traded goods. The information it gives is a rich source for interpreting colonial and intercontinental trade. The study focuses on the documentation of tax by the Real Caja de Veracruz at the New-Hispanic port of Veracruz, which served as the re-shipper of the goods negotiated in Mexico. It gives us information about incoming and outgoing ships, their destinations or origins, and the amount paid for almojarifazgo, without distinctions. The total value negotiated in the port between 1587 and 1650 has been calculated as a percentage charged on the value of the merchandise. In spite of fraud and contraband during this whole period, these calculations can be considered a source of reliable, if approximate, information of the new Spanish trade. It establishes the supremacy of imports over exports and intercontinental trade with Spain over colonial trade.

**Keywords:** *Almojarifazgo*, tax law, trade commerce, Veracruz, New Spain

## 1. Introduction

The maintenance of the Spanish trading system with America in large part was based on the collection of a series of taxes levied on the value of goods traded there, such as the breakdown, the duty of tonnes, the Admiralty, the market or the *almojarifazgo*. Each of them took on a specific function within the system. The breakdown was the source of funding for the navies protecting the Convoys of the Race of the Indies. The right of *tons* financed the expenses of the University of Mareantes de Sevilla, while the Admiralty did the same with the salary of the admirals of Castile and the *lonja* with the Consulate.

Of all these taxes, the *almojarifazgo*, or income of the sea, was the only one that was not collected for a specific purpose, but rather, financed the bureaucracy and expenses of the Castilian Crown in general, both in America and in the Metropolis. Its origin dates back to the time of the Arab domination of the peninsula. With the conquest of the city of Seville in 1248 by Ferdinand III the Holy, this tax was increased by the *Hacienda Real* and was later regulated by Alfonso X. From the outset, the system of collection of this tax varied from port to port and was carried out through the lease of this tax by third parties.

To better understand what colonial taxation was in general we must highlight a recent work on taxation, coordinated by Pilar Martínez, Ernest Sánchez and Matilde Souto [2], in which they study the works of Bartholome Yun, on taxation within the context of the nation state [3]. More specifically, for the *almojarifazgo* we highlight the research essays of Emiliano Gil, who has also worked on the history of the port of Veracruz and its trade [4–7], by Manuel Moreyra Paz-Soldán [8], by Manuel J. Ayala [9] or Luis Salas Almela, about the *almojarifazgo* in Seville and Sanlúcar de Barrameda [10, 11]. There is, as can be seen, a sparse historiography about the *almojarifazgo* for the sixteenth and seventeenth centuries for the New Spain viceroyalty. The same is not true of other taxes, such as Ernest Sánchez's studies on New Spain [12], Guillermina Valle on its management and the Consulate of Mexico [13] or Yovana Celaya on tax administration in the seventeenth century [14], or the breakdown of the classic study of Guillermo Céspedes [1, 15]. On the contrary, the eighteenth century has been studied more deeply, not only in New Spain, but in other American areas that began their expansion in that century, as is the case of Río de la Plata. Most use other tax sources or vessel registrations [16].

## 2. The tax

In 1497, after the discovery of America, the Catholic Monarchs extended the collection of the almojarifazgo to the trade of goods sent to that continent, exempting from the payment of this and any other rights to intercolonial trade and to all products Americans exported from the new territories annexed to the metropolis without exception ([17], pp. 209–210; [18], p. 105).[1] Initially, the collection of this tax was intended for the financing of the colonial administration, although the Crown initially imposed it to justify the high costs of its policy.

The exact date of its implementation in America is unknown to us, but the advance of the conquest and colonization of the new colonies was matched by the implementation of the *Real Caja*. In this way, the Caribbean islands were the first to see the Castilian fiscal power deployed, having been the first territories discovered and conquered, later to New Spain and then to Central and South America. We have news that in 1528 the *almojarifazgo* was already collected in the viceroyalty of New Spain and in 1543 in that of Peru [19].

From the *Caja Real* of February 28, 1543, ([17], pp. 210–211), the collection of this duty was extended to all products imported from Europe, with export and intercolonial trade remaining free of charge. At the same time, this *Real Cédula* introduced another tax in America on the value of goods, the alcabala, which taxed the first sale of items in American markets. The collection rates of the *almojarifazgo* were established in 2.5% of the goods declared from Seville and 5% for entry into the Americas (p. 21; [18], pp. 105–106).

[1] Merced given in Burgos on 6 May 1497 and ratified by the Consejo de Indias. We also use as a source the book of Antúnez, *Memorias histórcas...*, although it is not a very reliable source, but it includes tax legislation and other issues relating to existing regulations in the tax season.

As can be seen, the *Caja Real* of 1543 did not change the system established in 1497. The novelty was based on how to raise the *almojarifazgo*, a portion in the port of departure and the rest in the arrival port, when it was previously collected in its entirety in the Sevillian port. To this 7.5% of *almojarifazgo* we must add 10% of first sale alcabala, which in fact was taxed on goods at 17.5% of their value at destination. In cases where products imported from the metropolis were re-exported to other American ports, the *Caja Real* re-taxed them with another 5% [20].

This tax was applied once certain American agricultural products began to be exported, which was the beginning of a much bulkier trade to Europe. After a series of consultations with the king, held between 1559 and 1566 ([21], p. 218), and after consulting the Council of the Indies. The king decided to reorganize the collection of *almojarifazgo*. The *Caja Real* was issued on 29 May 1566[2] and the *Real Provisión* of December 28, 1568.[3] The Crown sought an expansion of its revenue in American trade, as it was hardly exposed to the fiscal pressure of the time, and also because it obtained great benefits and privileges.

The *Real Cédula* of 1566 doubled the percentages that they charged as *almojarifazgo* for intercontinental trade, looking at a 5% departure from Seville, previously it was 2.5%, with 10% entry into ports enabled for trade with America. In addition, Andalusian wines, which constituted one of the most exported products to the American colonies, were also traded with an additional 10% in both Seville and America.[4]

The *Real Provisión* of 1568 imposed the *almojarifazgo* for the first time on intercolonial trade, which in New Spain began to be applied within the general reform of Viceroy Martín Enríquez ([22], pp. 217–228) and in Peru by the Bachelor Lope García de Castro (1564–1569) under the viceroy Francisco de Toledo. The instructions for developing the new contributory system, as established by Moreyra ([8], p. 17) and Borah ([21], p. 218), did not reach the major ports until 1571.

According to this *Provisión*, goods exported to other colonial ports were required to pay the *Caja Real* 2.5% of the declared value, at the port of departure, as stipulated for export trade to Europe. Goods introduced or imported from colonial origin had since then paid 5% of their value at the port of destination. Whereas, European products re-exported between the same American colonies paid the Royal Treasury 5%, not on their declared value at the port of destination, but on the price difference between the latter and the port of origin manifested in the vessels' records. In order for the collection of the *almojarifazgo* to be carried out faithfully, the Crown necessarily extended the elaboration of records for intercolonial traffic.[5] With this *Real Provisión*, the circuit was closed for collecting the rights of *almojarifazgo* of Indian trade until the end of the eighteenth century.

[2] This Real Cédula refers to the collection of the almojarifazgo from intercontinental trade and was issued on June 24, 1566, received by the Real Audiencia de México on September 21 of the same year, sent to Veracruz the following day and settled in the books of the Real Caja of the port by treasurer Rodrigo Fránquez on August 27, 1573. Archivo General de Indias (hereinafter A.G.I.). Contaduría. Real Caja de Veracruz. Leg. 878. *Recop. Leyes de Indias...* Book VIII. Tit. XV. Law I.

[3] This Real Provision establishes the almojarifazgo for intercolonial trade. Its development is produced by the Cédula of October 11, 1570. In New Spain, Viceroy Enríquez imposed it on Provision of April 6, 1571 given in Mexico City on September 30, 1571. A.G.I. Contaduría. Caja Real de Veracruz. Leg. 878. *Recop. Leyes de Indias...* Lib. VIII. Tit. XV. Law I.

[4] A.G.I. Contaduría. Caja Real de Veracruz. Leg. 878. Transfer of Her Majesty's Card where the scarping rights of the goods of Castile are sent to collect to X per cent and the wines to XX.

[5] A.G.I. Contaduría. Caja Real de Veracruz. Leg. 878. The collection of the new almojarifazgo rights at two and a half percent.

The imposition of these new tariffs was by no means accepted by those most directly affected by merchants. In New Spain the merchants maintained a relationship with Viceroy Enríquez, who in turn sent them to Castile, in which they explained the possible consequences of the new collection on trade due to such a substantial increase in taxes ([22], pp. 221–222). In the Peruvian viceroyalty the opposition of traders and the *Real Audiencia* to the new almojarifazgo was such that its application had to be delayed until 1566 reducing it to 1% instead of the stipulated 5% ([8], p. 17). Also, as a result of these protests, the tariff on Sevillian wines was reduced to 7.5% ([17], p. 212).[6]

In fact, the economic repercussions of the increase in almojarifazgo in American trade were very different from the alarmist relations of traders on both continents.

## 3. Exemptions and reductions in the collection of *almojarifazgo*

Despite the mandatory charge of tax on all products, there were always exemptions at certain ports for political or economic reasons. Of course, there was no *almojarifazgo* on any of those products for the service of the Crown, both in America and in the Iberian Peninsula, as well as ammunition, bastimentos and equipment for the boats of the *Carrera de Indias* ([17], pp. 215 and 218).[7] Its application was initially carried out on the ships that were escorting the convoys and then extending to all those who participated in Indian Ocean traffic.

From early on, the personal belongings of travelers were exempt from tax, as long as they were not sold at the destination. The royal officers were tasked with enforcing these rules. In the case of the sale of any belonging, it was penalized with the collection of double the percentage of the respective almojarifazgo. When there were intermediaries of third parties, the goods were seized along with half of the assets of the complainant, which were distributed to third parties between the Crown, the judge and the complainant.[8]

Another article partially exempt from the payment of the *almojarifazgo* were books, continuing an ancient privilege established by the Catholic Monarchs (1480) that exempted from tax on all books introduced in Castile by sea and by land ([18], p. 106; [17], p. 218).[9] In America they were taxed by the *avería*, as was done with the importation of *azogue*. For the former there was a second customs office in Veracruz, that of the Inquisition, in order to filter those not in accordance with the governing doctrines of the Catholic Church of the time ([23], p. 75).

Certain ports also saw the *almojarifazgo* reduced in order to boost their trade. The Crown's policy of creating a monopoly trade capitalized by a single port of exit and another of entry meant that the rest of the colonies, with exceptions, were kept away from the trade routes until the Free Trade Decree of 1778. This gap was filled by smuggling with foreigners and by a few trade contacts that the Colonies maintained with each other. To this end, the Crown would grant reductions in the tax, especially leaving port, during certain periods to boost "legal" trade. This privilege was only directed to products exported to the metropolis according to Antúnez ([17], pp. 213–214), Lorenzo ([19], pp. 371–372) and Haring ([18], p. 107), referring to the documents of February 2, 1561 and May 8, 1577.

[6] Cédula of January 25, 1567.

[7] Goods shipped by the Crown have been exempt from 1507. April 27, 1574, ratified by the Cédulas of September 14, 1613 and December 12, 1619. Recop. Leyes de Indias... Lib. VIII. Tit. XV. Law XXVI.

[8] December 15, 1531 for clergy and February 28, 1543 for the rest of the passengers. Recop. Leyes de Indias...Lib. VIII. Tit. XV. Laws XXVIII and XXIX.

[9] November 4, 1548 contained in the Recop. Leyes de Indias... Lib. VIII. Tit. XV. Law XXVII.

These reductions are also found in several Venezuelan ports at the end of the sixteenth century. Specifically, tax rates for intercolonial trade were halved. Cumaná obtained this privilege in 1589, Margarita in 1592, Caracas in 1592 and 1597, Río Hacha (New Kingdom of Granada) in 1596 and Nueva Andalucía in 1597 ([19], pp. 371 and 372; [18], p. 107; [24], p. 39). Cartagena would receive permits to reduce the collection of taxes by 1535, 1539 and 1540, in this case for goods that encouraged local agriculture and livestock ([25], p. 62).[10]

Puerto Rico received this benefit in 1567, 1606, 1611, 1625, 1632 and 1636 ([26], pp. 224–225; [19], pp. 371–372). Specifically, the *almojarifazgo* was reduced in half to give incentive to the island's trade in leather and sugar. The Cuban port of Havana was also granted this right for the years 1569, 1577, 1589 and 1595 ([19], pp. 371–372).

## 4. Evaluation of the value of goods and revenue

Royal officers calculated the tax on merchandise value from the prices at the port of origin or destination within thirty days of being shipped or landed ([17], pp. 235 and 236; [27], pp. 479–481).[11] The source for his calculation was the records of the vessels or affidavit produced by the merchant. As noted by Antúnez ([17], p. 233) and Lorenzo ([19], pp. 378–379) in reference to the accounting of the *Caja Real de Veracruz*,[12] they included, with day, month and year, the goods they transported and their value, declaring bale to bale and crate by crate. This statement was not systematically verified, nor was purchased and sale invoices required, unless there was evidence of fraud or reporting.

This non-verification of the declared was a privilege of Indian traders and shippers ([28], p. 165). Very rarely were they checked by the royal officers. To avoid this, there were the respective consulates who with their donations and petitions to the Crown managed to wipe out the most jealous official and obtain greater privileges for their trade. The delays that would result from such inquiries in the loading and unloading of fleets and vessels were in their favour, as this delay would create increments in their profits and in the collection of taxes. In order to grant these privileges, the Crown issued a certificate in 1586, urging its officials not to open the loaded bales and to speed up the dispatch of fleets and vessels ([17], 1797, pp. 237–238).

This privilege was met with the opposition of some royal officials. Thus, we can see how in 1596 the *Casa de la Contratación* objected to royal officials investigating the contents of bales and loaded crates. The same situation was repeated in 1604, but this controversy ended in 1609 with a certificate prohibiting the inspection of what was stated in the records ([17], p. 241). A relationship of two officers from the *Real Caja de México* of this time confirms this situation.

As can be gleened from the text, this privilege favoured fraud in legal trade. The amounts reported as evasion by the two New Spain officers may be exaggerated, but the reality was that the omission of goods or their undervaluation in the registers amounted to between 75 and 80% of what was traded in the fleets ([19], p. 378). One way of circumventing fiscal control was the loading and/or unloading of goods out of port or the exchange between ships on the high seas, claiming that they were registered on other vessels or could not be because of the haste of departure of the fleet or vessel.

[10] Real Cédulas of December 8, 1533, November 8, 1539 and February 11, 1540.

[11] Ordenanzas of 1554 and Cédula of December 22, 1579.

[12] A.G.I. Contaduría, Caja Real de Veracruz, Leg. 878.

The existence of this fraud would not be understood without the participation of the same royal officers and even the authorities, since many of them bought their positions from the Crown, particularly in the seventeenth century, and needed to make them profitable in order to compensate the expenditure made to attain them.

To curb tax evasion, the Crown drafted a number of rules. Merchants or travellers often did not declare goods they brought to America in order to pay for their journey with their sale, or to concel their existence from the *Caja Real,* in order to pay less *almojarifazgo* tax. From this moment on, they had to be declared in the corresponding register of the vessel. Thus, in 1574 all undeclared goods were obliged to pay the *almojarifazco* on arrival as if they had actually been registered, including those rescued from shipwrecked vessels ([17], p. 216).[13]

In 1624 the Consulate and the *Hacienda Real* changed the system of collection of the *almojarifazgo*, in a clear attempt to prevent fraud in the records. From this year a fixed value was imposed for each crate or bale loaded, according to weight and goods contained within. This measure contributed even more to enhancing fraud, as traders did not load declared goods, but rather goods of higher value. In addition, the need to weigh bales before being loaded on the ships lengthened the loading period and, therefore, that of their departure. This system of capacity was replaced in 1695 by that of *palmeo* ([17], pp. 246–247).

Initially, the payment method of the *almojarifazgo* was in merchandise, from the same products traded, but from 1568 it was collected in cash with no exception. In 1620, it was converted back to the more primitive form of payment, suggesting that both ways of complying with the *Real Caja* were used in parallel for many years ([17], pp. 214–215).[14]

The Crown did not allow the payment of this tax to be postponed,[15] although the reality was another by allowing royal officials to trust in Seville and America. Payment was made in advance of the sale of the goods, withholding them in case of non-payment. Nevertheless, the major cash-flow problems that the established commercial system originated in traders made delay, installments and credit in paying the tax, function on a daily basis. For the Sevillian case they had to wait for the return voyage to be able to pay the *almojarifazgo*. At other times, traders anticipated 5% of the total goods tax, and the rest was paid on the return of the fleet or vessel. It could also happen that the payment was deferred for 4 years, paying 70% of the total the first year and the rest in the following three.

These "illegal" forms of payment of the tax were not condoned by the Crown, hence between 1550 and 1627 five *Real Cédulas* were issued to combat it,[16] in which for the first time they sanctioned those officials who transgressed the rules with the payment of 4% penalty.

How was *almojarifazgo* charged in Veracruz? There were usually two officers of the *Caja Real*, a treasurer and an accountant, and, in very rare cases, an agent appears. Their attitude was solidary and collegiate, as can be assumed, before the Court of Auditors of Mexico. Once the boats arrived at port, the masters handed over the records to the royal officers. With the records in hand, they authorized the unloading of the merchandise, which was stored in the warehouses of the *Caja Real* as a guarantee of future payment of the tax. In order to have independence and be

---

[13] April 21 and 27 1574.*Recop.* Leyes de Indias... Lib. VIII. Tit. XV. Laws VIII and XIX.

[14] Cédulas of December 28, 1568 and March 9, 1620. Recop. Leyes de Indias..., Lib. VIII. Tit. XV. Law I.

[15] Recop. Leyes de Indias... Lib. VIII. Tit. XV. Law V.

[16] Cédulas of April 16 and August 4, 1550, May 10, 1554, August 24, 1619 and January 23, 1627. Recop. Leyes de Indias. Lib. VIII. Tit. XV. Law V.

able to calculate the value and tax of the declared goods, the officers had to agree and remained isolated to evaluate them. The value of the merchandise was calculated, as we have already mentioned, according to the value it had in the port thirty days after its arrival, taking into account the average price of its wholesale value ([17], pp. 235–236; [19], p. 380).[17] To carry out this calculation and check or set the prices, they had at hand the regulations of the *almojarifazgo* and were accompanied by three witnesses, not merchants.

Once the value of the goods had been established, it was sent to Mexico for consideration by the *Caja Real de México*. This was composed of the viceroy, hearers, prosecutor of the *Real Audiencia* and officials of the *Caja de México*. The calculation of what traders had to pay for *almojarifazgo* was then calculated. Once the tax was calculated, it was again sent to Veracruz for the royal officers of that port to effect the payment. This system was created by Viceroy Enríquez in 1573 after consultation with all those involved in the New Spain trade, including royal officers, and accepted by the Crown in 1593. For the reforms of Viceroy Martín Enríquez see García-Abasolo ([22], pp. 226–227). For the acceptance of the conditions by Enríquez, *Real Cédula* of January 17, 1593, go to Antúnez ([17], pp. 239–240) and Lorenzo ([19], p. 380).

But the value of the goods calculated according to existing prices in the port of Veracruz was fictitious, since very few were sold in that port. Veracruz was only a distribution point and Mexico was in charge of its sale and redistribution to the rest of the New Spain territory. That is why in 1576 Viceroy Enríquez ordered that the price of merchandise be calculated according to the highest, medium and lowest value that had occurred in its sale, taking into account that it was produced on credit ([22], pp. 227–228). When this calculation was made, they took into account shipping costs and damage to goods during transport or from storage in the port warehouses.

The fact that the real market of unloaded goods in Veracruz was the capital of the viceroyalty influenced its collection of *almojarifazgo*. The merchants resided in the latter city, negotiated the goods there and paid their taxes. The officers of the Veracruz *caja* had to record these payments as made in the same port,[18] along with all the data of the vessels. For each period of accounts of each royal-service officer four relationships were established: 10% *almojarifazgo* for entry of vessels from Seville; 5% for the entry period from the American colonies; a 2.5% departure fee bound for the first; and a 2.5% departure tax to colonies. They included, in addition to the paid *almojarifazgo*, the type and name of the boat, its master, the origin and destination of the same and the date of entry or departure from the port. Sometimes they also recorded the person who paid the tax at the *Caja*, but this was done very rarely.

## 5. Fundraising

During the period between 1587 and 1650, notwithstanding gaps in documentation,[19] a total of 5,433,564.8 pesos were collected at the *Caja de Veracruz*, as an *almojarifazgo*, of which 4,957,826.4 pesos were collected (91.2%), and the

[17] Real Card of December 22, 1579.

[18] A.G.I. Contaduría. Caja Real de Veracruz. Leg. 878.

[19] Existing documentary gaps are from June 14, to December 17, 1594, from May 6, to August 31, 1601, from May 17 to November 29, 1602, from June to October 31, 1607, from July to October 1627, from August, 9 1628 to November 7, 1630, from November 4, 1632 to August 6, 1633 and from September 5, 1636 to August 11, 1637.

| Years | Hamilton | Lorenzo |
|---|---|---|
| 1571–1575 | 5,250,848.60 | 6,961,106.70 |
| 1576–1580 | 4,452,950.00 | 7,071,426.70 |
| 1581–1585 | 7,638,402.80 | 10,010,691.00 |
| 1586–1590 | 6,315,767.20 | 6,003,871.10 |
| 1591–1595 | 9,812,990.50 | 6,174,575.60 |
| 1596–1600 | 7,974,421.90 | 9,231,595.60 |
| 1601–1605 | 5,901,535.90 | |
| 1606–1610 | 7,542,324.20 | |
| 1611–1615 | 6,060,319.70 | |
| 1616–1620 | 8,759,988.50 | |
| 1621–1625 | 8,847,808.80 | |
| 1626–1630 | 4,270,502.30 | |
| 1631–1635 | 2,722,946.40 | |
| 1636–1640 | 4,649,319.60 | |
| 1641–1645 | 2,188,833.70 | |
| 1646–1650 | 2,223,195.50 | |
| Total | 94,612,155.60 | 45,453,266.70 |

*Source Hamilton and Lorenzo Sanz.*

**Table 1.**
*New Spain exportations of silver from private owners, merchants and assets of deceased persons.*

remaining 475,738.4 pesos for exports (8.8%).[20] From these two quantities and their evolution we estimate that the total value of the goods of the trade of Veracruz was 72,836,207 pesos, of which 53,798,475 belong to imports and 19,037,732 pesos to exports. The port's trade balance, as can be seen, was negative at 19,037,732 pesos. This was compensated with the export of numerary, already studied by Hamilton ([29], pp. 47–56) and Eufemio Lorenzo Sanz ([19], pp. 252–253) and which we present a comparison in **Table 1**.

Export superiority over import was substantial, with exports not reaching 10% of what was traded. However, during the seventeenth century the trend changed compared to the sixteenth century and exports have a higher share in Veracruz trade, 9.1% versus 7.58%, respectively. The reasons for this dispute are that import trade from Seville, the fleets, was mainly composed of European manufactures of high value and quantity; while exports, raw materials for the most part of lower value, are compensated by the silver output. As we know, American colonial trade was characterized by a monopoly on European manufactures and by the lack of a local industry that generated its own merchandise.

## 6. Evolution and stages of global revenue

At the beginning of the reign of Philip II, the *almojarifazgo* raised in the port of Seville amounted to between 54,000 and 62,000 pesos per year.

[20] A.G.I. Contaduría. Caja Real de Veracruz. Legs. 878, 879, 880, 881, 882, 883, 884B, 884A, 885A, and 885B.

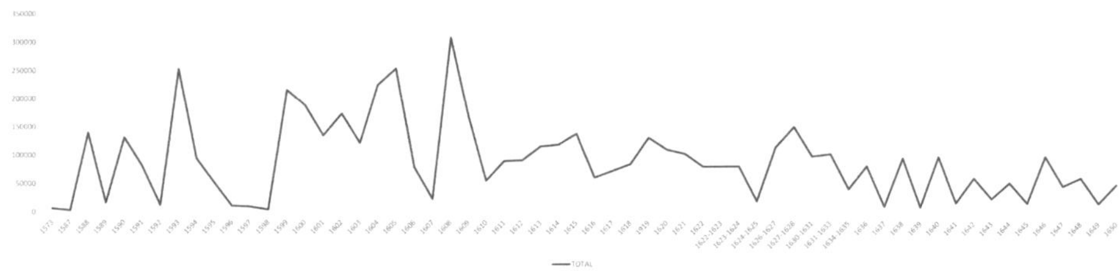

**Figure 1.**
*Almojarifazgo Real Caja de Veracruz (1573–1659). Annual distribution (in common gold pesos). Data extracted from* **Table** *3 annexed at the end of the present work.*

By the middle of the seventeenth century, this reached 600,000 ([18], p. 109). In Veracruz, between 1568 and 1571, 322,899 pesos were raised ([30], p. 1)[21]; while in the mid seventeenth century (1646–1650) the figure reached 291,246 pesos ([30], pp. 18–19).[22] The fact that the quantities were so unequal between the two centuries does not mean that there was a commercial or revenue superiority between one and the other. The characteristics of the evolution of the collection of the *almojarifazgo* in the *Caja de Veracruz* contradict this difference by its irregularity, which was influenced by the fleets. Thus we see that it was in the first 15 years of the seventeenth century that almost 40% of what was collected was concentrated. A symptomatic fact of this tax irregularity can be seen in the annual average, which we have set at 89,899.45 pesos, compared to the total collection (**Figure 1**).

According to data from the annual collection of the *almojarifazgo*, in Veracruz we have established five different stages in **Table 2**.

### 6.1 First stage of boom: (1587–1593)

After the epidemic of yellow fever, which ravaged New Spain during the years 1576 and 1580 and which left a lull in the economy of the viceroyalty ([22], pp. 67–86), there was a boom[23] in the collection of the *almojarifazgo* and, therefore, of trade at the port of Veracruz.

In these 8 years the amount paid for this right amounted to 642,638.9 pesos, 11.83% of the total collected. Although fleet traffic was not constant, there was no arrival in 1587, 1589 and 1592, nor of departure in 1587, 1588, 1589 and 1593. 581,949.1 pesos, 90.56% were raised for this concept; while trade on the side lines only totaled 60,689.8 pesos (**Figure 2**).

At the time, The *New Spain* economy suffered a series of manufacturing shortages that, as we have explained above, were filled from Seville, such as Andalusian wine and oil. These imports were mostly intended for the population of European origin. The evolution of this traffic conditioned the development of intercolonial traffic, since Veracruz acted as a re-exporter of the leftover fleets towards the area of influence of its trade, the Caribbean.

---

[21] A.G.I. Contaduría. Caja Real de Veracruz. Leg. 878, branch 1, from Septembre of 1568 until June of 1571.

[22] A.G.I. Contaduría. Caja Real de Veracruz. Leg. 885B, branch 7, from October to December 31, 1650.

[23] A.G.I. Contaduría. Caja Real de Veracruz. Legs. 878, branch 3, from August 11, 1572 to June 30, 1573; 879, branches 1 y 2, from June, 1587 to June 13, 1591; y 880, branches 1 a 4, from June 30, 1590 to June 14, 1594.

| | Importation | | | Exportation | | | |
|---|---|---|---|---|---|---|---|
| **Quinquennios** | **Flotas** | **Sueltos** | **Total** | **Flotas** | **Sueltos** | **Total** | **Total** |
| 1573–1593 | 558,836.50 | 46,539.30 | 605,375.80 | 23,112.60 | 14,150.50 | 37,263.10 | **642,638.90** |
| 1594–1598 | 120,030.50 | 15,740.30 | 135,770.80 | 30,075.20 | 5,179.30 | 35,254.40 | **171,025.20** |
| 1599–1615 | 2,241,184.20 | 108,384.40 | 2,349,568.60 | 135,022.90 | 24,437.20 | 159,460.10 | **2,509,028.70** |
| 1616–1635 | 1,048,877.90 | 95,120.80 | 1,143,998.70 | 185,191.90 | 19,394.10 | 204,586.00 | **1,348,584.60** |
| 1636–1650 | 507,808.50 | 215,304.00 | 723,112.60 | 30,905.00 | 8,269.80 | 39,174.80 | **762,287.40** |
| Total | **4,476,737.60** | **481,088.70** | **4,957,826.30** | **404,307.60** | **71,430.80** | **475,738.40** | **5,433,564.80** |

*In common gold pesos. In the concept "Sueltos", the name used in the handling of documentation. Included is the revenue from colonial, African and Sevillian commerce that were not connected to fleets, but rather ships that carried official documentation.*

**Table 2.**
*Evaluation of the collection of the almojarifazgo tax at the port of Veracruz (1573-1650) by the tendency in homogeneous periods.*

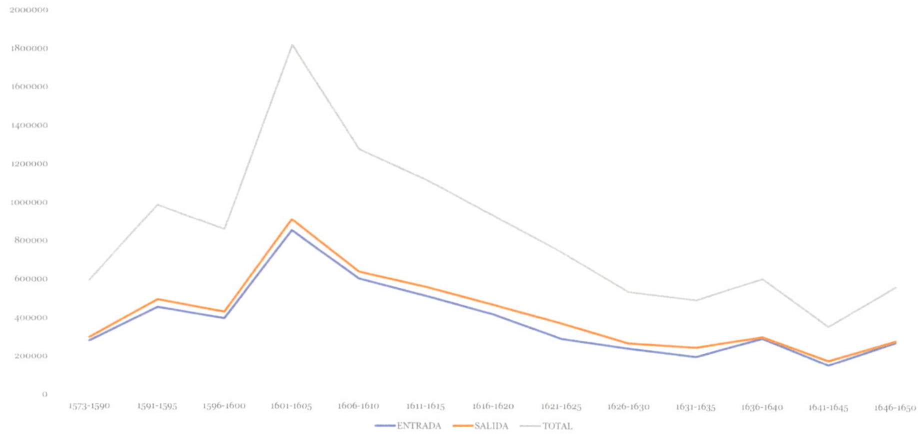


**Figure 2.**
*Almojarifazgo Caja Real de Veracruz (1573–1650). Distribution by quinquenios (in common gold pesos). Data extracted from* ***Table** 2.*

### 6.2 First stage of crisis: (1594–1598)

The European policy of the Castilian Crown conditioned the evolution of commercial traffic between the two continents and between the same colonies. Thus the wars of the late sixteenth century with Holland and France, allied with England, would influence the traffic and the collection of *almojarifazgo*. Fleets suffered harassment by these countries and by pirates, some English. During this period we see how the volume and value of what was negotiated between Seville and Mexico was reduced, leading to a short term crisis.[24] After the signing of the Treaty of Vervins (1598), this trend would change.

At this stage, collection is reduced to 171,025.2 pesos, 3.15% of what was entered in the *Caja* for the whole period, a quarter of the amount established in the previous stage. Of this figure 150,105.8 pesos came from intercontinental trade goods, 87.77%, 120,030.5 pesos from imports and 30,075.3 exports. The trend of intercolonial trade in the collection of these years is slightly higher than the previous ones, from 9.44 to 12.23%, 20,919.4 pesos, a third below that.

While the tax charge for inbound fleets and intercolonial trade was reduced, exports of the former saw a 30.13% increase over the previous stage, constituting the beginning of a phase of export expansion of Veracruz to the metropolis in the fleets, that would last until 1616.

### 6.3 Second stage of boom: (1599–1615)

The political problems that interfered with the normal development of intercontinental trade disappeared from 1599[25] the collection of *almojarifazgo* collected by the *Caja de Veracruz* shows an upward trend. The influx of fleets to New Spain was steadily reduced, except in 1607 when there was the presence of a Dutch fleet

[24] A.G.I. Contaduría. Caja Real de Veracruz. Legs. 880, branch 4, from October 20, 1592 to June 14, 1594; y 881, branches 1 to 5, from October 19, 1594 to January 1, 1600.

[25] A.G.I. Contaduría. Caja Real de Veracruz. Legs. 881, branch 4, from May 26, 1598 to January 1, 1600; 882, branches 1 a 11, from May 7, 1600 to October 14, 1609; and 883, branches 1 to 7, from October 14, 1609 to June 12, 1616.

on the coasts of the Iberian Peninsula[26], and instead an *armadilla* was sent with the necessary *azogues* for the *New Spain* mines and some merchandise.

The reality could well be another: the saturation of the markets. Already in 1606, there was a significant reduction in fleet tax collection compared to the previous year, from 240,837.9 pesos in 1605 to 69,643.5 pesos in 1606 and to 2,962.3 pesos in 1607. The Mexican Consulate argued that the dangers of navigation were a cause of this decrease.

In these 17 years a total of 2,509,028.7 pesos, 46.18% of the total were entered into the *Caja*. Of this amount, 94.7%, 2,376,207.1 pesos corresponded to intercontinental fleet trade, while the remaining 5.3% was collected from intercolonial trade.

Although the margin of share of intercolonial trade in income was less than in the previous stage, 5.3% versus 12.23%, the average annual value of intercolonial trade, increased by double, or 7813 pesos versus 3486.6. During these years, fleet trade eclipsed non-fleet commerce, even if the latter was prosperous.

### 6.4 Second stage of crisis: (1616–1635)

The saturation of colonial markets led to a reduction in imports from the metropolis. This fact caused Sevillian merchants to opt for cut-offs of colonial markets in order to be able to place their products. This undersupply favored alternative ways to alleviate manufacturing shortages, such as smuggling, the emergence of an indigenous industry capable of competing with imported products in fleets, or sourcing them through the Manila Galleon.[27]

This was reflected in the collection of *almojarifazgo* in Veracruz, which at this stage is reduced to 53.75% compared to the previous, 1,348,584.6 pesos, 24.82% of the total collected, of which 1,234,069.8 pesos correspond to intercontinental trade or 91.51%, and 114,514.9 pesos to intercolonial trade.

This decline in tax revenues was more noticeable in imports, which fell to 1,048,877.9 pesos; while exports on the other hand increased by 37.15%. This increase would confirm the good health of the *New Spain* economy.

### 6.5 Crisis: (1636–1650)

The depression produced in the previous stage was worsened by the changes in frequency of fleets, from annually to every two years.[28] There were no entry fleets in the port of Veracruz in 1637, 1639, 1641, 1643, 1645 and 1649, nor were there departures between 1634 and 1638 and in 1640, 1642, 1644 and 1646. These absences would significantly lower the income of the port *Caja*, which in those fifteen years accounted for only 762,287.4 pesos, which represented 14.03% of the total and a reduction of 43.47% less.

The consequences of this decline in intercontinental commercial activity would affect, by half, the intercolonial exchange of the *New Spain* port in its exports. By contrast, imports from colonial markets increased by 126.35% because of the emergence of Venezuelan cocoa in New Spain and the ban on trade with Peru (Arcila,

26 A.G.I. Consulado. Libro I. Folios. 162–165.

27 A.G.I. Contaduría. Caja Real de Veracruz. Legs. 883, branches 7 a 14, from June 11, 1615 to October 14, 1622; 884B, branches 1 a 9, from September 5, 1622 to September 14, 1627; and 884A, branches 1 to 10, from September 14, 1627 to September 4, 1636.

28 A.G.I. Contaduría. Caja Real de Veracruz. Legs. 884A, branch 10, from November 19, 1634 to September 4, 1636; 885A, branches 1 to 6, from August 12, 1637 to October 4, 1646; and 885B, branch 7, from October 5, 1646 hasta December 5, 1650.

1950, pp. 251–252; [31], p. 586; [32], p. 5). This activity raised this trade by 29.33%, compared to 8.49% during the previous period.

## 7. Conclusions

Colonial trade was taxed by several tariffs levied by the *Real Caja*, such as the *avería*, the duty of *tons*, the *almirantazgo*, the *lonja*, the *consulado* or the *almojarifazgo*, among the most important. The latter has served for the present study and for a later one in which we explained how the trade of the New Spain port of Veracruz functioned.

Taxes were collected by royal officials appointed by the *Real Hacienda* in all ports, creating *Real Cajas*. It was done from the ship records that merchants were obliged to keep. The information they give us is very rich. Not only does it inform the origin and destination of the boat, type and its master, but it also relates the different goods and their merchant, with their value and the tax paid. There were exemptions in the collection of *almojarifazgo*, either for political or economic reasons, of goods or ports, such as those of Cumaná, Margarita, Caracas, Rio Hacha, Nueva Andalucía, Cartagena, Puerto Rico or Havana. The stipulated high percentage of *almojarifazgo* encouraged cases of fraud and smuggling. However, the information provided by the documentation on *almojarifazgo* of the *Real Caja de Veracruz* shows us the trend of New Spain trade through the aforementioned port.

Although Veracruz was only a mere redistributor of the goods that were negotiated in the capital of the viceroyalty, all traffic with Spain and the rest of the American colonies of the Caribbean passed through their docks. This had an influence on the calculation of the value of the declared goods. At first, the average prices calculated in Veracruz were fictitious. For this reason, a different form of calculation was established in 1576, using the average price of its highest, average and lowest value of its value in Mexico.

During the period studied (1573–1650), 5,533,564.8 pesos were collected at the *Real Caja* de Veracruz for the concept of *almojarifazgo*. We have calculated that 91.2% came from import trade and the rest from export trade **Table 3**. This meant, according to our calculations, the value of goods exchanged at the port was 72,836,207 pesos.

Based on the evolution of the collection we have established five well differentiated stages, two of boom and three of crises, the last of them being the one that was felt the most by the economic and political situation of Spain. The first boom stage, between 1588 and 1599, arises as a result of a commercial take-off following the yellow fever epidemic in New Spain (1576–1580) and is characterized by the introduction of European goods for consumption by Spaniards and their re-export to other Caribbean markets. Then there is a crisis phase, between 1594 and 1598, of reduction of collection in the course of the European wars of Spain and that will have a positive consequence in the increase in trade towards the metropolis, with an increase of 30.13%. A second moment of boom (1599–1615) appears with peace in Europe, in which a regularity is established in the predominance of the fleet trade over the rest of the Veracruz trade. Then there is a second and long stage of crisis in the collection (1616–1635) caused by the saturation of the New Spain markets and that the Sevillian traders cause more criticism by deliberately undersupplying traffic. Thus, smuggling would arise and the development of an internal, local industry, which would supply the New Spain market. The collection shows us a reduction in imports, but not exports. Finally, this crisis would be exacerbated between 1635 and 1650 because the annual fleets become biannual. This was a major disruption of incoming *almojarifazgo* in the port of Veracruz, especially that originated by colonial exports, which are reduced by half. The revenue of colonial imports, on the other hand, would double with an increase of 126.35%. We leave the study of the different markets, goods and their negotiated value for future work.

| Year | Input | | | Output | | | Total |
|---|---|---|---|---|---|---|---|
| | Flotas | Sueltos | Total | Flotas | Sueltos | Total | |
| 1573 | | 964.3 | 964.3 | 5084.5 | 161.1 | 5245.6 | **6209.9** |
| 1587 | | 2801.6 | 2801.6 | | 268.3 | 268.3 | **3069.9** |
| 1588 | 126,927.5 | 7776.1 | 134,703.6 | | 4842.4 | 4842.4 | **139,546.0** |
| 1589 | | 14,440.4 | 14,440.4 | | 2233.6 | 2233.6 | **16,674.0** |
| 1590 | 118,482.0 | 7313.5 | 125,795.5 | 2899.3 | 2484.0 | 5383.3 | **131,178.8** |
| 1591 | 67,303.5 | 3113.1 | 70,416.6 | 8614.4 | 1972.0 | 10,586.4 | **81,003.0** |
| 1592 | | 5019.3 | 5019.3 | 6514.4 | 800.9 | 7315.3 | **12,334.5** |
| 1593 | 246,123.5 | 5111.0 | 251,234.5 | | 1388.3 | 1388.3 | **252,622.8** |
| 1594 | 80,333.0 | 3119.0 | 83,452.0 | 10,555.8 | 364.6 | 10,920.4 | **94,372.4** |
| 1595 | 39,697.5 | 2568.5 | 42,266.0 | 8208.8 | 1682.6 | 9891.4 | **52,157.4** |
| 1596 | | 4016.3 | 4016.3 | 5744.4 | 1052.8 | 6797.2 | **10,813.4** |
| 1597 | | 2500.6 | 2500.6 | 5566.3 | 1372.3 | 6938.5 | **9439.1** |
| 1598 | | 3535.9 | 3535.9 | | 707.0 | 707.0 | **4242.9** |
| 1599 | 205,662.4 | 4656.8 | 210,319.2 | 3975.5 | 1335.4 | 5310.9 | **215,630.0** |
| 1600 | 168,578.0 | 5336.6 | 173,914.6 | 11,582.5 | 2828.1 | 14,410.6 | **188,325.3** |
| 1601 | 110,862.1 | 9029.0 | 119,891.1 | 12,935.0 | 2254.3 | 15,189.3 | **135,080.4** |
| 1602 | 156,331.0 | 6337.8 | 162,668.8 | 9067.6 | 1886.8 | 10,954.4 | **173,623.1** |
| 1603 | 101,031.8 | 8233.3 | 109,265.0 | 10,958.5 | 1649.8 | 12,608.3 | **121,873.3** |
| 1604 | 204,846.0 | 7352.3 | 212,198.3 | 10,651.6 | 1814.6 | 12,466.3 | **224,664.5** |
| 1605 | 240,837.9 | 7054.5 | 247,892.4 | 4457.8 | 1516.1 | 5973.9 | **253,866.3** |
| 1606 | 69,642.5 | 6318.3 | 75,960.8 | 2348.9 | 1124.1 | 3473.0 | **79,433.8** |
| 1607 | 2,962.3 | 6863.6 | 9825.9 | 12,425.6 | 1261.4 | 13,687.0 | **23,512.9** |
| 1608 | 293,263.9 | 9188.5 | 302,452.4 | 4574.5 | 1762.3 | 6336.8 | **308,789.1** |
| 1609 | 157,472.1 | 5911.0 | 163,383.1 | 5533.4 | 916.8 | 6450.1 | **169,833.3** |
| 1610 | 44,837.4 | 5134.4 | 49,971.8 | 5094.6 | 826.4 | 5921.0 | **55,892.8** |
| 1611 | 75,833.4 | 7096.5 | 82,929.9 | 6607.5 | 1203.1 | 7810.6 | **90,740.5** |
| 1612 | 79,082.3 | 4014.5 | 83,096.8 | 7456.1 | 1500.4 | 8956.5 | **92,053.3** |
| 1613 | 100,806.3 | 5341.9 | 106,148.1 | 9693.1 | 1019.9 | 10,713.0 | **116,861.1** |
| 1614 | 105,920.3 | 5671.0 | 111,591.3 | 7308.8 | 919.4 | 8228.1 | **119,819.4** |
| 1615 | 123,214.8 | 4844.6 | 128,059.4 | 10,351.9 | 618.5 | 10,970.4 | **139,029.8** |
| 1616 | 52,942.0 | 2546.6 | 55,488.6 | 5819.8 | 619.6 | 6439.4 | **61,928.0** |
| 1617 | 63,053.3 | 3039.1 | 66,092.4 | 7165.0 | 621.2 | 7786.2 | **73,878.6** |
| 1618 | 72,956.8 | 3100.9 | 76,057.6 | 9234.9 | 552.8 | 9787.6 | **85,845.3** |
| 1919 | 116,363.5 | 3079.6 | 119,443.1 | 12,176.8 | 586.6 | 12,763.4 | **132,206.5** |
| 1620 | 94,834.4 | 4140.8 | 98,975.1 | 11,463.5 | 885.6 | 12,349.1 | **111,324.3** |
| 1621 | 86,818.0 | 5551.6 | 92,369.6 | 10,664.9 | 944.6 | 11,609.5 | **103,979.1** |
| 1622 | 62,353.0 | 2454.1 | 64,807.1 | 15,626.1 | 1032.6 | 16,658.8 | **81,465.9** |
| 1622–1623 | 56,686.0 | 4622.0 | 61,308.0 | 19,133.0 | 1192.0 | 20,325.0 | **81,633.0** |

| Year | Input | | | Output | | | Total |
|---|---|---|---|---|---|---|---|
| | Flotas | Sueltos | Total | Flotas | Sueltos | Total | |
| 1623–1624 | 58,622.0 | 6839.0 | 65,461.0 | 14,724.0 | 1781.0 | 16,505.0 | **81,966.0** |
| 1624–1625 | | 5813.0 | 5813.0 | 13,611.0 | 1137.0 | 14,748.0 | **20,561.0** |
| 1626–1627 | 90,269.0 | 10,863.0 | 101,132.0 | 12,263.0 | 2155.0 | 14,418.0 | **115,550.0** |
| 1627–1628 | 129,885.0 | 8778.0 | 138,663.0 | 11,693.0 | 1419.0 | 13,112.0 | **151,775.0** |
| 1630–1631 | 77,254.0 | 10,067.0 | 87,321.0 | 11,140.0 | 1352.0 | 12,492.0 | **99,813.0** |
| 1631–1633 | 57,127.0 | 13,616.0 | 70,743.0 | 30,477.0 | 2969.0 | 33,446.0 | **104,189.0** |
| 1634–1635 | 29,714.0 | 10,610.0 | 40,324.0 | | 2146.0 | 2146.0 | **42,470.0** |
| 1636 | 81,783.0 | 965.0 | 82,748.0 | | 236.0 | 236.0 | **82,984.0** |
| 1637 | | 11,067.0 | 11,067.0 | | 754.0 | 754.0 | **11,821.0** |
| 1638 | 80,518.4 | 15,924.9 | 96,443.3 | | 492.9 | 492.9 | **96,936.1** |
| 1639 | | 4795.4 | 4795.4 | 5547.4 | 429.9 | 5977.3 | **10,772.6** |
| 1640 | 88,625.4 | 10,463.1 | 99,088.5 | | 543.4 | 543.4 | **99,631.9** |
| 1641 | | 8490.3 | 8490.3 | 9331.0 | 446.4 | 9777.4 | **18,267.6** |
| 1642 | 48,385.6 | 13,186.8 | 61,572.4 | | 554.8 | 554.8 | **62,127.1** |
| 1643 | | 20,366.0 | 20,366.0 | 5151.3 | 405.4 | 5556.6 | **25,922.6** |
| 1644 | 32,652.8 | 20,495.4 | 53,148.1 | | 760.1 | 760.1 | **53,908.3** |
| 1645 | | 11,531.5 | 11,531.5 | 5515.0 | 1140.1 | 6655.1 | **18,186.6** |
| 1646 | 71,670.0 | 28,827.5 | 100,497.5 | | 307.1 | 307.1 | **100,804.6** |
| 1647 | 26,785.9 | 18,408.6 | 45,194.5 | 2812.9 | 553.6 | 3366.5 | **48,561.0** |
| 1648 | 45,783.5 | 15,766.9 | 61,550.4 | 1146.4 | 342.0 | 1488.4 | **63,038.8** |
| 1649 | | 16,556.1 | 16,556.1 | 753.8 | 661.0 | 1414.8 | **17,970.9** |
| 1650 | 31,604.0 | 18,459.6 | 50,063.6 | 647.4 | 643.1 | 1290.5 | **51,354.1** |
| Total | **4,476,737.6** | **481,088.7** | **4,957,826.3** | **404,307.6** | **71,430.8** | **475,738.4** | **5,433,564.8** |

*In common gold pesos. The concept "Sueltos" includes the collection of colonial, African and Sevillian commerce, apart from fleets.*

**Table 3.**
*Annual revenue from the almojarifazgo tax from the port of Veracruz (1573–1650).*

## Acknowledgements

My acknowledgment to Maria Ruth Giesbrecht for her support and collaboration in the translation of this work.

## Documentary sources

Archivo General de Indias (A.G.I.).

- Audiencia de México, Leg. 351. Cartas y expedientes de oficiales reales de Veracruz.

- Contaduría. Caja Real de Veracruz. Leg. 878. Cuentas de Real Hacienda de lo remitido a España desde 1568 a fin de junio de 1573 con los comprobantes del cargo.
- Contaduría. Caja Real de Veracruz. Leg. 879. Cuentas de Real Hacienda desde 1587 a 1591.
- Contaduría. Caja Real de Veracruz. Leg. 880. Cuentas de Real Hacienda desde junio de 1590 a diciembre de 1594.
- Contaduría. Caja Real de Veracruz. Leg. 881. Cuentas de Real Hacienda desde 17 de diciembre de 1594 a fin de 1599.
- Contaduría. Caja Real de Veracruz. Leg. 882. Cuentas de Real Hacienda desde 1°de enero de 1600 a 14 de octubre de 1609.
- Contaduría. Caja Real de Veracruz. Leg, 883. Cuentas de Real Hacienda desde 14 de octubre de 1609 a 3 de septiembre de 1622.
- Contaduría. Caja Real de Veracruz. Leg. 884B. Cuentas de Real Hacienda desde 6 de septiembre de 1622 a 8 de agosto de 1637.
- Contaduría. Caja Real de Veracruz. Leg. 884A. Cuentas de Real Hacienda desde 6 de septiembre de 1622 a 8 de agosto de 1637.
- Contaduría. Caja Real de Veracruz. Leg. 885A. Cuentas de Real Hacienda desde 9 de agosto de 1637 a 4 de octubre de 1646.
- Contaduría. Caja Real de Veracruz. Leg. 885B. Cuentas de Real Hacienda desde 5 de octubre de 1646 a 27 de noviembre de 1653.
- Consulado. Libro I. Libros de las Juntas y acuerdos del Consulado.


## Author details


Emiliano Gil-Blanco
Universidad San Francisco de Quito, Ecuador

*Address all correspondence to: emigilblanco@gmail.com

## References

[1] Chaunu P. Serie: Filosofía y Letras, Sevilla, Sevilla y América, siglos XVI y XVII. Publicaciones de la Universidad de Sevilla; 1983. p. 65

[2] Lorenzo Sanz E. Comercio de España con América en la época de Felipe II (Tomo II). Valladolid: Institución Cultural Simancas; 1980

[3] Yun B. Imperio español, entre la monarquía compuesta y el colonialismo mercantil. Metodologías, contextos institucionales y perspectivas para el estudio de la fiscalidad y la movilización de recursos. In: Martínez P, Sánchez E, Souto M, editors. La fiscalidad New Spain en el imperio español. Conceptualizaciones, proyectos y contradicciones. México: Instituto de Investigaciones Dr. José María Luis Mora/Universidad Nacional Autónoma de México, Instituto de Investigaciones Históricas; 2015. pp. 29-67

[4] García-Abasolo A. Martín Enríquez y la reforma de 1568 en Nueva España. Sevilla: Diputación Provincial; 1983

[5] Gil Blanco E. El almojarifazgo como índice de interpretación del comercio del puerto de Veracruz, 1600-1622. Estudios de Historia Social y Económica de América. 1986;**2**:89-119

[6] Gil Blanco E. El tráfico del puerto de Veracruz en 1572. Estudios de Historia Social y Económica de América. 1990;**7**:19-26

[7] Gil Blanco E. Auge y crisis del tráfico comercial veracruzano visto a través de la cuenta de almojarifazgo, 1573-1650 (Tesis doctoral inédita). Alcalá de Henares: Universidad de Alcalá; 1993

[8] Miranda J. España y Nueva España en la época de Felipe II. México: Instituto de Historia, Universidad Nacional Autónoma de México; 1962

[9] Ayala M. Diccionario de gobierno y legislación de Indias. Madrid: Ediciones Cultura Hispánica; 1988

[10] Moreyra Paz-Soldán M. Estudios sobre el tráfico marítimo en la época colonial. Lima: Libreria e Imprenta Gil; 1944

[11] Salas Almela L. Nobleza y fiscalidad en la Ruta de las Indias: el emporio señorial de Sanlúcar de Barrameda (1576-1641). Anuario de Estudios Americanos. 2007, (julio-septiembre);**64**:13-60

[12] Salas Almela L. Los antepuertos de Sevilla: señorío, comercio y fiscalidad en la Carrera de Indias (s. XVI). In: Vila Vilar E, Lacueva Muñoz J, editors. Mirando las dos orillas: intercambios mercantiles, sociales y culturales entre Andalucía y América. Sevilla: Fundación Buenas Letras; 2012. pp. 105-127

[13] Tepaske JJ, Klein HS. Ingresos y egresos de la Real Hacienda de Nueva España. México: Instituto Nacional de Antropología e Historia; 1988

[14] Celaya Nández Y. La cesión de un derecho de la Real Hacienda: la administración del impuesto de la alcabala novohispana en el siglo XVII. Tres estudios de caso. In: América Latina en la Historia Económica. 2010, enero-junio. pp. 91-125

[15] Céspedes del Castillo G. La avería en el comercio de Indias. Escuela de Estudios Hispano-Americanos: Sevilla; 1945. p. 187

[16] Hausberger B, Ibarra A. Comercio y poder en América colonial: los consulados de comerciantes, siglos XVII-XIX. Madrid, Frankfurt del Main y México: Iberoamericana/Vervuert/ Instituto Mora

[17] Antúnez RA. Memorias históricas sobre la legislación y gobierno del

comercio de los españoles con sus Colonias en las Indias Occidentales. Madrid: Imprenta de Sancha; 1797

[18] Hamilton EJ. The decline of Spain. In: The Economic History Review. Vol. VIII. 1938

[19] León Borja D, Szasdi Nagy A. El comercio del cacao en Guayaquil. Revista de Historia de América, LVII. 1964:57-58

[20] Vila Vilar E. Historia de Puerto Rico: 1600-1650. Sevilla: Consejo superior de investigaciones científicas, Escuela de Estudios Hispano-Americanos; 1974

[21] Borah W. Comercio y navegación entre México y Perú en el siglo XVI. México: Instituto Mexicano de Comercio Exterior; 1975

[22] García de León A. Tierra adentro, mar en fuera. El puerto de Veracruz y su litoral a Sotavento, 1519-1821. México, D.F.: F.C.E. Universidad Veracruzana; 2014

[23] Martínez P, Sánchez E, Souto M. La fiscalidad novohispana en el imperio español. Conceptualizaciones, proyectos y contradicciones. México: Instituto de Investigaciones Dr. José María Luis Mora/Universidad Nacional Autónoma de México, Instituto de Investigaciones Históricas; 2015

[24] Arcila E. Hacienda y comercio de Venezuela en el siglo XVI. Caracas: Banco Central de Venezuela; 1983

[25] Borrego MC. Cartagena de Indias en el siglo XVI: contribución a la conmemoración del V Centenario del Descubrimiento. Sevilla: Escuela de Estudios Hispano-Americanos; 1983

[26] Valle Pavón G. Gestión del derecho de alcabalas y conflictos por la representación corporativa: la transformación de la normatividad electoral del Consulado de México en el siglo XVII. In: Hausberger B, Ibarra A, editors. Comercio y poder en América colonial: los consulados de comerciantes, siglos XVII-XIX. Madrid, Frankfurt del Main y México: Iberoamericana/Vervuert/Instituto Mora; 2003. pp. 41-72

[27] Fuentes García A. Los ingenios de azúcar en La Habana del siglo XVII (1650-1700): estructura y mano de obra. Revista de Historia Económica, IX. 1991, invierno;**1**

[28] Haring CH. Comercio y navegación entre España y las Indias en la época de los Habsburgo. México: Fondo de Cultura Económica; 1979

[29] Gil Blanco E. Interpretación del comercio de un puerto colonial novohispano durante un periodo de crisis, Veracruz (1587-1650). Estudios de Historia Social y Económica de América. 1997;**14**:75-123

[30] Sánchez E. La mirada fiscal sobre el comercio interno: las alcabalas novohispanas. In: Martínez P, Sánchez E, Souto M, editors. La fiscalidad novohispana en el imperio español. Conceptualizaciones, proyectos y contradicciones. México: Instituto de Investigaciones Dr. José María Luis Mora/Universidad Nacional Autónoma de México, Instituto de Investigaciones Históricas; 2015. pp. 165-187

[31] Calderón F. Historia económica de la Nueva España en Tiempos de los Austrias. México: Fondo de Cultura Económica; 1988

[32] Jumar FA. El comercio atlántico de Río de La Plata, 1680-1778. El circuito legal español. Las fuentes utilizadas y su tratamiento. América Latina en la Historia Económica. 2004, enero-junio:11-36